Broken to Beloved

You may be thinking that this book is about me; it is, after all, my complete autobiography. Let's make this clear right at the start, this book isn't about me, it's about what God has done and is still doing in my life.

Brendan Conboy

Published by
Yellow Dog Publishing

BROKEN to BELOVED
First published May 2025
Originally published as:
The Golden Thread
First published September 2015
Second edition published May 2021
Third edition published December 2023
I'm Still Valued
First published November 2023

www.brendanconboy.co.uk
Printed and bound in Great Britain

A catalogue record for this book
is available from The British Library
ISBN: 978-1-7393684-7-0

Cover design
Brendan Conboy via DALL-E

Introduction

In case you haven't realised by now, this is two books in one. It is now almost ten years since I first wrote and published *The Golden Thread*. This book, *Broken to Beloved,* celebrates those ten years of my life and all that God has done.

The second part of this book is *I'm Still Valued*, which talks about some of the major life-threatening battles I have endured and matured through.

These stories are the same; it is my story, though some edits have been made. People tell me I have a powerful story, and I question – What makes a story powerful?

Our stories, indeed our testimonies, are made all the more powerful through the power of God. I hope and pray that as you digest each chapter, you will sense the presence of God.

At the end of the book, you will find a bonus of a third book I published called 'My Foundation for Life.' In this short book, you will learn about The Bible verses I have stood upon and built my life upon.

The Golden Thread
A true story of Fear, Forgiveness & Faith
Brendan Conboy

Acknowledgements

(The Golden Thread)

Writing your life story is a challenge. Figuring out what to include and what to leave out isn't easy, especially when it stirs up memories, issues, and struggles. This isn't the whole story of my life, not even close, but it's a window into parts of the journey I've taken. And through it all, I've never been truly alone. I'm so grateful for the Golden Thread—God's hand, guiding me every step of the way.

I've got to thank Heather, my wife. Honestly, I don't feel like I deserve someone so beautiful, kind, and thoughtful—but I'm incredibly blessed that I get to do life with her.

To my family and everyone mentioned in this book, thank you. Without you, the story would look very different.

And finally, thank you to those who've put even a little faith in me by supporting this book financially. Everyone listed on the next page contributed to the first edition, helping bring it to life and laying the foundation for future books. You believed in me, this story, and the legacy I'm building as an author. I'm deeply thankful.

Abbie Warren,
Alisdair Longwill,
Andrew Filer,
Andy Jarrett,
Andy Morris,
Ann Cresswell,
Anne Griffiths,
Annie Watkins,
Anton Wynn,
Ash Santini,
Berith Sandgren-Clarke,
Caro Denny,
Carol McDonald,
Cheryl Shears,
Christine Knighton,
Colin Cresswell,
Darren Weyman,
Dave Shears,
David Rose,
Dawn Salmon,
Debbie Bird,
Diane Rowe,
Fiona Parker,
Fiona Spring,
Gareth Zimmerman,
Gavin Smith,
Grant Harman,
Jane Mann,
Janet Townsend
Jarred Price,
Jason Parker,
John Read,
John Thompson,
Jon Schofield,
Jon Trim,
Karen Burridge,
Kate Sackett,
Lucy Houghton,
Martin Pearson,
Martin Shannon,
Md Shamsudduha,
Mel Reed,
Mervyn Cave,
Mike Juggins,
Nick Burne,
Paul Newbould,
Paul Wilcox,
Phil Coysh,
Phil Jones,
Roger Spiers,
Rosemary Cave,
Rosie Richter,
Steve “Scotty” Scot,
Sarah Clifford,
Steve Woodcock,
Tracy Spiers,
Trecia Filer

In memory of Jim & Eileen Conboy
Without them, I would not exist.

For reasons of anonymity, the names of some people in this book have been changed.

THE GOLDEN THREAD

Faith, Hope and Charity

I hope this blesses you.

Since 1986, I have considered myself to be a visionary.

I know that my visions are God-given. The Bible tells us that young men will see visions and old men will dream dreams. I do have some odd and weird dreams on occasion, and these are becoming more frequent, therefore confirming that I am getting older, but I also still have visions. The visions I have been given have become reality, but they have only come into being as a result of the mission.

Mission is the practical outworking, bringing about the fulfilment of the vision. I now realise that the mission, to succeed, needs to be supported by faith, hope and charity.

I have heard these three words mentioned by various people for many years, but it is only now that I begin to realise just how powerful a combination of these three things is.

Charles Swindoll says:
"Vision is essential for survival. It is spawned by faith, sustained by hope, sparked by imagination and strengthened by enthusiasm. It is greater than sight, deeper than a dream, broader than an idea. Vision encompasses vast vistas outside the realm of the predictable, the safe, and the expected. No wonder we perish without it!"

I first wrote this book when I was 54 years old and had been a Christian for 28 of those years. The day that I invited Jesus into my life, it was like a switch was thrown, and I became a channel to be used in such a way that God had planned for my life.

The time now feels right to share my story. This book has for some time been another part of the God-given vision. I hope that it will inspire you and others to step out and do even greater things.

Chapter One

Mixed Memories

Let's start at the very beginning; it's a very good place to start. Some of you may be saying that sounds like a line from the musical, The Sound of Music, and that's because it is. I can distinctly remember visiting my grandmother's house every fortnight and listening to the songs that accompany the amazing story of the Von Trapp family and their struggles to overcome the oppression of Hitler's Nazi army. At eight years old, I didn't understand what oppression was, but I was old enough to sing and learn the words of these songs. I knew them all and so looked forward to these visits, to be able to play music on a Dansette record player. I didn't realise it at the time, but music was to become a major part of my life.

I now recognise the power that there is in music. Music stirs up something in each of us. When we are feeling low, the right tune can lift us out of the depths of despair. When we are confused, again, music and lyrics can direct and guide us, influencing our decision-making. I have so often used the expression, "I don't sing because I'm happy, I'm happy because I sing." This is so true, as I have witnessed the lives of young people transformed through the power of singing. Singing releases self-belief and helps to maintain our sanity. Music has an amazing ability to carry a powerful message, something that I would realise more seriously in my twenties.

The Sound of Music, however, was not my first introduction to music. I grew up with two older brothers, and later a younger one came along when I was eleven years old. I can remember an occasion when I was five years old and went to Severn Beach with my grandmother and my two older brothers, Mike and Chris. Gran gave us all some money to spend. Chris and Mike decided to club together and buy the latest Beatles song 'A Hard Day's Night'. The price was seven shillings and sixpence, but they only had five shillings between them. They realised that if they could influence me, they could also use my buying power and together the three of us bought the seven-inch, black shiny disc – my first single ever purchased and what a classic.

I later realised that the strength of supporting each other was very powerful and that we would need to support each other through some very dark episodes in our lives.

So, let's start at the very beginning.' It is a good place to start. I now understand that the first eight years of any child's life are the most impressionable and the most influential. Any amount of trauma can leave deep, long-lasting effects. Our earliest memories form a foundation for our development. Positive memories and experiences will, in most cases, result in a positive development for a child. Whereas a negative and traumatic memory could lead to disaster and, almost certainly, some level of help will be required to understand the confused feelings which could be experienced later in life.

My earliest memory was one of my dad returning from the pub on a Sunday, at about three in the afternoon. Mum had kept his Sunday roast warm in the oven (no such thing as microwaves then) but it had been so long it had dried up and was not fit for consumption. I'm not sure if I had reached my fourth birthday, but I clearly remember my dad's drunken anger. He was so angry that he threw the plate and contents at the lounge window, smashing the large centre pane, with the plate landing in the front garden. I don't remember what happened next, but I do remember the feeling of fear. That feeling would remain with me for at least the next ten years, which is how long it would take before my dad admitted that he had a drinking problem. The power of any addiction can be all-consuming, and alcoholism slowly and gradually took over my dad's life.

At times, I will say that I didn't have a proper upbringing and that my childhood started when I was fifteen years old when my dad stopped drinking. Although I did play childhood games, the big change was realising that my now constantly sober dad loved me. He had always loved me, but the power of alcohol, with associated anger and aggression, had built up so much fear in me that I couldn't see any love.

Silly Games

By the time I had reached my fifth birthday, the family had moved from the house in Stonehouse (where I was born) to Chalford Hill. Dad discovered this picturesque Cotswold village whilst working, laying sewer pipes and had fallen in love with it. The house on Silver Street was the first of many houses my parents bought to renovate. They were both hard workers and not afraid of a challenge. I'm sure that is where I get it from. The houses that we lived in were not fit for human habitation, but my parents ignored this, believing that hard work would provide the right rewards. Looking back, it is amazing that they saved two houses in Chalford Hill from demolition.

As children, we were expected to help as best we could

with these building projects. We all learn from our parents, and both Chris and I later went into the building industry ourselves. You could say 'following our father's footsteps', but not all of his steps were good ones. We also learnt how to argue and fight with each other. We learnt this through the many continuous and seemingly endless nights when we would hear Dad shouting, swearing and arguing with Mum downstairs.

The fear grows as you lie awake in the dark... listening ... listening... waiting... waiting... for it to end.

By the time I was twelve years old, I would sleep with a knife under my pillow. I never had to use it, but in my head, I was prepared to, if I needed to defend myself. Dad never did attack us like that, though. Mum protected us and she prayed... she prayed... for protection. She prayed for it to end.

In every school, you will sadly often find a school bully. I had my first experience of being bullied at primary school. I was about eight years old, and a ten-year-old called Peter decided to pick on me. I don't think it was just me though, he picked on anyone he could use his strength and his power over. It didn't take long before he pushed me too far. I didn't care if he was bigger and I didn't care if I hurt him more than he had hurt me. That day, in that playground at the age of eight, I decided to fight back. Peter came off much worse and as far as I was aware he never bullied anyone ever again. It seemed as if he had learnt his lesson. On the other hand, I had also learnt a new lesson. I had for the first time, realised that I did have power. The power to fight back would remain in me. I became like a dormant volcano. The power, destruction and hate were bubbling away just under the surface.

My brother Chris soon realised there was a volcano inside; he would tease and antagonise me 'pushing my buttons.' Mum used to say "Don't let him wind you up," but I had no control once the eruption point was reached.

One day Chris asked me if I wanted to play a fishing game. I was eight years old and he was ten. He had a fishing rod with proper barbed hooks. "You can be the fish," he said, probably with a smirk look. So, I rather naively put the hook in my mouth. He didn't hesitate to give a sharp tug on the line and the hook sank in deep to my top lip. I ripped it out and Chris laughed. I didn't retaliate immediately; I cunningly planned my revenge.

It was some time afterwards that I carried out the premeditated act. Chris would come home from school every day and run down the garden to a large plum tree. He had tied a rope from a branch and every day he would swing on it. It hung over a pile of old wooden floorboards that had been ripped out of the old unfit-for-habitation cottage. These boards were all carefully placed so that no nails were sticking up. That is until I decided to turn them over and just to make sure that he fell on the bed of nails, I cut into the rope to ensure it would snap. The plan worked well and Chris still has the scar (he tells me) on his bottom today. The other amazing thing about that incident was that he didn't realise that it had been sabotaged and there was no retaliation... this time! As we grew older, the games and violence increased but not always towards each other.

At eleven years old I started Marling Grammar School for boys. We had also moved to a larger house with two fields but it was even less fit to live in. There was no water and the toilet was a bucket in the shed, which we shared with rats.

One day a group of us were playing in one of the fields. 'Playing' though, is not exactly the right word. We were smoking cigarettes (I started at the age of seven) and setting fire to dry grass. This dangerous game soon turned into a very serious situation as the wind got up, the fire spread and rapidly became out of control. We all panicked, taking our tops off to beat the flames out. The destructive power of the wildfire struck fear in us all. We fought that fire for what seemed like a lifetime and when it was out another fear struck... What would Dad say? To our amazement, when Dad found out he said "OK let's go and burn the rest of it!" He wanted it done and he wasn't in the slightest angry, but he also wasn't in the slightest drunk. If he was, I am certain that it would have been a different story.

Having two fields also meant that we could have motorbikes. We had an old Zundap which Chris rode and I rode the BSA Bantam 125cc. Mike was old enough to ride on the road with an old Suzuki 125cc. Chris liked to show off on his bike; he would ride standing on the seat and he would pull exceedingly high wheelies. I'm not sure whether he had been winding me up or if it was just pure jealousy but one day, I resorted to sabotage again. I loosened his front wheel and his seat so if he tried one of his tricks it would almost certainly result in disaster. The sight of his front wheel coming off was both funny and frightening. In a split second, reality dawned. He could be seriously injured or he could survive and I could be seriously injured. He was injured and I think he gained another scar to keep the other one company, the one gained from the nail incident. To my surprise, he didn't retaliate. I think he just thought that he had badly maintained his bike but he later must have realised the truth as he plotted his revenge.

Our motorbike track was a figure of eight. This consisted of a lap around the field, up a jump into the garden, around the garden, taking the tight hairpin bend by the lounge window and back down the garden path to return to the field. Chris was much better at sabotage than I ever was. He decided to fix the Bantam so that the throttle would stick open, adjust the brakes so that they didn't work properly and also loosen the handlebars. It wasn't until I wanted to slow down for the hairpin that I realised something was wrong. I made it around the bend but at such a speed, control was easily lost. The loosened handlebars flew off as my arm went through the lounge window. Chris was in there watching football and he started shouting at me for interrupting the game (I think it was West Ham playing). My elbow was now resting on the window frame and I thought, apart from a broken window, everything seemed all right. As I lifted my arm off the frame, I realised that I had been leaning on a sharp point of glass. It had penetrated my arm by at least 50mm and I had just pulled it out. Now basic first aid training will tell you never to remove a foreign object as it is plugging the hole. The hole rapidly became a leak and I remember using a pillowcase as a bandage. It was a grizzly sight and all the result of silly games. Mum couldn't drive and Dad was nowhere around so a neighbour drove me to the local Doctor's Surgery. The doctor laid me down and told me to bite down hard on a rolled-up bandage. He told me that it would help with the pain as he stitched me back together. He said that I had been very lucky and that he could see the artery in my arm. Maybe my Guardian Angel was watching over me. The seven stitches were more painful than the cut. The room must have looked like a scene from a war film or a cowboy film.

This though was the second time that I had been in this room, on the same bed, with the same doctor, having the same arm stitched up. A year earlier I had fallen from the scaffolding that was on the house. As I fell, a bolt ripped a gaping hole out of my armpit. This injury again just missed the artery. My Guardian Angel was working hard. I also started to realise that each time I had a serious injury, resulting in a visible dressing or a sling, I would get sympathetic attention. I was thirteen years old when I realised that fighting was the answer to my problems. If I won, I would be glorified and revered, if I lost and was injured, I would get sympathetic attention. Either way, it was a win-win situation. I started to look for fights to feed and meet this need, but there is a fine line between fighting and bullying and I crossed it.

The silly and dangerous games continued. Chris was given a .22 air rifle for Christmas or Birthday and he was a crack shot. On one silly game occasion, he had me pinned down behind an old apple tree. As I placed my hand on the ground to stabilise myself, I felt the sharp sting of pain from the pellet and I still have the scar on my thumb today. Weapons had now become normal! So, it wasn't surprising that on one occasion, when Chris had been 'pushing my buttons' I retaliated with the best weapon that I could find. He had bent over to tie his lace (I think) but it could have been he was picking up rocks to throw at me. In that split second, I picked up a cast iron drain pipe. It was over a metre long and 75mm in diameter. Without even thinking I smashed it across his back. The pipe snapped in half and Chris dropped to the ground. I ran, he chased, but I don't think he caught me. That time!

How far would Chris push my buttons? He found out when I was fourteen years old. I feel this age was probably my craziest age! Chris and I had spent the afternoon at a friend's house. We had been playing cards and Chris had been cheating. He was good at cheating and then bragged about how good he was. The combination of cheating and bragging was another wind-up, another form of 'button pushing.' I would often react by sulking. He would notice the sulk and push even harder. The card game had long finished and I was in one of my deepest sulks. It was a bit like the calm before the storm. Chris knew this and loved seeing the storm arrive, and the unpredictability of what it would look like. He wasn't expecting the hurricane. I often wonder, 'Would he have stopped pushing if he had known what was coming?' Honestly, I don't think he would have.

We were making our way back home and had to walk through Brownshill allotments. Chris was still winding me up ... pushing ... pushing. In my mind, I'm thinking, 'Don't make me angry.' A little bit like Doctor Banner before he turns into the Hulk. Our card-playing friend was there and that may have egged me on, as an audience can often do. The point where a person passes into that uncontrollable anger is often referred to as 'red mist.' It is a point where anger takes over, and to regain control without any form of incident is rare. The mist can be calmed with the right level of calming intervention. I know this now because I have had to calm many 'red mist' situations.

One moment the brick was on the ground, the next it was in my hand. I heard my own fearsome roar as I charged towards my brother. Stopping with the brick raised above his head, I waited for that calming intervention. It didn't come. Our friend watched, probably stunned with mouth open wide. Instead, what came was the button being pushed again. "You wouldn't dare, go on I dare you?" It seemed as if time had stopped. I slammed the brick down hard. The hurricane hit Chris in the head. Blood poured down his face from the fresh wound. Fear struck me, just before the fist that followed, one hit and the light went out in my right eye; I couldn't open it for a whole week. The fear subsided, calmness returned, and we both looked like a mess. Reality hit us; the concern of brotherhood returned. We both had the same thought out aloud, "What would Mum say?" She had enough problems of her own; she didn't need to know the truth. Chris's blood washed off and his hair hid the wound. We made a story that I had fallen whilst playing football and an elbow had hit me in the eye. The story protected both of us, but it also protected Mum from the truth. She may have suspected that it was a lie but at least she didn't know the truth about the hurricane.

Although the first eight years of a child's life are the most impressionable and influential, the adolescent years can be the scariest and the most unpredictable. Chris had started to realise this and he never pushed my buttons as hard as he did on that day ever again. My unpredictable anger found me getting involved in more fights at school. Now it didn't bother me how old or how big a person was. I had a power in me that I could use to take control. I couldn't control the drunken arguments at home but I could take control of other kids in the school. It wasn't until later on in life that I realised that this is what is referred to as 'bullying' and that was what I had become, a BULLY. I even picked on teachers; they were a new level of challenge. With a bigger audience, I was going to show them all that I wasn't scared. All the time though, looking back now, I know that the rage was driven by fear.

In the 70's at Marling School, some teachers would try

to exercise their authority by throwing something at you. This was usually if you were talking in class which I tended to do a lot. I decided that whatever was thrown, I would throw it back. In my head, I figured that was fair. The chalk hit me; I threw it back. The board rubber just missed me; I threw it back. On one occasion instead of throwing the board rubber back, I threw the stool that I was sitting on. The teacher just told me to calm down and I did, which proved that calming intervention does work. It was no surprise then, that when I was fifteen, I was called to a meeting with the head teacher. I'm not sure if everyone had one of these meetings, but I can still remember every word of that conversation as if it were yesterday.

"Come in Conboy and sit down."
"Yes Sir."
"What are your plans for next year?"
"Don't know Sir?"
"Well let me help you. You're not coming back here."

I didn't want to stay on to the sixth form and I can remember being excited to be told this. Looking back now though, I feel annoyed that my choice was taken away, my power was taken away. I believe that this is now one of the underlying reasons why I empower young people to make positive choices, based on information available, using the decision-making power that is within. Little did either of us know that I would return twenty years later to teach a few lessons in drug education.

Chapter Two

Easily Led

Before I go any further, I want to point out that I am not proud of any of the bad stuff that I did. I am especially ashamed of the bullying, but I will go into that later.

You will probably not be surprised to hear that I did have a few run-ins with the law and I was surprised that I was only arrested twice. Either I was very good at not getting caught or my Guardian Angel was watching over me again. My first arrest happened when I was just thirteen. I was just getting off the bus at the bus station after school and Nigel came up to me. We had been friends since starting primary school and had been stealing cigarettes from his grandmother's shop since we were seven. He was with two slightly older lads that I had never met before, Malcolm and Jack.

"Hey Yob, what you up to tonight?"

I was given the name Yob as a shortened form of Yobnoc, which if you haven't worked it out is my surname spelt backwards. I now believe that if you call someone something for long enough, they will over time become what they are being called. My nickname was 'Yob' and I was rapidly becoming one!

In response, I answered his enquiry, "Not a lot, why?" "E's just sold his bike for thirty quid," he says pointing at Jack, "an look what 'e's bought. Show him."

Jack opened the bag to reveal a thousand bangers (fireworks, not sausages), a hundred packs with ten in each pack. Another bag contained 24 air bomb repeaters, each one with two highly- charged explosive flares.

"There's plenty to go around if you want to join us," came the invitation from Jack.

Later that dark November evening in 1973, Chalford Hill was terrorised. To us, it was just a little bit of fun. We threw bangers everywhere, every garden along every street was a target, but the people that were 'special targets,' such as teachers, had two air bomb repeaters with a total firepower of four explosions. These lethal devices were aimed tactically at doors and windows. This was such a foolish thing to do and it is a miracle that no one was injured. That is until PC Ted Moore caught up with us. His arrest technique was most brutal. I could see a dark figure looming behind me, torch in hand, slightly out of breath, slightly overweight.

"Don't move," he shouted as he pushed me against a wall that was covered in a thick layer of ivy. I disappeared into the ivy and his torch came in hard, hitting me on the right cheek and splitting my face open.

"Don't move!" WHACK, "Or I'll hit ya!"

No matter how many times I play it back in my head that WHACK always comes before hearing those words, "I'll hit ya." It was the early 70s and good old-fashioned policing was very effective. To be fair to Ted, he was in the process of a single-handed apprehension of four youths armed with explosives. However, by the time he caught us, the air bombs were all gone and we only had a handful of bangers left. We were all charged with contravening the Explosives Act, which sounded extremely serious but at the time was just fun.

Soon after the arrest, my parents were called to Brimscombe Police Station to collect me. As soon as I saw them, I said, "Dad, he hit me... look!" As I pointed to the cut, the only reply that came was, "Damn well serves you right! Now get in the car!"

In court, we were all found guilty and I never really had much to do with Jack after that.

From about the age of 12 to 15 I took quite an interest in football. I played in goal for the 1st Chalford Hill Boys Brigade. Our big rivals were the Scouts and we were always guaranteed a match full of fouls on both sides.

For me, football was associated with aggression. It was the early 70s and there was an increasing problem of football hooliganism. A group of us would catch a coach from Stroud to Swindon for every home game of the 'Robins.'

The acronym 'STAB' was everywhere around Swindon and you could even find it scribbled on the walls in Stroud. STAB – Swindon Town Agro Boys! I was drawn to that acronym, like a moth to a flame. My trips to Swindon were not about football, it was just another way of being able to fight, of letting off steam and putting myself at risk again. I can't recall one game of football although I was there, but I do remember chasing the away team supporters through the town on many occasions.

I dressed as if I was looking for trouble... short jeans, tall boots and braces. We had strength in numbers. The police would watch, but we were untouchable... or so it seemed.

I remember West Ham United being drawn to play Swindon in the FA Cup. It was an evening match, so probably a replay. My brother Chris is an avid West Ham supporter and as he too had been used to travelling to Swindon in the supporters' coach, he decided to travel the same way for this game. Chris and a friend of his were the only ones wearing claret and blue. They stuck out very obviously within a sea of red and white.

The journey up to Swindon was fine, but West Ham won, and on the way back, the minority of claret and blue became an easy target. Small objects were being lobbed at Chris and his friend, as the hate was rising.

Suddenly a Swindon fan in front of me was jumping up and down, shouting that he was going to kill the West Ham fans (or words to that effect). He had strength in numbers and he felt safe, but something then snapped in me. My brother was being threatened! Chris could have easily looked after himself, but some form of primaeval protection instinct took over and I punched the Swindon supporter in the face. The sharpened snake ring that I was wearing did what it was designed for; slicing the cheek; blood appeared instantly.

The coach stopped at Chalford and it was time to get off. Perfect timing! We quickly made our way from the coach and as it headed off, we realised that one of the ring-leaders of the aggression towards Chris and his friend also left the coach with us. Now with the odds of three to one, we made sure that he would live to regret what he had started. I don't think we ever caught that coach to Swindon again.

I started to follow Liverpool FC for two reasons: One, I had a red and white scarf from following Swindon and two, the sight of the Anfield Kop End was an impressive, powerful sight and I also wanted to be associated with that power.

Liverpool was a long way to travel, but the opportunity arose for me to go to an away game at Derby County. Meeting up with Liverpool fans from Gloucester at the train station, we looked like a mini version of the Kop End. We felt powerful, nothing could stop us, the train was ours, throwing every light bulb out of the window and arming ourselves with toilet rolls for the match.

The transport police waiting at the Derby station didn't have to look very hard for someone to arrest. I was dressed for trouble and now with a British Rail toilet roll sticking out of my pocket, they grabbed me.

In a small police office, in a not-so-obvious part of the station, I denied that I had stolen the toilet roll. They told me to look closer at the toilet roll and pointed out that it had printed words on every sheet... 'Property of British Rail.' I could deny it no longer! They processed me so quickly and let me go on to watch the match. As I left the room, I realised that they had many others to process and that we would all meet up together again for our day in court. I was 15 years old and it was the last football match that I ever went to. I think I may have started to learn a lesson; I may have even started to change, ever so slightly, although some of those I was with have since gone on to commit far more serious crimes. I often look back and think that I could have gone that same way, but now realise that once again my Guardian Angel was watching over me in that Derby train station.

I never told my parents about this latest arrest and thought that it would just go away. Then about three months later a policeman arrived at our house. By this time my dad had stopped drinking and we had moved to yet another house – a new start my parents called it.

It seemed like it was different. Dad now seemed more concerned and supportive. He accompanied me to court, back in Derby. I had the day off school. My dad liked to gamble on the horses and looking at the newspaper, I picked two horses to have a gamble on. 'Village Thief' and 'Head Master' were the two horses that I picked. The names seemed appropriate. Placing the bet before court and collecting my winnings afterwards, I won enough to pay my fine and I had what I regard as one of the greatest days out with my dad. He was there for me. He was supporting me. I could see that he did care for me, even if he did influence me to gamble at an early age!

A thread of goodness

My mum's influence was a complete contrast. Her father, my grandfather, who had died before I was born, was a Methodist Church Lay Reader. His contemporaries would have referred to him as a 'true man of God.' His influence on his daughter, my mother, was now influencing me.

A friend of mine recently told me that she had been praying about me writing this book. She told me that God had shown her a picture of a tapestry, with a silver thread running through it. The tapestry is my life and the thread is God's influence. The thread ran through the whole tapestry she told me. I have since then grown this picture in my mind. There are times when we look at the tapestry of our lives and perhaps wonder where God's hand is in it, but turn the tapestry over and there you will find the continuous thread. In my mind, I have also increased the value of this thread, of God's hand in my life. I now see this thread as a 'Golden' thread and I am so thankful that God has watched over me since the day I was born.

Looking back now, I can see that the thread of God's influence was in the Methodist Church Sunday School that I attended. Every Sunday I was there with my mum and two older brothers. Dad only ever went on special occasions such as the Christmas service or the annual Sunday school play (where I first started to perform). He was born and grew up in Ireland, an Irish Catholic who had married an English Protestant.

A child doesn't understand or even care to understand about such things. What they do understand is that those times when both parents are there watching and supporting you are very special times.

I was seven years old when one morning a new kid arrived at Sunday school. Mark had recently moved with his mum from Devon. His mum became friends with my mum and the two of us started a friendship that still exists today, decades later.

When Mark turned up at school and was walked into the class, with Miss Poulton teaching us, he was asked if he knew anyone. He pointed at me and spoke, "I know him, he goes to my church." I remember thinking at the time, 'Actually, it's MY CHURCH, I was there before you!' I now know that none of us own the Church, as we are the Church, the Body of Christ, God's Church. As children though, we have an interesting perception.

I previously mentioned that I was a member of the 1st Chalford Hill Boys Brigade. Most of the children in the village either went to Boys Brigade or Scouts. It seemed that if your parents went to church, you were more likely to attend Boys Brigade, as it was then compulsory to attend church if you wanted to attend Boys Brigade.

Every week we would gain points for our squads for the way that our uniforms looked. We were being inspected, just like the armed forces, but if you were not in church on the previous Sunday, you instantly lost your squad ten points! This would lead to peer pressure to attend church, to be the top squad of the year. Although I now disagree with this incentive method, which I don't think exists any more, the Gospel seeds that were sown were many. I now forever think back over scripture and remember that I first heard this at Sunday school or later in Bible Class.

Bible Class was a place where you didn't have to fight to prove yourself. The only fighting was in Bible searching quizzes. The friendships grew and everyone always looked forward to the annual Boys Brigade Display or church parades which involved a march with the band around the village. Then of course there was the annual camp. This was always at Charmouth in Dorset and always with the Girls Brigade. We were always joined by Bath and Romsey BB & GB and needless to say that at the end of every camp, I always had a new girlfriend.

Momentous occasions are what help to shape and develop us for a more positive future and it was in 1975 (the same year that I was arrested in Derby) when the Chalford Hill BB & GB had a chance to perform at the

Royal Albert Hall. The day left a lasting impression and I still love it when I have a chance to tell people that I performed there. They are usually surprised to hear it and even more surprised to hear that I was dancing. Every young person that took part formed a bond, as part of a team and we all keep those memories.

John and Brenda Evans ran the BB & GB and looking back, I now regard both of them as my positive role models, my mentors and much more.

Mum had struggled with Dad's alcoholism for around twenty years. The problem slowly and gradually increased. At times of high risk, Mum would seek sanctuary standing outside the house. She would wait until all of the lights had gone out, wait another half an hour or so, then slip back indoors. She now knew though that she could not do it alone any longer. Her love for Dad had not diminished and when you love someone, you want to do what you can to help them. Alcoholism is a disease and diseases can be healed. Mum had been praying for around twenty years for Dad to be set free from this addiction and for life to change.

Twenty years is a long time to carry the burden alone, but now Mum decided it was time to share this need for prayer. Shame had prevented her until now... Pain though had become too much and she asked Brenda Evans to pray. The Bible tells us that where two or three are gathered, there He (God) is in our midst. It also says that if two of you agree about something, it will be done by our Father in Heaven (Matthew 18:18-20). Within a year of Mum sharing her burden, Dad had stopped drinking.

I was fifteen years old when Dad walked into Stroud

Police Station. He was drunk, but had also realised that he had, 'reached the bottom of the Pit.'

He asked a young police constable for help and was told to go away. An older and wiser Sergeant stepped in and asked if Dad was serious. Having convinced him of his desperation, the Sergeant gave a drunken Irishman a bed (in a cell) for the night. The next morning breakfast was provided, followed by a sober conversation. That conversation led to Dad getting the help and support that he needed. The closest clinic for alcohol addiction was in Birmingham, but with help from a sponsor that he met through Alcoholics Anonymous (AA), Dad went there and change was almost instant.

The clinic played its part, but the main work and the reason for the dramatic change was answered prayer. God had won this battle. Dad had changed, but it would be years before I would recover from the lasting, impacting effects.

Chapter Three

Hanging On

I will often refer to 1975, the year that Dad stopped drinking, as the start of my childhood. It was the start of peace at home and the start of having a dad who wasn't scary.

However, the previous year of 1974 was probably the darkest of my teenage years. It was the year that my grandmother died. She had been so reliable, always there! From the early days of 'Sound of Music' until now, when I would cycle down to Stonehouse with my friend Mark. She would make us egg and chips which were amazing. Was her death the tipping point? Probably not, but it was a definite contributing factor.

I was fourteen years old... impressionable... confused... angry... seeking... looking for love... looking for answers... looking for a release! SEARCHING FOR HELP!

I searched in many places. In complete contrast to what I was being shown at church, I drifted into the occult. I was drawn to the dark power, the thought of being able to 'tap into' a spiritual realm.

At church, I was learning nice, interesting Bible stories, but they weren't enough. I needed power! With power, I may be able to take control of the things that I had no control over. Those things in my life that were out of control!

It started as a bit of fun. A derelict house was a perfect setting. No electricity, just one candle on a tea chest as a makeshift table. A single word on each side of the table was written on a piece of paper, 'Yes' on one side, and 'No' on the other. An upturned glass was placed in the centre and we all placed our hands on it. We asked questions but had no answers. There were at least four of us there and someone started to push the glass. We asked questions... We made up the answers. It was all a bit of fun (or so it seemed). We met regularly to conduct these 'pretend' séances. Nothing ever happened and someone always pushed the glass. We all had a laugh, pretended to be scared and saw it as a bit of fun.

Finding a book of Voodoo on the shelf of the school library was a real find (I hope it's not still there). The spells and incantations were a lure to someone like me. I started to cast spells and aimed the worst ones at teachers. I'm not sure if anything happened to my teachers, but my life continued to be one of fighting and bullying at school. I soon became bored of Voodoo, but little did I know that I had taken another step to expose myself to spiritual darkness. More about this shortly, but those who can remember cast your mind back to 1974.

It was the era of platform shoes and I had four-inch heels with three-inch platform soles. Needless to say, these were some of the biggest and most dangerous. By now I was even more into music and would help out as a 'Roadie' for a band. I would then dance to help to get the crowd going. Three times I fell off my platform shoes and three times I ended up in plaster. Now you are probably thinking that a plaster cast was a little excessive for a twisted ankle. The problem though was that, by the time I went to hospital, the injury had become more than just a twisted ankle. I suddenly realised that if I made the injury worse, the loving attention would be more. I had experienced this following my genuine accidents resulting in injury, but now I could control the level of injury and as a result, feel better.

I would sit on my bed at the end of an evening with a twisted ankle and wrench my foot as hard as I could. This progressed to hitting the swelling with a hammer. There was a release every time I hit. I wanted to be released and now I had found an exit for the pain in my life. By creating a more intense temporary pain, the other constant pain and fears seemed to subside. At last, I was in control of something. When I was bullying other people, I was taking control, but this behaviour always resulted in trouble for me. Now, I could channel my anger, my fears and anxieties on myself.

I carried on injuring myself in this way until I was about seventeen years old. Every small accidental injury was transformed into a more serious injury. No matter whether I had an arm in a sling or a leg in plaster, I was always able to tell a story of how it happened. However, it wasn't until I was thirty-seven years old that I realised what I had been doing was referred to as self-harm and I had done this. To me, I just knew it as FREEDOM!

I often wonder if I pursued the road of self-harm because of my involvement in occult practices. Quite possibly.

It was the summer of 1974 when I met up with some girls from BB and GB summer camp. They lived in a house with an attic room and it seemed the perfect setting for another 'pretend séance.' By now I was well-practised and familiar with the process and knew it would be fun. I also knew that it would be a little exciting for the two girls who had never done it before. How wrong I was.

The room was cluttered with old furniture. Dust lay on every surface. It looked spooky. I sat opposite a wardrobe with a full-length mirror. The girls sat on either side. The usual items were laid out on the table. I was already thinking, 'This situation shouldn't be any different to the previous times. I'll just push the glass and frighten the girls a little, it'll be fun.' At least that's what I thought.

I now believe that each of the previous times and the combination of Voodoo had lowered my resistance and made me vulnerable. This time was different. Almost immediately after asking the first question, "Is there anyone there?" an apparition of an old lady, all grey looking, appeared in the mirror opposite me. I panicked, I freaked out, wanting to hide. This was suddenly scary, now it was real! The figure disappeared almost as quickly as it had appeared, but where had it gone? It would be another fourteen years before I would find out the answer to that. I decided that was the last time I would touch anything to do with the occult. However, the horoscope remained a daily, innocent topping up. I didn't understand or realise that this too is linked to the darkness of the occult.

More silly games

My friendship with Mark had by now grown over seven years. His mum had told my mum once that they had called him 'Mark' because it couldn't be shortened. Of course, we all saw this as a challenge and thought, 'No it can't be shortened, but it can be changed.' The Methodist hymn book had a composer of hymns in it called Percy Dreamer. Mark did seem to be a bit of a 'Dreamer' so we decided to call him 'Percy.'

During the long boring summer holidays of 1974, we borrowed our mother's twelve-inch carving knives and headed to the playing field. The game was 'Chicken,' throwing the knife at your opponent to see how close you could get without hitting him. This soon progressed to cutting some hazel branches and fashioning a bow each. A short piece of string completed the weapon, whilst the thinner, straight hazel growing at the bottom of the tree made perfect arrows. Finally, sharpening the arrow tips with the knives, we were ready to do battle.

I remember the game took on a Robin of Sherwood type of theme. Percy was the Sheriff of Nottingham and I was Robin Hood. Fantasy was taking over. The role-play became real. Percy ran to the sanctuary of the tall slide. There were fewer health and safety restrictions then and the cage at the top of the steps was some twenty feet in the air.

"You'll never get me up here," shouted Percy from his fantasy castle.

Waiting for my moment and taking my aim, I didn't hesitate or even think, instincts took over and I released the arrow. The sharpened point found the soft penetrable target of the cheek. The arrow was embedded, protruding from Percy's face. The game was over, Robin Hood had won again as he always does.

Percy just pulled the arrow out, went home and put a plaster on the wound. He probably told a story to his mum that he had cut himself shaving. We had all started shaving at the age of 14 and none of us were very good at it.

This had been a dangerous game. I could have hit his eye. It could have killed him.

Interestingly years later, when I met up with Mark after being out of touch for years, he could not even remember the incident. What was even more interesting was that my friend had now become the Reverend Mark, a church minister. The most incredible thing though was the fact that there was no visible scar.

Pushed to the edge

By the autumn of '74, I had discovered Minchinhampton Youth Club. A group of us would catch the bus from Chalford Hill down to Brimscombe, and then catch another back up the hill on the other side of the valley to what had become known as the best youth club to hang out at. Disco nights would see over 200 young people and the atmosphere was incredible.

Under the lights of the disco and with a bit of alcohol, every girl looked attractive. At the end of the evening, arrangements would be made to meet up again with the girl that you had met on the following Sunday afternoon. This was the pattern of trying to find the love that seemed to be missing in my life.

Often, I would meet girls on a Sunday afternoon and in the reality of daytime with a sober mind I would realise that it was a mistake. That was however until one particular girl who seemed different. She seemed special. Was she what I was looking for? I had been seeing her for about six weeks. This was the longest I had ever stayed with one girlfriend; was this love?

I had even started walking the long trek from Chalford Hill to Minchinhampton, a distance of about two and a half miles each way down into the valley and back up the other side. I did the journey about three or four times each week, but she seemed worth it.

Previously I had broken off with many girlfriends and some had broken off with me. The decision had been ours and I was okay with that. As I mentioned earlier, I am a great believer in allowing people choices and letting them make their own informed, educated decisions. Now, long before the head teacher decided that I was not good enough for his school, someone else was about to make a decision that would make a greater impact, more than anything else had done before now.

We were now in the dark evenings of October 1974 and I arrived at my girlfriend's house, but something immediately felt different. She wouldn't let me in. She told me that her dad had found out who she was going out with. Her dad knew my dad and he had made the decision... I wasn't good enough for his daughter.

The rejection... the hurt... the pain... the confusion...the embarrassment... the hate... the tears... the anger... the overwhelming surge of emotions... they all hit with catastrophic impact. I was already beating myself up with a hammer. The hospital had become my sanctuary, the place where I knew help could be found.

This time though, the pain was at a new level, the feeling of being out of control was overpowering, and the desire to live left me in an instant. I turned away from the doorstep and within seconds I had made my plan. The train ran through the valley every hour. I would be down there and dead within two hours. Everything was happening so fast. Decision made; I was back in control. I would make the ultimate and final decision in my life. Nothing could stop me. Rage had taken over again, only this time it was inward. This would be the end. Rain and tears mixed on my cheeks. On the wet dark October night, no one was around to see me. No one would care. Although that Golden Thread, the hand of God is still in our lives, even when we can't see or feel it.

I had made my plans and walked two hundred metres from the doorstep where it seemed life had already ended. The light from the red phone box gave an attractive glow. I was drawn to that light shining in the darkness, on that cold wet October night. A sign next to the phone read, 'Suicide, Lonely, Despair? Contact the Samaritans.' The number was free to dial. I had nothing to lose.

I talked to someone who called themselves Peter. I can't remember what was said, I just talked and he listened. He made me feel valued. The desire to live returned almost as quickly as it had left. I left the phone box where I had found a new hope and walked past the train line, home to the warmth of my bed.

I am alive today because of the Samaritans. I am alive because someone took the time to listen. It didn't take long, but that phone call saved my life.

I sum up this chapter simply by saying that I now realise that suicide is a 'permanent end to a temporary problem.' My dad and his addiction were the root of my problem, but less than a year after the call to the Samaritans, my dad had stopped drinking.

Later on in life I would look back at this incident and picture it as me standing on the edge of a cliff. In my imaginary picture, there is a fence. That fence is there to protect. I had been driven beyond the fence to the edge of oblivion but then came back. However, I would also find myself back at the edge of that imaginary cliff later on in life.

Chapter Four

Love is a Roller-Coaster

Another friend that I grew up with was Tomo. I can recall the time that I had gone to his house straight from school. I was about eight years old. It hadn't occurred to me that I should tell my parents. I can't remember the exact time that I arrived back home, but I do remember the rage of my dad. His patience had expired and grabbing me by the ear, he dragged me up the stairs, threw me on the bed and gave me several whacks with his leather belt. This whole scenario did teach me how important it is to tell your parents where you are, but I also learnt more about temper, aggression and the effectiveness of weapons.

I was now 15 years old and I had become close friends with Percy and Tomo. This may have been partly because Percy's birthday was exactly a week after mine and Tomo's was a week later. I was the oldest of the trio.

1976 was the year when my life would start to change. My dad had already stopped drinking, but now Percy and Tomo arrived with an exciting discovery. They had travelled to Brownshill, the next village and met some girls.

"Do you fancy coming over to Brownshill?"
"What for?"
"Girls, three of them and there's only two of us. We need a third person, so one isn't left out."

With everything to gain and nothing to lose, we walked the nearly mile-long journey. Brownshill bus shelter was the agreed rendezvous point and we arrived first. Shortly afterwards the girls arrived. I never was quite sure who Tomo and Percy had identified as 'theirs' or 'the one that I fancy,' I didn't ask.

I rapidly assessed the choices, number one? No. Number two? I don't think so and number three? YES. Little did I realise how important that choice would turn out to be. The decision was so quick that I could have just been selecting my favourite chocolate bar out of a choice of three.

It is said that beauty is in the eye of the beholder and it was as if my mind said, 'Behold this beauty.'

The other two seemed slightly disgruntled, although by the end of the afternoon, we were three couples and I had no doubt, I was certain, I had made the right choice.

I was nearly sixteen years old and Heather was only twelve. Her friends all told her that she was crazy to associate with me. My reputation was not a good one. I had a history of violence but that, I am glad to say, did not deter her.

We quickly found out that we had so much in common, yet we were also so different.

The feelings that I was now feeling were all new to me. I had never felt like this in the presence of any other girl. Something happened deep inside of me every time I met her. I began to wonder, 'Is this what love is?' Having never really loved and struggling to recognise if I had ever been loved, the feeling was new, it was alien, but it felt good.

With so many insecurities though, could anything last? A tumbleweed never puts down any roots and I had been tumbling through life, never entirely seeing the good things that life had to offer.

I passed my 16th birthday and I had been with Heather for six weeks. This was my longest relationship ever with a girl, but temptations were looming. I was now able to access the money that my grandmother had left me when she died and I decided to buy a moped. With a faster form of transport came a new-found freedom and it wasn't long before doubt crept in... 'Do you really love her?' Temptation won the battle and at the start of the summer of '76, we went our separate ways.

It took less than a month for me to realise what an idiot I had been, what I had thrown away, but it was too late. Temptation had won the first battle and now pride was continuing the fight. That fight would continue throughout the summer and beyond, nearly six months would pass before we would reunite. That summer would be long and crazy.

With no job and no school to attend, the summer became one long alcohol-fuelled party. Some older friends were left at home whilst their parents went away on holiday and the house parties started.

First Percy's mum went away for a couple of weeks and we had the freedom to do what we wanted. Each night we would drink several cans of cheap beer and stack the empties in a triangle against the wall. Before long the triangle touched the ceiling and covered half of the wall. That was a lot of cans, especially for a bunch of sixteen-year-olds. Off licences and pub landlords seemed to ignore the law and we were served in any pub that we walked into. If we didn't have a house to go to, we would just hang out each evening in a local pub beer garden, drinking and laughing.

One of the craziest parties during this time saw me stay at Nathan's house for the best part of the week. At the height of the party at the weekend, the house was packed. Nathan didn't know half of the partygoers.

People were beginning to act more foolishly. Inhibitions had flown away and dares were being dished out. They started small and innocent such as "I dare you to drink this." It was usually a mixture of everything going. Gradually the dares became bigger, riskier and more illegal until someone said, "I dare you to drive Nathan's dad's van!" This was the last dare of the night.

Before anyone knew what was going on, someone had found the keys and had now stormed out of the driveway. Nathan panicked... we all panicked! "Who had taken the van?" No one knew him.

Tom grabbed his crash helmet and jumping onto his 250cc Kawasaki, headed off hastily in pursuit. People were shouting at him, escalating the confusion as he approached the fork in the road at the small green. At the last moment, he realised that the onlookers were telling him that he was going the wrong way. The change of direction came too late and hitting the kerb, Tom was thrown from the roaring motorcycle.

The danger and severity of the situation was increasing rapidly and out of control. Alcohol was the reason for the accident, in which Tom escaped unharmed, but the crowd who were also fuelled by alcohol immediately blamed the unknown joy rider of the van.

It was less than five minutes before the van suddenly returned undamaged and the driver just came out of it smiling. His smug look was saying, 'There you are everyone, I did it,' but it disappeared in an instant.

The alcohol-fuelled crowd had already passed the sentence and the joy rider was guilty, he had crossed the line. The sentence it seemed, had also been decided as someone shouted, "Hang him;" a rope appeared as if from nowhere.

The frightening reality of what was now an incident way out of control was sobering. Something prompted me that what was about to happen needed to stop. Yes, this unknown person had done wrong, but if the roller-coaster ride of events didn't stop, he could die.

God's Golden Thread that is running through my life suddenly surfaced again, as I was the first to speak out against what was in progress. Nathan agreed with me that the prisoner should be released.

The party crowd quickly dispersed but the party continued for a few more days with just a handful of Nathan's friends.

Seek and you shall find
(Matthew 7:7)

The Bible tells us that if we have lost something, we should go out and find it. This next section is all about trying to retrieve the most valuable thing that I had ever thrown away... my relationship with Heather.

Every so often Percy and I would take a ride over to Brownshill on our mopeds. At times when my moped wasn't working, I would ride on the back of Percy's moped illegally. Riding up into the playing field, we would terrorise the younger children. All of the time, I would be looking out for Heather. Where was she? What was she doing? Who was she with?

The summer came to an end and with it some of the craziness. As I started my apprenticeship, I settled down to train as an engineer... my first job. I had struggled to learn in school... too many other issues to fill my mind, but now I was learning. Life at home was happier... I was happier... my thinking was changing... perhaps I was growing up?

It had been some five or six months and my mind had changed, but I had never stopped thinking about Heather. I decided to track her down on a Saturday afternoon at the end of October or November. She seemed pleased to see me and told me that I could go with her later that evening as she had made arrangements to go babysitting. What she had forgotten to tell me was that she was now going out with an older lad. To make matters worse, our paths had crossed when we were younger. We had fought and I had suffered from his beating.

Any cares and concerns soon disappeared, as I was now with Heather. We soon settled into the cosy warmth of the small cottage with the wood-burning stove casting a romantic glow around the room.

The knock at the door startled us and Heather went to see who it was. I could hear Ian demanding to come in. Heather was telling him to go away. I recognised his voice as I listened from behind the door. I waited less than a minute, but it seemed like hours. I had to fight for the girl who I hadn't stopped thinking about for months. Ian was much bigger than me though and had already proven that he could beat me in a fight. The odds were stacked against me. In my mind, I had learnt that weapons were made to improve the odds.

I approached the door where the argument was taking place. Making sure that Ian could see the knife, I simply said, "She's with me, now go away!" He responded as I had hoped I am glad to say, but it could have been a completely different story and what did Heather think? What was she taking on? Would she calm the anger of the beast within?

So much had happened in the months that we had been apart, but the most important thing was that I had realised that I didn't want to lose this girl. Now in 2015, thirty-seven years later, I am still with her, married and even more in love with her. I am so glad that I went in search of that which I had lost!

Chapter Five

Leaving School

The shock of being told that I was no longer welcome at Marling school had motivated me, strangely. I remember being in an interview with a careers adviser.

“What do you like doing?” came the one probing question.
“Messing around with engines,” was my short answer. I didn’t think about it, it just came out. I had been playing around with motorbikes for at least four years.
“Engines? Then you would be good as an engineer!”

Looking back, I now consider this as bad guidance. I was misled and not given any choices. I think that I wanted to be a mechanic, but I was given a list of different engineering companies to apply to. There were thirteen in total and I wrote to all of them. Surprisingly twelve of them offered me an apprenticeship and I chose the closest one to home. Benson’s International was also where my mum and dad both now worked, but it was where I would be ‘imprisoned’ for the next four years.

I never really enjoyed the engineering industry, but what it did teach me was attention to detail and the importance of accuracy. I carried those skills on in all areas of my life and I always tell people that no experience is ever wasted!

In the same way that I would fall off of my platform shoes and then enhance my injuries, I would now do the same at work. A slip of a spanner would result in a bruised and swollen knuckle. The accident would be immediately followed by a trip to the toilet. The spanner would be in my pocket and several more whacks with that spanner would ensure that I had an injury that was serious enough for me to visit the First Aider, often then to be sent once again to the hospital. Mum would joke about how I was accident-prone and my hospital file was getting bigger all of the time, but every injury had a legitimate reason, an excuse; it had been an accident.

My apprenticeship involved attending Stroud College and surprisingly, I never had one physical fight whilst I was there. The inward aggression towards myself though continued, with regular visits to the hospital with my self-inflicted painful wounds. I was in control of this; I controlled the pain, unlike the deeper emotional scars that had compounded over the years of childhood. My dad had stopped drinking and was now what I later learnt in life was referred to as a recovering addict, but I was also on a road to recovery.

It has been said that 'Behind every great man, there has to be a great woman.' Now looking back, I believe that some of what I have achieved could be regarded as 'great,' but I could not have done anything by myself.

My strong belief in giving people choices was given another foundation stone on an occasion when Heather said to me, "I don't like you smoking, it stinks, in fact I hate it!"

Although she didn't say it, to me it sounded as if she was saying, "It's your choice, smoking or me." So, at the age of seventeen years old, I quit smoking. I had tried to stop on so many occasions, but never before had such an incentive. Interestingly, it was around the same time that I stopped harming myself. I now believe that smoking is just another form of self-harm and that by stopping the one, the other left me as well. The choice to stop smoking empowered me to stop purposely putting myself in the hospital. One small choice had impacted other areas of my life...but I also believe the power of God's Golden Thread was also influencing my life again.

Committing to more

We all need to feel security in life and by the time I was twenty years old, I had known Heather for nearly five years. My apprenticeship was ending and my parents had been offered redundancy payments at work. They were leaving Bensons and planning to start life afresh. Their plans were tempting me away from the 'prison-like' factory. Their decision was a big step though. With their redundancy payment, they wanted to make a new start in Cornwall. They planned to buy a small farm, but where would that leave me? Where would it leave Heather?

It was decision time again...

Choice number one – I stay here and try to find somewhere to live, but I couldn't afford that, especially if I was escaping Benson's 'Prison.'

Choice number two – we just split up and go our separate ways. We didn't even consider that... we had been together for so long and were already engaged.

Choice number three – Heather comes to Cornwall and we all live on the farm. We both liked this choice, but it was a long way, a big step. It meant Heather leaving her job and family, but how much security would she have? I had demonstrated my commitment, and my loyalty and gave her the security that she needed. She was only seventeen years old and I was twenty, yet we both instinctively knew that we should be married.

We married with just over three months to plan for it. I wore an old suit with a shirt that didn't fit and a pair of shoes that my brother had thrown in the bin. Heather's mum made her dress and she looked beautiful. We married on 17th January 1981 and four days later were on our way to Cornwall.

People will often say that getting married, moving house and buying a car are some of the most stressful things in life. I made all three of these in one week, as I also bought Chris's car from him.

We made so many big decisions in such a short space of time, yet there was no stress. It all felt perfect.

Later in life, I would hear this decision-making and step-taking process as, 'Taking a step of faith.' This is something that I have now done so many times. It is now an intrinsic part of my makeup and the whole process of getting married had helped to build this in me. Looking back, it is easy to see where God had his hand on us both in our decision-making. We didn't even know him then, but he was guiding us, with his continuing Golden Thread.

Our first home was a mobile home on the farm. It was like being on holiday and without any work, it really was a holiday or even a honeymoon.

We lived in Cornwall for exactly a year and in that time, I had six weeks of employment in a factory. I hated it, but it was what I knew. I also ran a disco with my brother Mike. We had brought our mobile disco down with us to Cornwall, having been running this previously in Gloucestershire. Before the disco and being a DJ, we had been in various bands, but there were always too many arguments. I had been the drummer but the drums had been sold to buy disco equipment. This was now helping to bring in a little extra income, but it was never enough.

A visit back to Stroud for the weekend made us realise what we had given up. We didn't have to think about it for long, as we stood on Rodborough Common, we both said, "Isn't this view beautiful? Let's move back!"

We were amazed to find out that there was a grant available for skilled engineers who wanted to move to Gloucestershire. The county had a shortage and this was a government initiative to boost the labour force. It didn't matter that I had only left a year ago and I quickly found myself working in the factory where my mum and dad had met. RHP Ltd. was not just another factory, it was yet another 'prison.'

We used the £1,000 grant for a deposit on our first house and following my parents' footsteps, we bought a house that was unfit for human habitation. This was the start of my building career and I started to fall in love with this new trade.

I would start my day with work in the factory at 7.00am until 4.00pm and then go straight to my night job of house renovation. What I hadn't learnt from watching my dad, I learnt from reading books. My working day would end around 10.00pm. Fifteen hours of work followed by seven hours of sleep.

We lived with Heather's stepdad, Roger, where she had grown up in Brownshill. That was until Roger decided to move to Stroud and we moved with him. Our house was being completely gutted and we were technically homeless but Roger gave us a roof over our heads, whilst we kept him company and cooked for him.

We moved into our new home in September 1982, making it the third time that we had moved house in less than a year. At last, we had security; our own house, with good money coming in, but how long would it last?

Two months later I was called into the office at work. I was told that my job was being made redundant and that I was no longer needed. I had only been there for ten months, but the sum of money that they gave me to be rid of me was enough to set myself up in business. I could now break out of this prison and do something that I now loved doing. I could become a builder. As my foreman gave me the news, he looked confused. He had expected me to be disappointed, but instead, I was overjoyed. I was FREE!

My redundancy money was used to buy equipment and at the start of November 1982, I was a builder, self-employed and no longer with the security of regular income. Was this another step of faith? Was this another twist of the Golden Thread? I would now have less than a year before God's hand would reach out and seriously touch my life, but I still wouldn't recognise him!

I was self-employed when Heather told me that she was pregnant. We had been trying for this since getting married and even though work wasn't always secure, plus we would now have another mouth to feed, we were once again overjoyed. Life couldn't get any better! I had my own house, my own business and now I was going to be a dad. I had made it. What more could anyone want? Everything was perfect.

Chapter Six

A wake-up call

I was twenty-two years old, my own boss and first child on the way. There were some weeks when work had been short and not much money coming in, but that would give me the freedom to do whatever I wanted to do. We always had enough to get by, even though on some weeks we did only just get by.

Now as the summer approached, the work was increasing. I was glad to be given a job on the busy London Road running through Thrupp. A three-storey house was in great need of some tender loving care. Heather's auntie had recently moved in and the first job on the list was the dormer windows, almost thirty feet above the ground. The paintwork had almost completely peeled off, over at least ten years of neglect and deterioration due to weather. This was my opportunity to restore them and for them to stand out as the best on the terrace. This one job could lead to me doing the whole row. This was my lucky break; the moment had come.

The tower scaffolding was a very cheap, thin tube construction. It didn't have any adjustable feet, but the hire company assured me that it would be fine at a height of thirty feet.

With no adjustable feet and uneven ground, I needed to place some blocks flat on the ground and level up the base with appropriately sized pieces of wood.

The height didn't bother me I had been on scaffolding when I was just a child. Now I was king of my own castle, I was on top of the world.

The paintwork scraped off easily and I moved on to the process of sanding. I knew that a good paint finish required good preparation; the attention to detail was in me from my engineering apprenticeship. My mind was now focused on the detail of the work, the job in hand, so much so that other details were being missed.

The scaffolding was wobbling! If you have ever laid a rope or a hosepipe on the ground and lifted one end up and down fast, you will have seen the movement transferred along it until it reaches the other end. My physics teacher probably gave this process a name. Now, as the energy of movement was transferring through the feeble tower, the movement at the top was being mirrored at the bottom. Every small fraction of swaying on my small platform resulted in the base being gradually walked off the makeshift packing.

That moment, when the scaffolding toppled, was another moment when it seemed that time had stopped. I had experienced it briefly in the allotments with a brick in my hand, ready to smash into my brother's head. This time, at the start of the moment in time, a thought hit me. I am going to die! I had heard about people seeing their lives flash before their eyes, now I was experiencing it. I pictured Heather, pregnant, and imagined a child that I would never see. I pictured my parents, both still alive and I was about to die before them. I pictured my house and pictured Heather again. The pictures do just flash by. From the thought of, 'I am going to die,' flash, flash, flash and at the end of the flashes another thought, 'I want to live.'

I remember my hand reaching out to the sky. Everything seemed to be happening in slow motion.

FLASH....... FLASH........ I grabbed the plastic guttering... FLASH.... but that had given way from my weight. Why did everything seem so slow... FLASH......?

By now the feeble frame of the tower scaffolding had completely buckled. A twisted hazardous mess of deadly steel, 30 feet below and my body was going to be reunited with it any second.... any second.... time seemed slow. My hand was reaching out to the sky. There was nothing to grab hold of, although it felt as if something had hold of me. Slowly, slowly I fell.

I landed and my back slumped across one of the steel tubes. Slightly winded, slightly dazed, I looked back up amazed. I was alive!

A pot of paint had landed in the busy road and a passing motorist had now stopped. He picked up the paint and cleared the damaged scaffolding. I watched in a daze, still in disbelief at what had just happened. The 'Good Samaritan', now helped me into his car, turned it around and drove me a couple of miles to Stroud Hospital. Here I was again, only this time it was a genuine accident and I didn't like it.

The motorist left me in safe hands. I never did find out who he was, was he an angel? I don't think so, but I do now believe that my 'Guardian Angel' lowered me to safety. Yes, I was hurt, but nothing too serious. This I now believe was my first encounter with an angel, but it wouldn't be the last.

On admission to the hospital, the staff took my clothes and dressed me in an open-back gown. What could they see that I couldn't? I felt fine and after a few hours, I told them that I wanted to go home. This visit to the hospital was out of my control and I didn't like it. I signed myself out. I must have looked so stubborn and so ungrateful for their help, but I didn't need it, I didn't ask for it and all that I wanted was to be at home.

The next day I decided to take the day off work and think about what had happened. The lawn needed cutting and the sun was shining. As usual, I stripped to the waist and took to the task in hand forgetting about the previous day.

It wasn't long before my neighbour leaned over the fence and asked if I was OK. "I'm fine," I told him, "Why do you ask?" He just pointed at my back and said, "You're all black." I went inside and looked in the mirror. Sure enough, my back was as black as ink, yet I was in no pain. I could have and probably should have broken my back, but instead, all I had was one huge black mass that covered my whole back.

Fear creeps in

Never wanting to allow a task to beat me, I went back to the dormer windows, but this time I contracted a professional scaffolding company. I figured that I had learnt the hard way on this job and now the profit had gone. I did finish the job but failed to make any money. To make matters worse, no more work came in. Perhaps the news of my fall had put people off using me.

A while later, my brother-in-law, Eric, asked me to help him with some work on his roof. He had recently bought his house and as I climbed up onto the roof ladder, to re-bed the ridge tiles, I started to shake.

Panic and fear came into my mind, rapidly taking over my thoughts. Flashbacks, the mind plays tricks, with memories of the fall that I had recently taken. I could barely do the work and Eric could see it. Heather was pregnant and I was going to be a dad in just a few months. Eric reminded me of this.

"You shouldn't be doing this kind of work now with a kid on the way; you need to keep your feet on the ground."

I didn't argue with him, fear had a grip on me. As I returned to the solid concrete path below, the fear left me and calmness returned. It was a little like sea sickness. When you are out at sea and you are ill, you just want it to end. Then when the boat returns to shore and you set feet on solid ground, all of the motion sickness leaves and normality returns.

I talked to Heather about the lack of work and consequently the shortage of money. I never did tell her about the fear that gripped me on Eric's roof.

Things became so bad that we didn't have any money to put food on the table. If this happened today, we would be able to receive charitable hand-outs from organisations like Food Bank, but there was nothing like that We had to work this problem out for ourselves. I can remember saying, "If we can't put food on the table, what's the point in having a table?"

We decided to sell the table and the money fed us for over two weeks, but what about when it would run out? There was no other option, I would have to go back to what I was qualified to do; I would have to go back to engineering.

I wasn't keen to return to the prison of the factory, but I knew it had to be done. Any job was better than no job at all. My building career had come to an abrupt ending. I had failed in business. I felt REJECTED!

I always could sell and this time, reaching for the telephone, I tried to sell myself. I didn't stop. I called one number after another. I was determined; soon there would be another mouth to feed. I know that motivation and determination will always pay off and by the end of the day I was offered a job. I had lost count of the number of phone calls I had made, but I had succeeded. I would now have a steady income. We would be able to pay the bills and put food on the table. We would have to buy a table again at some point though.

It has been said that we learn from our experiences and especially our mistakes. This would not be the last time though, that lack of finance would become my enemy.

Chapter Seven

New Beginnings

Springfield Engineering seemed different. This was not a big firm, but they were growing. They had allowed me to become part of that growth. There was a great atmosphere and friendships within the workforce. The relationships were fun and we enjoyed each other's company. Each day we would laugh together, but it was still engineering. Locked up! I missed my freedom.

It was November 1983 and our son Chris was born. Suddenly, becoming a dad made me think a little about the miracle of creation. Questions started to come to mind such as, 'What is life all about? Why are we all here? Where does God fit into the equation?' Becoming a parent had thrown a switch in my mind. The thoughts and the questions were looking for answers, but I didn't know where to look for them.

With a regular income and a family, we decided that we should move to a bigger house, but finding the right house proved to be harder than we had imagined. We went for one house after another, only to lose out to someone else. The house that we eventually moved to was our fourth choice. It almost felt as if we were led there, guided by some unseen force. Interestingly, in 2015, we had moved four more times since and each time we were guided by that same unseen force. Nowadays that force has a name, but right then we didn't recognise Him.

The house was a more modern design. There wasn't much room to improve it. We weren't going to climb many steps up the ladder with this one. Why were we here?

The neighbours were very friendly on one side. They introduced themselves as Kim and Paula Brown. They were about the same age as us and had a son about the same age as our son Chris. Kim had also been a DJ and had a similar record collection to mine, all labelled and indexed in a manner that any song could be found within seconds. This was going to be an inevitable friendship.

It was a few months later that a lady living a few doors up the hill, stopped me in the street and commented, "You live next to Kim and Paula Brown, don't you?"

She seemed friendly enough so I answered, "Yes, do you know them?" I've always liked answering a question with a question, it's the art of conversation.

"Yes, I know them," she answered, "but they're a bit weird!"

"What do you mean, 'weird'?" The tone of the conversation was changing. She seemed to be on the attack, wanting to find fault in our 'apparently' perfect neighbours. "Weird? In what way are they weird?" I asked again, almost in defence.

"They call themselves 'Born Again Christians'!"

The conversation ended and I can remember walking home and thinking, "Is that really weird or is it really interesting?"

Kim and Paula were very interesting and we would watch them from a bedroom window, particularly on a Sunday morning. At times they would leave long before 10.00am and often not return until mid-afternoon. What sort of church were they going to? We were inquisitive, intrigued, more questions... where were the answers?

*****

Having moved and been given a new mortgage, it seemed a perfect time to consider another career move. I missed the freedom of being my own boss, but didn't want to return to building work.

An advertisement in the local newspaper caught my eye. It was intriguing in the sense that it didn't at all say what the job was. I expected that it was some form of sales work. It said that I could earn loads of money, no experience was needed and all training would be provided. It talked about fast-track promotion and other temptations. I made a phone call and was offered an interview almost immediately.

The office was a new environment for me. The old wedding suit came out for the first time in three years. The interviewer was only a few years older than me. It was September 1984 and I was offered the job as a 'Financial Consultant,' which was just a fancy title for Life Insurance Sales Person.

I would be in this role for the next eighteen months and would do exactly as the advertisement had said. I would become fast-tracked to become a manager with my own sales team. I would become a top salesperson and find myself listed in the top ten sales consultants for the company. I would rise high, only to be dropped, but before the drop, I would interview someone for a job. That interview and that 'person' would change the course of my life.

Now, for eighteen months, I immersed myself in my new career. Every day was spent in the office in Bristol making appointments and most evenings would be out visiting those appointments. I would leave the house around 7.30am and work until at least 9.00pm. The pay was commission-based, which translated in my mind as effort-related. If I didn't earn enough in one month, I would aim to bounce back the next month and make up for it.

Our second child was born during this working period, in December 1985. Ellie was a beautiful-looking baby, but after her birth, I had hardly stopped to notice. I now always look back and feel that I missed most of the first year of her life. Work had taken over and if I stopped for too long, the money would also stop. Here we were again with financial insecurities, no regular income, the only way to increase our security it seemed, was to work harder and harder.

I did find time to relax at weekends and we would often find ourselves chatting to Kim and Paula next door. Eventually, we were invited round to their house for a meal. Lasagne and salad were dished up, followed by a dessert that I can't remember (probably Lemon Meringue). At the end of the meal, we sat drinking coffee and chatting. Until now, we had never talked to Kim and Paula about what the lady up the road had told me. Likewise, they had never pushed their beliefs onto us. Now as we sat relaxed, I asked a question. At the time it must have seemed as if it had come from nowhere. However, later we realised that my question was an answer to prayer. Kim and Paula had been praying for us since the day that we had moved in.

Now I asked the question, "I'm interested in

something," I started tentatively. I didn't want to upset them, but I was puzzled. "We just ate a meal and neither of you said Grace beforehand, yet we have been told that you are something called 'Born Again Christians'?"

They both explained that they didn't want to offend us, so had both just prayed in their heads. That one question led to question after question. The conversation lasted about three hours, ending in the early hours of the morning. This couple had something special. The details of the conversation have long been forgotten, but the feeling of hearing the truth of the Gospel was exciting. This pair were talking about things that I had heard at Boys Brigade and Bible Class, but this time it was more than just a story. It was real and it was alive in them.

By March 1986 we had had numerous conversations with Kim and Paula. Heather had also had long daytime chats with Paula alone. Her questions were being answered. I, however, was spending more time at work and building my team. This meant that Kim did not have the opportunity to speak to me individually. If God was going to get inside my head, he would have to use someone else, some other method.

I was using a two-stage recruitment process. Stage one was to fill a conference room in a local hotel with possible candidates. I gave them a slide show and a sales pitch. At least 50% of those who came to my presentation requested an interview to come and work for me.

Peter hadn't attended any of my presentations. He just phoned me up and arranged to come into the office for an interview. He told me that he was already selling life insurance, but was looking for a new team to join. On the phone he certainly could sell himself, so we met.

As Peter had told me that he was already in the industry, I asked him the typical question that would always be asked, "How's business?" I wasn't prepared for the answer.

"Great! In fact, it's never been better, since I found The Lord!"

The rest of the interview was a conversation about what Jesus had done for him. He explained that Jesus was just one step away, that he had taken that step and that his life had changed instantly. I told him about my neighbours and the reaction was as if he already knew. He continued to tell me more and more that I didn't know, that I hadn't realised.

I was so impressed with him that I gave him a job. "You can start next week," I told him, but that was the last I saw of him.

At the start of the following week, the whole team were told to clear their desks. The Government had brought in new legislation, and new rules that stated our direct sales force could no longer function legally. We were all out of work.

Peter though, had planted more seeds in me. Within a few weeks, those seeds would grow. I would have my eyes and heart opened to God's forgiving grace, love and mercy. Later I would look for Peter. I would try to track him down, but could not find his telephone number in my diary. I would contact others from the office to ask them if they remembered him, but none of them had seen him! I now believe that this was yet another encounter with an angel. Kim and Paula had given me a lot of answers, but I was blind. God sent Peter to break down the remaining barriers and I listened.

It's interesting that the Samaritan helpline worker who I had phoned, all of those years ago, on that dark wet night when I was fifteen years old had also called himself Peter!

Chapter Eight

Turning Point

Conversations with Kim and Paula were now becoming more frequent. Suddenly I had more time on hand. Unemployment also raised the question of, "What next?"

I was offered jobs with various companies, asking me to go to them and sell insurance products, but it was time for a change.

Could I go back to the building trade? I decided that the answer to that question would only be known if I just tried it. To try to run my own building business seemed just too risky. I would start by going on a short college course at the Gloucester Skill Centre, the 'Work Related Skills Assessment Course – WRSAC'. This was a course that looked at a whole range of skills and trades, but I was only interested in one trade, bricklaying.

I spent six weeks teaching myself, as it seemed that I knew more than the tutor. As I did this, my confidence grew. My work was different, creative and imaginative. Before long the students on the bricklaying course were coming to look at my work. They were impressed, with some even saying that they couldn't do what I was doing. I took photographs of everything that I built and this became a portfolio that I could use to help me find work. I still strongly believe in the power of a good portfolio and have seen it open many a door for young people who are trying to find work. Whilst on this training programme I went on a crash diet and lost over two stone very quickly (wouldn't recommend this now). I was almost fasting and now understand how our spirits are stronger when we are physically weaker (Matthew 26:40-43).

Even more time was being spent talking to Kim and Paula. I remember attending a local church, as we wanted to have Ellie christened. Chris had been done, so why not? It was tradition. The 'done' thing.

The church minister explained that we may want to consider a 'dedication' rather than a christening. It sounded less formal and I suppose less religious. It sounded better, so we agreed.

We didn't want to just turn up out of the blue one Sunday, with people wondering who we were, so we started to attend the church every week. Very slowly we started to talk to people as they all seemed friendly and welcoming, at least on the surface. We had been turning up every Sunday for about four weeks, Ellie's dedication was booked for two weeks, but at this service, we left feeling very upset. It was announced that there was going to be a meeting in the following week, we couldn't believe our ears. The meeting was to discuss the increasing number of people who were using the church, for things such as weddings, funerals, christenings and of course dedications. There was concern over the fact that these people were not committed to the church. I often think about that church and how it communicates to the world now.

I went home and had a moan at Kim. It was more than a moan, I was angry! We would have likely stayed attending this church, but this judgemental, petty attitude drove us away. We never went back after the dedication service.

Kim described what I was feeling as, 'Holy Anger.' He explained that Jesus had become angry with the hypocrites and of what had become of 'His Father's House.' His anger had resulted in tables being turned over. Had I thought of it, I may even have turned over a few tables. That Holy Anger can still affect me today. Another seed had been sown or was it another stitch of the Golden Thread being sewn?

Having finished my short training course, I considered what the next rung of the ladder should be. 'The lowest level on any building site is the labourer,' I thought to myself, 'so that is where I should start.'

I found a job advertisement that was asking for someone to help with labouring on a huge extension project. The original cottage consisted of just one room upstairs and one room downstairs. The extension though was the size of a hotel, with woodland on one side and a lake on the other.

Arriving on site I introduced myself to the foreman, Tom. He didn't know much about construction and was just a trusted friend of the owner. His job was to make sure that the stonemason and the carpenter had everything that they needed to do their jobs. Right now, they both needed extra help with boring, strenuous, repetitive tasks, so I was there to help both.

I was keen to make an impression and so arrived on site every morning at 7.00am. This was a good hour before Andy the stonemason would arrive. By 8.00am I had loaded out the scaffolding with a selection of stone, mixed the mortar and loaded that out ready to go. Andy was old and slow, which meant that I would find myself standing around, waiting for him to catch up. It seemed to me that because of this, my boss was wasting money, so I suggested that he let me lay some stones, instead of just hanging around waiting. Andy felt slightly threatened, I'm sure that he wanted to make the job last until his retirement, but my work ethic wouldn't allow that.

Now the job was progressing well and I was given my own little projects. It was whilst I worked alone on these projects that I started to think about the conversations with Kim and Paula, about my 'Holy Anger' and other things.

On 4th May 1986, I went home and read through a small booklet that Kim had given me. It was called 'A Journey into Life' by a man called Norman Warren. Now, after so long of searching... questions... answers... seeds being sown and a lot of prayers (mainly by others), things were beginning to make sense.

I went to bed contemplating what I had read. The next morning, I made myself some breakfast and sat eating it whilst looking at my fish tank. I wasn't just watching them I was admiring them, admiring 'my fish.' I was almost worshipping them! I did this every morning, but this morning seemed different. I was still thinking about what I had read during the previous evening. I couldn't rid my mind of it; even if I tried it was still there. Norman Warren's words had left a strong impression.

Now mixed in with these impacting thoughts, my usual thoughts also appeared. 'These fish are amazing, they are so graceful and so beautiful,' but as I thought this something happened.

This was the first time that I ever heard God speak to me. It wasn't a loud, booming, thundering voice, it wasn't even audible, but it was a gentle, touching presence. The words were placed directly into my mind, just like a computer download and I remember as clearly now as I did on that 5th May morning in 1986.

"Yes, they are beautiful aren't they, but don't forget that I made them." It was as simple as that. God had taken what I was thinking and given it a fresh new meaning. He was giving me a fresh understanding.

There was a real presence in the room. I realised that I wasn't alone. Jesus was just one step away. He always had been, but now I realised that that step had to be taken by me! He had been speaking to me through his messengers for long enough and the final step was mine to take.

I skipped through the 'Journey into Life' book and stopped at page six. On that page, I had previously found a prayer, which I now knew that I had to say. The previous page had talked about sincerity and I couldn't have been any more sincere when I said that prayer. I invited Jesus into my life over breakfast, whilst worshipping my fish!

I didn't speak to Heather before going to work but did so upon my return. We had just finished eating and sat down for the evening. Norman Warren had told me in his book to make sure that I tell someone that I had chosen Jesus. He also advised me to do it within twenty-four hours. If I didn't tell Heather now, we would later go to bed and that important time period would pass. I knew that if I left it, it would just get harder to tell someone.

"Did you see the book that Kim and Paula had given us?" I asked just touching my toes into the water.

"Yes," came the reply, she wasn't giving much away.
"Have you read it?" I asked.
"Yes, have you?" No longer was it just toes in the water; we were paddling up to our knees.
"Yes... I have..." hesitation, waiting before I ask, "Did you see the prayer near the back?"
"Y - e – s," came the slow reply.
"Did you read it?"
"Yes."
"So did I... Did you mean it?"
"Yes."
"So did I."

Heather had probably invited Jesus into her life a couple of days before me but didn't know how to tell me. Although God made sure that we would both know what each of us had done.

At the weekend we would visit my mum and break the news to her. How would she react? Would she understand? She had been a regular church-goer, but that was all wasn't it? I had a few days to plan what to say.

Almost immediately, the people who knew me, my brother Chris and those that I worked with were asking questions. "What's happened to you? You seem different. You even sound different."

At least four people asked me this before I realised what it was. Previously I used a lot of bad language, swearing and profanities. I had stopped blaspheming, using the name of 'Jesus Christ' as an expletive, about a year earlier. I really did want to stop using such bad language. I didn't want my children to learn it. I had even introduced a swear box whilst working in the insurance office. The money was used to buy drinks for the monthly office party and it never stopped anyone from swearing.

Now, three days after inviting Jesus into my life, I was working alone on a small dry-stone wall project. Thinking about what people had been telling me, I now realised that I hadn't used any bad language for three days. Three days earlier, Jesus had come into my life and bad language left me.

The Bible says that 'God gives us the desire of our heart' (Psalm 37:4). I had desired to stop swearing and I was delivered from the habit! I was different, I DID sound different, the people were right and they had noticed it. I was a new creation, the old had gone and the new had come (2 Corinthians 5:17).

The weekend was nearly here and we had planned to visit my mum and dad. We needed to tell them of our decision to follow Jesus, but what would they say? Dad had grown up in the West of Ireland, an area with strong Catholic influence. He had previously told us stories that the priest would visit the school, line up all of the children and say to them, "If yas don't behave yasilves the Divil a put horns on yas!" He had grown up in fear of God and the church.

Mum, on the other hand, had always been a church-goer and encouraged us to go. She would be easier to talk to. Sitting in her kitchen I asked, "Mum do you know what a 'Born Again Christian' is?" It was a way to try to draw her attention.

She answered my question with a question, perhaps that's where I get it from, "What like Cliff Richard?"
I didn't hesitate, "Yes, like Cliff Richard, but also like me... like us."

Her reaction was totally unexpected, she was overjoyed. I now realise that I act the same way when I have had a prayer answered and she had just had one answered.

She went on to tell me that she had given her life to Jesus at the Billy Graham crusade, which took place in Bristol in the 50s. She had never told me this before. To us, she just religiously went to church each week, but now it seems there was a point of awakening and a conversion story. Why had she kept it quiet all of these years? Why do any of us keep it quiet? The answer to that is massive, there are so many reasons and that is probably another book in itself - maybe that will come next?

Though, for now, we talked about what had happened to us. This was just the start, as over the next twenty-five years we would have endless conversations about our relationship with God, through Jesus.

Mum had been what I now regard as a 'Closet Christian'. She had asked Jesus into her life, but never really moved on much or so it seemed.

Mum soon started to attend the church that we were going to, Minchinhampton Christian Fellowship. This was where Kim and Paula had been disappearing on those Sunday mornings when we would watch from the window. We were no longer puzzled about where they went.

Mum used to tell me, "I like your church as it is so lively."
I would always reply, "Lively is good, but the most important thing is that it is alive!"

This church certainly was alive. We quickly started to see what we now know to be the power of the Holy Spirit. Most weeks would include someone sharing a story about what God had been doing in their lives during the week. There was often a queue of people who were keen to share what God had done and each of them inspired others to look for the indicators of what God was doing in our lives. Every week prayers were being answered for someone, plus most weeks involved someone being prayed for and being healed or set free from their burdens.

Once a month the whole church organised a 'bring and share' lunch. It was during this time of fellowship that deeper friendships were formed. This group very rapidly became our extended family, with deeply rooted bonds. We were accepted by everyone and were quite surprised to find many others who were the same age as us. These friendships and this group of Christians would eventually give birth to what is now known as, 'The Door Youth Project.'

I soon stopped calling myself a 'Born Again Christian'' as I now realised that to be a Christian, a follower of Christ, meant that you were born again.

In the Gospel of John, we can find in chapter three, the story of Jesus chatting to a man called Nicodemus. Here Jesus explains that we are first born of flesh, our human birth and then later we have the choice of a spiritual birth. It is this spiritual birth that is often referred to as being 'born again,' but all Christians should have a spirit birth and continue to grow spiritually. Our spiritual growth comes from a continuous relationship with God and we were just starting on what has become a remarkable relationship and an incredible journey.

Here is the prayer that I mentioned earlier:

Lord Jesus Christ, I know that I have sinned in my thoughts, words and actions.
There are so many good things I have not done.
There are so many sinful things I have done.
I am sorry for my sins and turn from everything I know to be wrong.
You gave your life upon the cross for me.
Gratefully, I give my life back to you.
Now I ask you to come into my life.
Come in as my Saviour to cleanse me.
Come in as my Lord to control me.
And I will serve and follow you all the remaining years of my life.
Amen.

Chapter Nine

Guided, Directed and Moulded

Jeremiah 18:5 says, 'God is the Potter and we are the clay.' The potter works gently and carefully, moulding the clay. A push too much in the wrong direction and the whole pot will collapse into a useless mess.

I know that I have over the years been moulded by the hands of God, as he formed me to become his instrument. Although in that first year, there was such a lot to take in. I can't remember the exact sequence of events, but I do remember the stories. These stories built the foundation of my relationship with God.

A tale of two Duncans

Within the first three months of becoming a Christian, I was invited to attend a Wednesday morning prayer meeting. It started at 7.00am and it was for local Christian businessmen. Why I should have been considered for this, I wasn't quite sure. I wasn't in business I was just a labourer on a building site. Incidentally, in 2015, that same prayer meeting was still held on most Wednesdays twenty-seven years on.

We would always start with coffee and sometimes toast, it was very civilised. It was called a 'prayer' meeting, but at times the Holy Spirit would lead someone to start singing. Everyone would join in and I quickly learnt the words to many songs.

Occasionally, someone would bring a scripture from The Bible and share something about what it meant to them. Then very occasionally someone might bring a prophetic word from God.

I had never heard about prophecy before. I had read about people in The Bible called 'Prophets', but didn't realise that there were still Prophets around today.

Duncan White (the 1st Duncan) was such a person. I didn't know Duncan and he certainly didn't know me. Now, during the prayer time, Duncan started to speak in a way that sounded different. This was God speaking directly through him. I was partly intrigued to hear this new thing and partly amazed to think that this was God's own words for us today. He talked a lot. Far too much for me to remember every word, but the gist of what he said was, "Two of you will do great things. You will become a team, which will reach out and touch thousands of lives. You will especially touch the lives of young people in this area of Stroud."

After the prayer meeting, I was outside standing on the pavement. Duncan asked if I could spare a couple of minutes for a chat. He told me he felt that the prophecy he had brought was for me. I remember sounding a little vague and asked him to repeat it.

"Can you repeat what you said in the meeting?" It was all new to me and so he repeated the gist of what he had said earlier.

Then he said, "I am absolutely convinced that one of these people is you. You will be used in a big way by God. You will touch the lives of thousands. You will speak to thousands of young people and I am not sure, but I think the other person is Andy Morris."

I had been a Christian just a few months and this was

all new to me. I listened to what he had to say. I still clearly remember the conversation that took place, but it was another four years before that prophesy started to be fulfilled. It would be four years before Andy Morris and I would open The Door Youth Project. It would then be several more years after the project was opened that this prophecy would be remembered and recognised as being fulfilled.

During these same Wednesday morning prayer meetings, we would often pray for someone called Duncan (the 2nd Duncan). He was known to everyone else, but I had never met him. I did know that he had gone through some difficult times and was greatly in need of prayer and so I prayed for him.

The more that I prayed for him, it seemed the more I got to know him, although I had never met him.

My time on the building site with old Andy and Tom was coming to an end. I was now beginning to have the desire to go back into my own building business. Not forgetting that God gives us the desire of our hearts, I took the step.

I needed four things to start myself off. Transport was number one. I couldn't work without a vehicle and I had that. So, next was a name for my business. I wanted to be near the start of the telephone directory, so it had to start with the letter 'A.' As I searched in The Bible for inspiration I read, "I am the ALPHA and the Omega." I liked the word 'Alpha' and thought about what the Alpha symbol looked like. It was similar to the fish symbol that is used to say "I am a Christian." So, I had a name and a logo, ALPHA BUILDING SERVICES α. Kim was a printer and a graphic designer. He produced some business cards and some headed paper for me. Now I was in business.

The third thing that I needed was a job and a very kind man called Derek Morris (yes, Andy's dad) gave me my first job, to paint his house. It was a big house, so therefore a big job. Some of it would require scaffolding.

I didn't want to go on scaffolding by myself, so the fourth thing that I needed was a labourer. I prayed about this, as I had never before employed anyone to work for my own business.

I remember that we had been invited to go to an event on the Three Counties Show Ground near Malvern. David Pawson was speaking and I was praying before going. I asked God what I should do about employing a labourer. I remember turning to my Bible after praying and reading the words, "You will know him when you see him."

Upon arriving at Malvern, I was introduced to Duncan, who we had been praying for. I had already come to know him through prayer. Now as soon as we met, I felt God say, "You will know him when you see him." Duncan was to be my labourer, the fourth part of my business plan. I had to give him a job.

I asked him if he was looking for a job, "Oh yes! Am I ever! What I wouldn't do for a job?" He sounded keen, yet desperate. "Come and see me tomorrow for an interview."

I had interviewed people for work before during my time selling insurance but never like this. I knew that I wanted to give him a job, that God wanted me to give him a job, but I also knew that he had to earn it. If he was going to work for me, he had to work his way into the job. We were friends immediately and at the end of the interview, I told him that he had a job. He couldn't believe what he was hearing. It was as if I had given him a new life and that is exactly what I had done, but that is his story to tell. He was even more blown away when I disclosed to him that God had told me to give him a job before I had interviewed him. God had answered his prayers and saved his life from the road that he was on.

Interestingly, I still often have the same feeling now, when I am interviewing someone for a job. I will often feel God say, "This is the one that I want you to employ."

Becoming a Capstone

We settled quickly into a new way of life and the Potter continued to mould us just like the clay. It wasn't long before we were attending mid-week small group meetings. These could be in the form of a Bible study, a short course, a prayer meeting or simply a social gathering.

A few weeks before Duncan gave me his prophetic word, another word from God was given to me. That same word still resonates with me, whenever I hear it.

It was given to me at another prayer meeting, which was this time being held at Derek Morris's house. I was still working there and he brought two scriptures. One was for me and the other was for Heather. We were being welcomed into this body of believers and Derek said, "I have been praying and asked The Lord to give me a word for each of you."

I don't remember the one for Heather, but he continued

by reading them both out. For me, he read a passage from the book of 1 Peter, but the part that really spoke to me and has stayed with me ever since is, "The stone the builder had rejected will become the Capstone" (1 Peter 2:7).

He knew nothing about my previous attempt to try to run a building business. He knew nothing about my fall and my first angel encounter and he knew nothing of the fear that I had first experienced on Eric's roof. He didn't know that I had (or so it felt) been rejected, but God knew and he understood. This was God speaking directly to me through his word and channelled via Derek's obedience, sensitivity and discernment.

That word would also be fulfilled, as over the next two years my business would grow on the wave of the building boom which was now in place. I always say that God's timing is absolutely perfect and this was the perfect time for the construction industry. By 1988 I would be employing a team of twenty-seven men and managing projects over nine different sites.

God was now leading and guiding us on an amazing journey. That journey would see many signs and wonders. We would witness miracles and see prayers answered, but through all of this, we would learn to trust God, grow in our relationship with him and be built up in faith.

Tested

The Bible tells us that you, "should not test The Lord your God" (Deuteronomy 6:16), although that doesn't stop him from testing us. I do believe that God tested me very early in my journey with him. At the time that it happened though, I didn't stop and say, "I think God is testing me?"

My test would teach me to, 'let go and let God.' I did know this, but would still frequently forget what I had learnt and do things my way. Then when something went wrong, I would say to myself, "I really must let go and let God."

We decorated every room in our new home next to Kim and Paula, except for the spare bedroom. This room had been used as a bit of a dumping ground, but it was now time to clear the mess and start making better use of the space. It would be Chris's room. Ellie had the smaller nursery room and was asleep in her cot as we worked.

Chris was there with us and getting into all sorts of things. He was naturally inquisitive, the same as any two-year-old.

It was time for a break and we both went downstairs to the kitchen. We wouldn't be gone long and Chris was safe. The stair gate was in place and there was nothing to harm him. At least that is what we thought until we returned just five minutes later.

Chris had found an old medicine cabinet and thought the contents were for eating. A two-year-old will naturally put anything in their mouths, with the favourites being snails and worms. The sight before us now though was more serious. The box contained potassium permanganate crystals. This is something that I had used for the treatment of 'trench foot,' which I had suffered from during building work in wet conditions. All it took was a few crystals in a bowl of warm water to help dry out the feet, but the feet would be stained a dark purple colour, like wearing purple socks.

Chris had poured the contents of the container into his mouth. This intensive dose had now turned his mouth, tongue and lips completely black.

Fear passes very quickly, followed by basic survival and protection instincts. Picking him up from the floor I ran to the bathroom and started to wash out the remaining crystals, pouring water into his mouth. Another natural reaction tends to be to look for blame and now, as I washed out his mouth I started to shout out, "God why have you let this happen? God this can't be happening!" Although, it was and I lost count of how many times I said it. In my head I knew that God was almighty and all-powerful, he could have stopped this. I had forgotten that we also have a responsibility as parents. We were the ones to blame, but I failed to see it!

I ran to the car and headed for Stroud General Hospital, which was just a short drive down the hill. At the same time, Heather phoned her mum asking her to come and pick her and Ellie up. Things were happening fast and the hospital called for an ambulance to transfer Chris to the much bigger hospital of Gloucester Royal, where there was a special poisons unit.

Whilst waiting for her mum to arrive, Heather discovered that some herbal sleeping medication had also been consumed. The situation immediately became even more serious than had previously been realised. She phoned the hospital with this new information and the nurse told her to head straight to Gloucester Royal. I heard the nurse pass this new information to the ambulance crew and we left with blue lights flashing.

My son looked a mess and was now beginning to lose

consciousness. This wasn't sleeping, he had passed out. Now at about three miles into our journey his body was limp. Until this point, I had not stopped blaming God. Outwardly I tried to remain calm, whilst in my head I was still shouting, "God why are you letting this happen?"

Now my thoughts changed. I remembered that Jesus said, "Let the little children come unto me" (Matthew 19:14). This wasn't God. Then maybe it was an attack? I had read about spiritual battles between forces of good and evil. If this was evil, it didn't belong in this ambulance. It was like a revelation.

My mind suddenly became calmer. In my head, I prayed, "Lord, please don't let Chris die. Don't let the Devil take him, but if he does have to die, please will you take him and look after him? I place his life into your hands. Please, Lord, PLEASE!"

I prayed like this for the remaining seven miles of the journey, but he never moved, he remained still, his body limp... I continued to pray.

The ambulance stopped. We stepped out into the summer air. His eyes opened. He spoke, "Ambulance". Heather appeared with her mum. We were rushed into the poison unit. The doctor arrived immediately. Chris spoke as he picked up the toy, "Lego." He seemed fine. God had heard and answered the prayer. I had given my son to God. He had given him back! The medics had never seen anyone swallow potassium permanganate before. His mouth, tongue and lips were still black and the doctor suggested keeping him in overnight for observation.

I said, "He's fine now, we'll take him home." I didn't

give God the glory for his healing. I was a young Christian, only a month old, but I have made up for it since.

"Okay," said the doctor, "you can take him home, but he is going to look awful for at least the next two weeks. The black will take at least that long to go."

We took him home and gave him a drink of blackcurrant Ribena. Within twenty-four hours the black staining had disappeared. So, I look at it like this, either the doctor had been wrong, Ribena has an amazing neutralising effect on potassium permanganate or God had healed him. I know which one I believe! Ribena would later play another part in a different story. That story would have a different ending, with a mixture of different emotions.

I later realised that a man in The Bible called Abraham had a similar story to tell, regarding his son Isaac (Genesis chapter 22).

I had grown massively through this testing time. The test didn't last long, but the memory is still strong. This would be my foundation to build upon and always to look back at. It would remind me that God is in control, but also that we have to more and more, "Let go and let God!"

God can heal

I had witnessed the healing power of God and wanted to see more.

When I was two years old, I cut the middle finger of my left hand. The nurse rushed the repair, as she was in a hurry to finish her shift. In her haste, she had stitched through the tendon. As I grew older, the tendon didn't grow with me and the result is a finger that is now bent. It has become something of a trademark, but when I became a Christian, I asked for prayer for it. I did this whenever there was an opportunity.

I can remember taking several photographs of my finger and thinking to myself, 'When God heals my finger, I will be able to show everyone how it was and then compare it to how it looks following God's miraculous healing.' Looking back now, I realise how stupid that sounds. The photograph could have been on someone else's hand. People would not believe it was mine.

Hardly a week went by when someone didn't pray for it. Sometimes the Holy Spirit would come and just gently knock me down. I found out that this is referred to as being 'slain' or 'resting' in the Spirit and whenever it happened, I just felt cocooned in the overwhelming presence and love of God.

On one occasion Kim was praying for my finger. The Bible tells us to pray whilst laying on our hands (when appropriate, touching the part that needs healing). As Kim prayed, we both felt the power of the Holy Spirit. The finger became hotter and then we both felt the crack, "Did you feel that?" Kim asked. He already knew the answer, as I showed him that I had movement at the end of my finger.

"I couldn't move that before!" I told him and both of us knew that God had touched my finger.

I continued to ask for prayer for my finger to be completely healed, but I stopped asking in May 1987. I had been a Christian for a whole year. I had seen my son healed and my finger had been touched by God, but never completely healed.

It's not that God couldn't heal my finger, but he chose not to. It is a rare thing for anyone to know why God chooses not to heal and in 1987 I just accepted it. I felt that by giving me movement in part of it, God was saying, "I can do it if I want to, but I want it to stay the way that it is for a reason." I would have to wait another nine years before I would find out the reason why God chose not to heal my finger completely.

Chapter Ten

A new gift I give to you...

It is important to know that becoming a Christian doesn't mean that life suddenly all becomes a 'bed of roses.' Yes, God provides all of our needs, but we still have to work, battle on and play our part. We would play our part by praying into situations and stepping out in faith.

Our time of living next to Kim and Paula was coming to an end. We had been there for just three and a half years and our neighbours had been praying for our salvation for most of that time.

Alpha Building Services was now becoming established with a good run of work.

The desire of our heart now was to live back up in Chalford Hill, so we put our house up for sale. Although finding a property back in the village where we had both grown up was now not that easy. Anything that we considered was quickly bought by someone else and usually for a lot more than we could afford. Would God give us our hearts' desire this time? It seemed impossible. Would the Golden Thread lead us to where we were meant to be?

We prayed about the situation. We had learnt to pray and read The Bible following prayer. Sometimes during praying, I would feel led to a certain book in The Bible, with chapter and verse. This was God speaking to us, directing us, using His word to speak into our lives. At times when a chapter and verse didn't come, simply opening The Bible at a random point and reading what jumped off the page, would often be an answer to prayer (but not always). God had directed us in this way when I was to employ Duncan. Now praying about where we were to live, he spoke to us again. The Bible fell open near the centre and Psalm 2:6 read, 'Yet I have set my king upon my Holy Hill of Zion.'

What did that mean? Holy Hill? Was that Chalford Hill? It wasn't that clear until the full picture was revealed. Nowadays, I realise how important it is to look at the full picture. This verse in the book of Psalms was just a road sign. We would need to keep it in mind and recognise the turning, the direction to take when the time was right.

We soon found a buyer for our house and in a strange coincidence, it turned out to be Tom with the Kawasaki motorcycle. Now, thirteen years on from the crazy party that nearly ended in a lynching, Tom wanted to buy our house.

The deal was done. A price had been negotiated and solicitors were notified. The sale was all going smoothly. We still didn't have anywhere to move to and a few weeks later were starting to wonder if we would ever find anywhere. What did Psalm 2:6 mean? What were we supposed to do?

The phone rang and it was Tom, with what seemed like bad news. He had a property to sell and the sale of that had fallen through. "I'm afraid that unless I can find another buyer, I won't be able to buy your house. I don't suppose you want to buy a building plot, do you?"

We had never considered a building plot. The risks were so high. We would be technically homeless again, but he had managed to grab my attention. I wanted to know more, "Where is it? How big? What's it like?"

"It's in Chalford Hill and big enough for a large four-bedroom house."

Now he had my attention, "OK what's the catch? What's it like?" It was very cheap and there was something that he wasn't coming straight out with.

"It's on an old thirty-foot-deep quarry which has been filled in with asbestos. It has been pile-driven though." He sounded desperate.

This was the other part of the big picture. This was also a great opportunity. My chance to become a house builder. Until now all of my contracts had been small projects. God's signpost of Psalm 2:6 mentioned the Holy Hill in Zion. It also referred to a king. The house that we could build would be our castle (fit for a king) on top of Chalford Hill. I don't really think that Chalford is a Holy Hill, but it is a great place and the house that we would build, we would call it, 'Zion House' and in 2015 it still had that same name.

I put down the phone after talking with Tom and discussed this option with Heather. We wasted very little time as we both knew that it was right.

The sale now proceeded quickly and we moved our entire belongings into storage at Andy Morris's Foundry.

In February 1987 we purchased a second-hand, very large mobile home and had it delivered to our new building site. With no electricity, we had to rely on a generator until the main connection was made. We had no water and had to visit my mum's for a bath and to fill up water containers.

The main sewer was nearby and we quickly made a temporary connection, but we would live without water and electricity for over a month.

The man from the local council arrived on the same day as the mobile home. "You don't have planning permission for this! You can't live here!" His tone was authoritative and he sounded rather impatient.

I thought back all of those years to a similar situation. My parents had moved into a house that had been condemned and was considered for demolition. The man from the council had arrived then and told Dad that he couldn't live there. My dad had just answered, "Okay then, you can find somewhere else for me and my family to live!" They never did and we just stayed there. So, I now used the same reply, "Okay you find somewhere else for us to live!"

He started to calm down and became more reasonable. I explained that the mobile home was not permanent. He then told me that we would have to apply retrospectively for temporary planning consent. We did however still have to have plans drawn up and submitted to gain full and detailed planning approval. This would be for a big house.

It would take us eight months before we would be able to move into the unfinished house and during that time, I would be visited by two very different Christian friends. Each of these would have a different approach to our situation.

We adjusted very quickly to living in a mobile home.

We had done this before in Cornwall which was all good preparation for where we were now. There was of course the added complication of two small children, both under the age of four years but they also adapted well.

With plans passed, we started the groundwork in April 1987. Every spare moment of my time was now to be consumed in building our new home. I had done this with our first house and knew what it would take. With our first house though, I wasn't a Christian. I wasn't going to church every Sunday morning. I couldn't now afford to waste time and decided that church would have to wait. Some may have said that I was 'backsliding' and 'falling away' from God, but that was not the case at all. His Golden Thread continued with me throughout the build. It may not have been visible, on the front of my 'Tapestry of Life,' but it was still there. All anyone had to do was turn the tapestry over.

At the start of 1987, my friendship with Andy Morris had developed and I was now helping him with youth work in the church. He had asked for anyone to help him and I just felt that it was right to offer a hand.

Andy was a practical, helpful friend and he knew just what he had to do, as he came to see me. My lack of attendance at the church meant that I hadn't been able to help him for a while, but he didn't judge me for not being there. "What can I do to help you? Give me a job. I'm here to help!"

I hadn't even asked him for help but he just knew that I needed it. He helped me to clean up asbestos, wheeling wheelbarrows and shovelling. He was the only one of my new-found Christian 'friends' who turned up to help me. I have always had a bit of a problem with asking for help, but they all knew what I was doing. I also have the attitude that a good volunteer is worth ten 'pressed men' and Andy worked hard. We were a team. He gave me a few days of help, which in the scale of the project, didn't sound like much, but it was enough. It was practical and it said, "I understand."

My second visitor was very different. He was one of the leaders of Minchinhampton Christian Fellowship. "We're concerned that we haven't seen you on a Sunday."

I couldn't believe my ears. We were standing in the small lounge space of our temporary home, staring out at a building site. Was he blind? I remember the anger that I had towards him. He had a zero level of compassion. Looking back now, I can see that this man lacked the essential pastoral skills that are required. The leaders were concerned that we were 'back sliding" but if Andy Morris hadn't given us his practical help and support, we may have done exactly what they feared.

One man had judged me and I felt, condemned me; whilst the other had helped. That help had tipped the balance and made me thankful. I wasn't just thankful for Andy's help, I was thankful for the provision of this house, this 'Zion House' that God had led us to. This house would become the 'jewel in the crown' for my business. It would be regarded as an excellent example of my work and it would lead others to me. They would also want houses built.

Eventually, we returned to Minchinhampton Christian Fellowship, but more importantly, we returned to return the favour to Andy. I now started to help him even more. I can remember thinking to myself, "I wish

I could be as good at youth work as Andy is." He was good and I don't think I was the only one with those thoughts.

Andy was aware of how people regarded him and he would often say, "People need to stop trying to be like me."

Eventually, I also heard God, as he spoke into my heart again, "Don't try to be like Andy, be like me." I don't know when that was, but I am glad that it happened.

We said goodbye to our mobile home and now found ourselves living in an unfinished house on a plot of land with asbestos fragments on the subsoil. Until then we had been watering the asbestos down for health and safety reasons. If it were allowed to dry out, the dust could be very dangerous to health. Our new priority therefore was to landscape the garden, burying the asbestos and making it safe. Heather was now pregnant again with our third child. Hannah would be born in February 1989 and our growing family needed somewhere that they could play safely.

We continued to learn more in mid-week Bible studies and more friendships were developed. It was a continuous juggling act of what we needed to do for family, house, work and church.

One Sunday afternoon, in the spring of 1988, we had been to church and returned. We hurried through lunch to carry on working in the garden. The project in hand was digging out a foundation for a dry-stone wall.

It was near the end of the afternoon when I decided that it was time to stop. I now sat briefly in the armchair in the unfinished lounge. Something didn't feel right, as I tried to move, the pain hit me. I couldn't stand up. My back had locked up completely! I did eventually manage to lift myself from the seat, but I was still in the sitting position. Now I was bent double, with my head looking straight down into the seat that I had just managed to get out of. The pain was unbearable. In desperation, I managed to lower myself back into the chair. I then asked Heather to phone around, asking some people to come and pray for me.

Geoff Sanders, Derek Morris and Basil Sands arrived and prayed for my back to be healed. I felt that familiar, warming touch of the Holy Spirit and the pain left me. Movement returned and I was able to stand. The three 'Prayer Warriors' told me that they would need to return later in the week for further prayer and we agreed to them coming back on the following Wednesday.

In the meantime, I thought it best to seek some medical advice, just to be on the safe side. I managed to book an emergency appointment with an osteopath the next day. She told me that it was highly likely that my spine was bent, as she could see that my left leg was about an inch shorter than the right one. She did various things to try to manipulate my spine, but it was still the same when I left. She asked me to return the following week.

Derek, Basil and Geoff returned on the Wednesday as agreed. I told them about my visit to the osteopath and showed them that my leg was shorter than it should be. They first of all prayed for this leg to grow and be healed. They laid on hands as they prayed. I sat on a chair and my leg was stretched out in front of me. I remember thinking, 'If my leg is going to grow, I want to see it happen.' So, I kept my eyes open throughout.

Once again, I quickly felt the healing warmth of the

Holy Spirit touching me. It didn't take long before my leg appeared to grow. I watched it, heard the creaking and felt it change. I quickly sat on the floor and put both legs out in front of me to check. Both legs were the same length and it felt amazing.

Derek next asked me if I had ever had any involvement with the occult. "No, not really," I replied. I had never worshipped the Devil or sacrificed animals, I was fine. He continued by asking questions about specific things that he suspected I may have 'dabbled' in. I told him about my teenage years and the séances, about the Voodoo and even the horoscopes that were mentioned. I told them about the detail of the séance that took place near Southampton, about the image of the old lady in the mirror and the fact that one moment it was there and the next it was gone.

Derek explained that the manifestation that I had seen was an evil spirit and that it had probably entered into me. He explained that we can breathe evil spirits in and I flashed my mind back to the moment in that room. That moment when fear struck me and I took a sharp intake of breath, then it was gone. Was I really 'possessed?'

Derek continued to explain that this spirit was now manifesting itself in my back problems, so I asked them to pray for it to come out. They did as I asked and I was delivered. There was no dramatic thrashing around, I just breathed out as I was told to. My mouth was suddenly filled with a stale, rancid taste. I breathed it out. The foul taste lasted just a second or two.

They prayed again and I breathed in the refreshing, cleansing power of the Holy Spirit. This new power of God would manifest itself in a new form and use me in a way that I never would have imagined.

Less than a month later I was asked if I would like to be involved in an outreach mission, aimed at young people in Chalford Hill. Now that I was helping with church youth work, it made sense to say yes.

I had also recently started doing school assemblies with Rob Burr at Archway School. He would sing his songs and I attempted backing vocals.

The mission was a week-long and full of fun games, music and a message. It was suggested that we use some drama with a message. Most of the material that we used for this was written by Dave Hopwood from Lee Abbey. The sketches were simple and powerful. Some of them were written in the style of 'rap', punchy, rhyming verse. Dave Hopwood explained in his books that a large group of people should all speak out the rhyme and clap their hands for a beat, whilst the story was told in the form of mime and actions. We didn't have a large group of people but we tried it anyway, with just two people rapping and clapping. I sat and watched, never really wanting to put myself forward. It didn't sound very good!

Dave Rose had been asked to have a go at it with someone else. I had seen Dave a few times at church, he was quite new as well and he told me that he had a musical interest, having been in a few bands. He was good, but the other person was struggling.

When I had become a Christian, soon afterwards I felt that God led me to get rid of my record collection. I had worshipped it for too long and it had become my false god. I felt that God was saying, "Get rid of that 'false god' and I will give you something much better." I had also been a drummer in a few bands and could sing reasonably well. Maybe performance was another one of my heart's desires.

Now, everyone in the room realised that this rap duo wasn't working. They all turned to me and asked, "Do you want to try?"

"I don't know if I will be any good," I tried to defend myself before I knew. Did I have the confidence to do this?

The person who had been partnering with Dave commented, "You can't be any worse than me, give it a go." It was the encouragement that I needed.

I asked if we could do alternating lines. I would take the first line and Dave the next. Instead of clapping we used 'human beat-box' (making drum beats with your mouth). Dave was surprised to find someone else that could beat-box. The piece was called 'The Prodigal Rap' and three people would mime the actions. To my surprise and probably everyone else's, it sounded good, it had potential.

A couple of weeks later Dave arrived at rehearsals with a backing track and suddenly the whole piece took on a completely different nature. It was now more dynamic, professional and polished. It was so good that Dave Hopwood found out about it and asked for a copy of the backing track. We gave him more than that, as by then we had also recorded it with a vocal track and we shortened the title to 'Prod Rap.'

Prod Rap

Now a few years back there was a wise old man,

Lived on a Ranch had a clapped-out van.
Had two strong sons and life was swell,
A hen, three gerbils and a wife as well.

But one fine day working in the rough,
The youngest boy said, "I've had enough!"
Threw down his spade on his brother's toe
And headed for his father just to let him know.

He packed his bags and he stood at the door,
Said, "Digging ain't what my right arm's for!
Don't try to stop me, cuz I'm gonna go,
Gonna get me some fun if you give me some dough!"

It was a mean old day for the poor old man,
Cuz, he loved his son and couldn't understand.
Why he wanted to leave his family and home,
But he gave him all his money and he watched him go.

Well, I'd be lying if I didn't tell you,
He had a lot of fun – for a week or two.
Laughing, dancing, drinking homebrew.
The cars were fast and the girls were too.

Till one fine day, he woke up in a daze,
Smelling worse than the neighbourhood strays.
His body was aching and his brain was bad,
His friends had run off with everything he had.

Nobody cared now that he was broke,
His life had become a mighty bad joke.
Lost all he had and when he fell asleep,
Someone stole the fillings from his two bad teeth.

Well, he felt pretty silly and he wandered around,
Till he got so thin his pants fell down.
So, he took a job dishing out pig swill,

And it smelt so bad that it made him ill.

Then suddenly he realised,
What a fool he'd been and he opened his eyes.
He saw the waste, his life had become,
Lost everything for a week of fun.

"I'll go on home", he said that day,
I'll scrub the floor for a servant's pay.
What a fool to reject my dad!
Couldn't see just what I had."

Well, he walked on home in the mid-day sun,
It was the hardest thing he had ever done.
He was a broken man now, nothing to lose,
The holes in his life like the holes in his shoes.

He threw himself at the feet of his dad.
Said "Dad I've wasted everything I had.
I know I've done wrong and you should send me away,
But if I work for you, will you let me stay?"

"Son, I love you," the father replied,
I thought you were lost, I figured you'd died.
It broke my heart when you went away,
And I've been waiting for you to come home today.
I don't care where you've been or what you've done,
I just want you back, cuz you're my son."

Performing felt good. It felt very good! I was now a rapper, but where would it lead?

Dave would soon come to work for me. He was the kind of person that changed his job every year. I was expanding my business and needed another labourer. Duncan had now left and moved on to nursing (he was better suited to that). Working with Dave would help us to develop a musical partnership with extremely strong chemistry.

The summer of '88 was coming to an end and plans were already being made towards Christmas. The Oasis Trust had launched a campaign called 'Christmas Unwrapped.' We had been looking at it briefly, considering whether the group of young people that we were now working with would want to get involved. It was enough to plant a seed of thought.

I found myself in another big prayer meeting at Derek Morris's house. As we prayed, the words of a song kept coming into my head...

It's Christmas, Christmas,
Christmas Unwrapped; Christmas Unwrapped.
It's Christmas, Christmas,
Christmas Unwrapped for you.

Whose party is it anyway?
I hear you say on Christmas.
I don't really care, just have a good time,
with turkey, tinsel and plenty of wine.

The words continued over and over in my head and I had a feeling that I had heard this song before. It had a certain familiarity to it. When I left to go home, it was still going around in my head. I was trying to think where I may have heard it, but could not come up with an answer. I found it quite frustrating.

The next morning Dave arrived at my house before we headed off to work on a site together. I asked him if he recognised this song. The words were still very clear in my head and now even stronger. I told him that this song had been in my head since the prayer meeting of the previous evening, but couldn't think where I may have heard it.

"I reckon you heard it last night when God gave it to you," Dave said with a smile on his face. I wasn't sure what he was saying, so asked him to clarify.

"God has given you a song, it's yours, I've never heard it until now, so I reckon you ought to get and finish writing it!" I had not recognised God's voice speaking these words into me. This was the first time I had ever experienced this, but it wouldn't be the last.

We went to work, but as we worked, I had to keep stopping. Every so often more words would come into my head. Verse after verse, until by mid-afternoon, when we stopped for a cup of tea, it was almost finished. One line was missing and together we wrote that. Dave wrote the backing track and together we finished our first song. Christmas Unwrapped would be remixed in different styles over the next twenty-six years and it would be heard by thousands of people.

Christmas Unwrapped

Chorus: *It's Christmas, Christmas,*
Christmas Unwrapped; Christmas Unwrapped.
It's Christmas, Christmas,
Christmas Unwrapped for you.

Whose party is it anyway?
I hear you say on Christmas.
I don't really care, just have a good time,
with turkey, tinsel and plenty of wine.
It's Christmas, Christmas,
Christmas Unwrapped for you.
There'll be gifts on the tree and mistletoe,

Toys, nuts, cards, cake, booze, holly and snow.
We'll party all night, we'll party all day,
Whose party is it anyway?

Chorus

We'll rock the house this time of year,
We celebrate with party cheer.
We'll party all night, we'll party all day,
Whose party is it anyway?
It's Christmas, Christmas,
Christmas Unwrapped for you.
Carol singers sing and sleigh bells ring,
There's plum pudding and everything.
There's party fun, for everyone.
What's that, I hear you say?
Whose party is it anyway?
Chorus

Well, I could tell you some more
about these joyous things,
But this you already know!
So, I'll tell you 'bout the truth and
I'll tell 'bout the way,
That you must surely go.
So, stop as I unveil to you what it's really all about,
'bout giving an loving an peace on earth an that's without a doubt.
It's Christmas, Christmas,
Christmas Unwrapped for you.
Just take a look at the Holy Book and
you will find the way,
God sent his Son into the world,
upon that Christmas day.
"Emmanuel" they called him, God with us!
He sent his Son into the world to save us.
It's Christmas, Christmas,

To recognise God's voice takes practice and unless we practise listening, we never will. I was now keen to hear God speak to me more. I was excited about the opportunity to have another song to perform. The 'Prod Rap' was good, it had been fun and whet my appetite for rap music, but it wasn't my lyrics.

The excitement was building and I was praying to God, asking him where it would lead. He didn't answer or at least I didn't hear, that is until I was trying to sleep. I realise now that God has a habit of doing things in his timing, on his terms.

Now, as I lay in my bed, new lyrics started to pour into my head. I knew instantly that it was new lyrics, words from God, a new song, but I was tired. As my eyes closed and sleep started to fall upon me, the lyrics would drift away. I remember thinking, 'I will write this song in the morning,' but God had other plans. I now know that when God speaks through you, you don't mess around, just get on with it. After all, God's timing is perfect.

I lost count of how many times I had woken up and as I did the lyrics would flood back into my head, it was at least six times, maybe more. I had no choice but to get out of bed and write. Making my way downstairs I sat at my desk and the pen flowed. Out came the words and I didn't stop until the song was finished. This time it was written in one fast-flowing, non-stop session, unlike Christmas Unwrapped which had taken me all day, with a bit here and a bit there. I wanted to listen. It was as if I was totally tuned in and I just wrote.

After I had stopped writing I didn't bother to read what I had written. I was tired, "Can I go to bed now please God?" No more words came. I knew it was the end, it was finished. Sleep!

The next morning, I read what I had scribbled out in my sleepy state of mind. I was amazed by what I had written. Yes, it was a new song, but it was more. God had given me a name that he wanted me to use as a rapper. The lyrics also reminded me that although God wanted to use me, he was in charge, he was the 'Master' and I was to be his MC (Master of Ceremonies or Mic Controller). The song that he had given me this time was 'The Master's MC'.

Master's MC

Ya'll listen right now cuz they've given to me,
The microphone and a chance to be free.
If you listen to the words, the things I have to say,
The smart ones among you are sure to find the way,

Chorus:
I'm the Master you see, of the ceremony
Now they've given me the MIC
I'm the Master you see, The Master's MC
Check it out!

Now the Master of The Master's MC
Is the Master himself, the Master JC
We all have a Master of some kind or another
But the Master I got, I can call my brother

Chorus

Some people worship the colour TV.
Listen to their music on the latest CD

There's football, cricket, all kinds of sports
Going to the pub drinking beer and shorts
Maybe your master's some kinda new drug
Or cigarettes, you've been hit by the bug.
You could have the master of crime,
Do time you slime and other words that rhyme

Chorus

So let me tell you bout the Master JC
He cares for you and he cares for me.
He's with you at work, he's with you at play,
He'll tell you the truth, he'll show you the way.
So, if you're sitting by the TV,
or you're sitting in the pub,
Remember Master JC,
he's the one that they call love.
If you're feeling kinda lonesome and
you want someone to care
Reach out to the Master, cuz he is always there!
And that's a fact!
Chorus

Chapter Eleven

Rise and Fall

Throughout 1988 and the start of 1989, Alpha Building Services grew. The building industry was experiencing a huge boom across the country. If work came in, I just increased the workforce to cope with the demand. At the peak of the boom, I was building five different executive-style houses and had smaller contracts on four other sites. In total I was running nine different sites and employing twenty-seven men, all working for me and all depending on me to pay their wages every week. My job now involved driving around the sites, checking on work standards, ordering materials and keeping the money coming in. The stone the builders had rejected had become the 'Capstone' – the word that Derek had given, had been fulfilled.

However, keeping the money coming in was becoming a problem. It doesn't take much to cause an interruption in cash flow and now I was experiencing a regular interruption. My biggest customer, a property developer started to negotiate over his invoice every month. This developer was struggling because the wave of the building boom was rapidly coming to an end. The whole building industry was heading in the opposite direction. It was about to crash.

Work started to dry up. All over the country building sites were being closed down, with half-built houses everywhere. Builders and developers were going out of business. People couldn't pay their mortgages due to soaring, high interest rates. Thousands of people had their homes repossessed by the mortgage company. I made a tough decision. Ten of my loyal workforce had to go. I was now down to seventeen men. Shortly after this move, I parted company with the developer who was bleeding me dry. I have since then, learnt a lot more about business, but you could say that I learnt the hard way. How much more could I handle? How much further would it fall?

I held out as long as I could, before laying off the next ten members of my team. This time it was harder. The first ten to go were the weaker ones; they didn't work so hard and didn't have families or mortgages. This second group of men would struggle. Some may not find another job and some may even lose their homes. I waited as long as I could, which I now know (with hindsight) was too long. I was paying wages, but didn't have the work for this fantastic gang of workers, I had no choice. This was another week, in which I added ten more to the rapidly rising number of unemployed. I should have done it weeks ago, as the delay had cost me hugely!

The stress and worry were growing. How much more could I handle?

Every time that I cut down my workforce, it just wasn't enough. The building industry was crashing faster and faster. Five more of my team had to go, which would leave just myself and Dave again – right back where I had started, only now I had two vehicles on lease hire. I couldn't afford to keep the pickup truck that also had to go. It was replaced by an old beaten-up truck, what a comedown! I asked myself, 'Is this it? Is this the bottom? Can I fall any further?' It wasn't long though before we realised that the lease hire car also had to go. It seemed as if everything was slowly slipping away, but now we experienced something new. Rob Burr knew of our escalating financial problems and that we now had transport problems, "I've got an old car that you can have and it should keep you going for a while." This was the first car that we had given to us, but it wouldn't be the last.

*****

There is a saying, 'It was the piece of straw that broke the camel's back!' We say it when problems and issues have piled up over a while and then it only takes one small thing, for everything to come crashing down. My piece of straw was a retaining wall that was moving. Dave and I had built it and we had to return on numerous occasions to carry out remedial works to stabilise it. The pressure was increasing as the problem was becoming unbearable. I tried not to show it, but all this did was increase the pressure even more.

I was starting to think, 'I can't take any more of this!' It had been fifteen years since I had considered going to the train track and ending it forever. Now I was considering it again. The trains ran past the problem job. From the viaduct, I could look down at my wall. I would put an end to this pain once and for all.

That is what I was feeling and that is what I was planning, but obviously didn't go through with it or I wouldn't be writing this now. Instead, I talked to people. God pulled me back from the brink again. How could I even have considered what I was thinking? I had three young children and had been a Christian for three years, but the pressure had built. It needed to be released. Talking may not sound like much, but it is an amazing way to release the pressure. Talking can be tough, but twice it has now saved my life.

I never did get another call about the retaining wall.

Perhaps we had solved the problem? It is still there and I am still here. It's easy to look back and say, "No problem is ever bad enough to turn to suicide." It is a completely different matter though, when your mind is overwhelmed and can see no other way out. Anyone who has ever been there will relate to what I am saying. To those who have never been there, I sincerely hope that you never will, but if you do happen to find yourself there, go talk to someone, anyone, just talk!

Psalm 23 tells us that we can walk through the valley of the shadow of death. I had walked in that valley. It also says, 'I shall not want and He refreshes my soul.'

A new plan I give you

A new feeling was building inside of me, one of a desire to give back. With less building work to do, I could now spend more time doing youth work. I was now working with young people at church on a Sunday morning and a mid-week meeting. We also met regularly for Sunday afternoon walks, games and tea, but I still wanted to do more. Boys Brigade had played an influential part in my teenage years. John and Brenda Evans had been my mentors and supported me when I was younger; now looking back I was beginning to see just how much they had helped me. So, I decided that it was time to go back and help out as a leader. It had been fifteen years since I had left and it did feel good to return.

There was a growing problem of young people hanging out on the streets getting bored; Boys Brigade gave a positive focus and hope. I would run the band sessions, teaching drums and bugles. I would also help with other activities such as first aid or planning a route for the Duke of Edinburgh Award expedition. The evening would always have a physical part such as football, circuit training or even aerobics, all of which I would organise. It was fun, but the best part was watching young people achieve something.

John and Brenda Evans were my mentors, but little did I know that I would go on into full-time Christian work. For now, I was working with them as a volunteer and mentoring young people. Interestingly at least two of those young people that I mentored at Boys Brigade have grown up to become full-time Christian workers. Anton would become a youth worker and Andrew would become a church minister. I believe that we all influence those that we meet, whether we spend a long time or just a brief period with them, we can plant a seed in their lives. I only stayed at Boys Brigade for two years before God called me into the next project.

The church youth group were keen to play an active role in making a difference and the Oasis Trust now had another project that they were promoting. Crackerteria encouraged groups of people to set up a temporary restaurant or cafe to raise funds for the developing world. It was held during December for the run-up to Christmas, hence the title 'Crackerteria'. The project had the theme of 'pay more eat less.' Our group made simple soups and curries and opened for the two weekends before Christmas. Alongside this, Andy and I would go out onto the streets with mince pies and entice people in.

It was so successful that we ran it for two years (1989 & 1990) and would probably still be running it now if we hadn't been led to do something even more challenging. I do know that other projects are still running all these years later.

It was during our second year that our experience out on the street took on a whole new dimension. It was the night of the local youth club Christmas disco and there were some two hundred young people on the streets of Minchinhampton. Some had been consuming large amounts of alcohol, which resulted in several aggressive situations developing. Fights were about to break out. Armed with a tin of mince pies each, Andy and I would walk into a heated situation as a punch was about to be thrown. Stepping between the potential fighters we simply said, "Happy Christmas, have a mince pie." This was such a random thing to do, it instantly defused the aggression, often with the pair of aggressors repeating what we had just said; "Happy Christmas," they would say and sometimes even hug each other.

I have, since this experience, used this method of diversion on the streets on many occasions. Many years on from the 'Crackerteria' project I would be involved in detached youth work and would adopt this same tactic. Mince pies would become lollipops and these would be used to divert young people from fighting, but also just as a great thing to share. I found that if I was sucking on a lolly and I gave one to a young person, suddenly we would have something in common. From that point, we could chat and be surprised that we had much in common. I have used various things over the years, to try to obtain that common link, but lollipops are my favourite as they last longer and are very cheap. I now often ponder over the number of fights and therefore arrests that have been prevented simply by sharing a lolly.

Whilst we were spending our time working with this great group of young people, working on 'Crackerteria' projects and other fun things throughout the year, the Stroud Town Council carried out a survey. This survey asked young people who were hanging around on the streets of Stroud, particularly on a Friday and Saturday evening, what they would like provided for them. Over two hundred young people then used the street as a social gathering place so it wasn't surprising that they asked for somewhere safe and friendly where they could gather. Their first choice was a Cinema for the town, which incidentally it now has. Their second choice was a coffee bar type of project, somewhere they could meet and not be hassled to buy anything or be moved on.

Those who were working with young people in the area were all very excited. At last young people were being asked what they wanted. Their opinions were being considered and someone would now provide what they were requesting. It was the talk of the town, but that was as far as it went 'talk' and no one did anything! Why ask? Why expose the need? Why bother if you can't follow through?

Andy Morris and I were two of those youth workers who were talking about what was going to be provided for young people. "Someone is going to provide a coffee bar for the youth of Stroud," but no one ever did!

Following the vision

I have now learnt to identify and act upon a God-given vision sooner than I did in 1989. I had only been a Christian for three years. Andy had only been a Christian for a few months more than me and we were both still spiritual babies. Even when God had given us both the same picture, we still didn't react.

It was the summer of 1989. The findings of the Town Council survey had been published in the local newspaper. Now, whenever either Andy or I drove past a particular building, we would see it as the place where the coffee bar would be set up. The young people of the town had asked for it, so it was surely going to happen.

Twenty-six Gloucester Street had recently become vacant and the two of us found it impossible to drive past without seeing the building overflowing with young people. This was not just an idea, more than just imagination running wild, this was a physical picture of what this place was going to become. Not what it could be, but what it would be! The two of us talked about this shared 'vision' that God had given us both. We agreed that this was going to be the place where someone would set up a coffee bar for young people. It would be fifteen months before we realised that God was speaking to us and eighteen months before we actually did anything.

Looking at our situation now I think that we were a little like Jonah. God spoke to Jonah and told him to go to Nineveh, but he went in exactly the opposite direction. Similarly, we did nothing about it, we just talked.

We were now doing various school assemblies that involved singing and acting. We did one song called, 'When God speaks you've gotta do it!' I often now think of that song and I tend to take steps of faith more readily nowadays.

When God Speaks You've Gotta Do It

There's a word in The Bible some people do ignore,
And others turn away.
This word is very simple it's easy to understand,
So let me tell you what this word does say.
Chorus:
You gotta do it, do it, do it not just hear it.

You gotta do it, do it from your heart.
When God speaks you gotta do it, do it,
do it not just hear it,
do it, do it from your heart.

A story in The Bible, a man walking down the road,
Some robbers came and punched him on the nose.
They took all of his money, let's clear off they said,
And left him there half-dead.

Then a priest came and saw him,
walked past ignored him.
Along came a Levite, who ran off in sheer fright.
Then a man from Samaria said,
"Here mate I'll take care of ya."
And the man said,
"I don't understand why you're doing this for me."
So, the man said, "Well when God speaks..."

Chorus

A man in The Bible, Noah was his name,
God spoke to him one day.
Said, "I'm gonna send down lots of water,
I think I'll call it rain,
So, build a big boat Noah and
you'll be saved that way."

So, Noah wasn't lazy,
but his friends thought he was crazy.
They mock at him and laughed at him and said,
"You must be a nutter Noah,
to build a boat this way!"
And Noah said, "Well when God speaks...."

Chorus

It was now 1990 and two friends, Ian Sadler and Rob Burr decided to re-launch the Stroud Youth for Christ organisation. This was giving Andy and me the motivational spiritual kick that we both needed. I was thirty years old, the same age that Jesus was when he started His ministry. What better age to start something new?

I don't remember much about the Stroud Youth for Christ re-launch. Someone from British Youth for Christ was speaking, talking about the 'Remnant.' I can't remember the exact Bible verses, but the gist of what he was saying is that we would rise out of the remnant of what was left previously. Stroud Youth for Christ had not been active for several years, but there were a handful of people who would soon actively make that change. The small church building was packed!

At the end of the meeting, people were asked to let their names be known if they would want to do something to support the youth of Stroud. Andy and I put our names down and agreed to attend a meeting that was planned for later that week. Interestingly, some of those who had been talking about doing something for a couple of years had failed to turn up. I do feel that it is important that we talk the talk and walk the walk, but sadly some will talk about doing and then never actually put words into action. Those that were present were the ones who would make something happen. We were the remnant with enough energy and enthusiasm to rise up.

On the evening of the follow-up meeting, we started in prayer and then Andy and I shared our vision for a coffee bar. Everyone present was excited about what they were hearing. Nobody else had anything else to offer as a means of restarting Stroud Youth for Christ. After talking things through for probably about an hour, we decided to pray some more. We were now seeking the finer details for the next steps. After praying, Andy spoke first and said, "I think we should call it 'The Door.'"

Tracy Baker (later married and became Spiers) was a BBC Radio Gloucestershire reporter and a very good person to be present. She suggested, "How about 'The Open Door?'" Other suggestions were now being thrown in for consideration such as 'Doorway.'

Just for a laugh, I said, "How about 'A Jar?'" Everyone then looked at me strangely so I said, "When is a door, not a door? The answer, when it's 'A Jar.'" My level of humour still hasn't changed much.

Andy spoke again, "No I feel that God wants just 'The Door,' as in Jesus said, 'I am The Door.' It should be 'The Door,' nothing else." When he had finished speaking everyone agreed, that we would set up a coffee bar called 'The Door.'

We were also planning our second Crackerteria, so nothing much happened until the New Year. We had no business plan, no money and not a lot of experience, but we had a huge heart and a pile of faith.

I talked briefly with Andy on the phone and agreed. "We've waited long enough, now it's time for action! It's time to make a phone call to the owner of twenty-six Gloucester Street, the building of our vision."

Andy made the call. We had cheekily decided on a very low offer of rent. We told the owner that we wanted it for a year and that we didn't want to pay anything for six months. We were very surprised when he agreed to all of what we had asked for. He was keen to see the building used, as it had been vacant for at least two years. He also wanted to see something done to support young people.

Andy called me back. As the phone rang, I remember thinking that it must be bad news, it was too quick. We were both blown away at how easily it had gone, but it could have been down to the amount of prayer that had gone on before the phone call.

Two months went by as legal issues were taken care of and we were given the keys at the start of March 1991.

The building was previously used as a pine furniture shop. The previous tenant had left in such a hurry that they just made a huge hole in the floor, through which they passed everything from the basement. The building was a mess, but we had the skills to do what was required.

Andy had previously renovated an old house and was a skilled pattern maker, who owned his own foundry. My knowledge of buildings saved us from having to employ a builder. We organised regular work parties, never paying for any labour and wherever we could, we would even scrounge materials.

Andy built the coffee bar and kitchen area, whilst Rob Burr made a window seat. We even roped my dad in to help with his plastering skills and he set to repairing a ceiling. An army of volunteers helped with decorating and together this great team transformed the ground floor and basement.

My work was now very sporadic and I would have

about three days paid work each week. This meant that I could give the rest of my time to work on the refurbishment works that were required to keep The Door project on track. I would take Dave along with me and pay him, but I was not earning anything. Floors needed laying, walls needed building and it seemed that every task was bigger than we had first realised.

The youth group from church arrived every Wednesday evening, as they worked their way through a list of jobs. Before long we were joined by other adult groups, all of them were keen to see this project come into being.

We were now attracting helpers from many local churches and word was spreading. We were seeing volunteers from two Christian Fellowships, the Baptist Church and the Anglican Church; people from a variety of backgrounds all with one common aim; to help young people.

The refurbishment work took us about six months to complete and about a month before we opened, we invited people from the local churches to come and visit. Our thought was that if every Christian in the area could give just £1 each month, we would be able to run this thing. We were about to start paying our rent and we had no money, just a lot of faith.

The Bible says, 'God shall supply all of our needs (Philippians 4:19).' People will often confuse their 'wants' with 'needs' and then wonder why they don't receive what they want. We had spent eighteen months running away from this project, so it would seem that we certainly didn't want it. Now though, we had been brought to the place of meeting the needs of young people and God was going to supply all of our needs!

In that first meeting, we were pleased to see about twenty people turn up. Most of these would become the volunteer workforce. The building work was coming to an end and the real work was about to start.

We knew of no other project like this in existence and therefore couldn't go and learn from anyone else. We, therefore, made it up as we went along. Nowadays, it's the complete opposite, as there are projects like ours all over the country. Many of those have visited us before setting up and I have always given them the same five key points for advice:

- *Always involve young people in the planning, preparation and refurbishment stage.*

- *Recruit an army of willing volunteers, some of whom must have the essential skills required to do the work.*

- *Find at least one local business to support you. DM Foundries continued with their support for years, as they supplied our toiletries and stationery.*

- *Unless you have your own charity number, set up under the banner of an existing charity. British Youth for Christ worked for us.*

- *Prayer – I usually only say this one if it is a Christian group that is visiting us, although prayer is the most essential ingredient. Without it, we would never have opened 'The Door.'*

Chapter Twelve

First Contact

We eventually opened on the last weekend of August in 1991. We had installed a pool table, pinball table and jukebox. It was all second-hand, but it was enough to attract every kind of young person who would normally be hanging around the streets. Initially, to attract young people we went out to them. We gave out vouchers for free coffee and cake. We had publicity through the local press and had mentioned it during Archway School assemblies, which I was now doing with Dave and Andy.

We didn't have to wait very long until our vision of the building overflowing with young people was fulfilled. Word spread quickly. This was something new. No membership or identification was required. It was un-territorialised; no one had claimed it. It was there for all young people.

The place could hold about sixty people and that would be very full but during our second weekend, we saw 120 to 150 people on Friday and Saturday. This was the vision, it was overflowing; however, if we had known in advance what we were getting into, we never would have stepped out on this journey. This was the start of what has now in 2015) been a twenty-four-year journey.

Reality started to hit us almost immediately. The demand was more than we had ever imagined. Now we began to realise just how much time this was going to take out of our lives. Andy and I both volunteered to work for three Saturdays out of four. This was a huge commitment. It took our family time. It took over our lives. Even when we weren't actually working at the project, we were still thinking about it and the young people that we were now forming relationships with. We were meeting young people with problems and struggled to switch off, unable to think about anything else. The work was all absorbing and none of us were getting paid. The project would be entirely dependent on volunteers for nearly five years.

The Stroud Town Council survey had highlighted a need for somewhere warm and dry where young people could hang out. Now we were quickly realising that some of the young people that we were meeting had much deeper needs. Some had so many problems that life had dumped on them that they just needed to unload.

None of us then, had any formal training. We just wanted to help these young people, to show them that someone cared about them and most of all, to demonstrate love in action. I would think back to my own childhood, my aggression, the pain, the harm that I did to myself, the problems with the police and my many personal struggles. Being a teenager was not easy, I knew that and I empathised with them. If they wanted to talk, I was willing to listen.

It was the second weekend of opening when a young girl asked if she could speak to a female member of staff. We hadn't met her before, and no relationship had been built, but she found herself in a desperate situation and recognised that we might be able to help. She suspected that she might be pregnant. She was fifteen years old and full of fear and worry. Thinking on our feet, someone ran to the local pharmacy and we offered her a free pregnancy test. The test was negative and her world was returned to normal. Lessons had been learnt on both sides. She learnt that she would take greater care in future. We realised that we needed to provide more to meet this kind of need. Later we developed links with the local Pregnancy Crisis Centre and they would carry out any tests that were required, plus provide the right kind of support and guidance.

Over the years we have always tried to identify and meet the needs of young people that we have met. At times this has been frustrating, as needs are identified, but we are unable to do anything to help. Often the reason that we can't help is due to lack of funding.

A month after opening we held our very first business meeting. This was the first time that I had the privilege to meet Di Rowe. She had moved into the area twelve months previously and she felt that God had told her not to get involved in anything in the area until now. She explained that she was a qualified, fully accredited Christian counsellor, with experience of working with young people and families. The timing was perfect but then God's timing always is. We agreed that Di should start and head up a completely free and confidential counselling service in the flat above the coffee bar. It was a drab space but with a lick of paint, a second-hand three-piece suite and an old carpet that didn't quite fit, it would soon become more comfortable. This new service would eventually grow to four counsellors, receiving referrals from social workers, doctors and schools, as well as general enquiries through the coffee bar. Another service that was completely free and confidential. We never would have reached the point that we are today if it were not for so many volunteers. We still rely so much on volunteer help but at the start, it was all that we had.

Our times of opening would change over the first five years, depending on the volunteers available. Initially, the coffee bar only opened on Wednesday and Friday after school, on Saturday in the daytime and on Friday and Saturday evenings. Each shift was manned by a different team and each team did their best to interact in a variety of different ways with the young people, but it lacked continuity.

This was a long way from Boys Brigade. It was informal, with no uniform, never knowing what to expect, no membership, no restrictions on gender. We all quickly learnt the skill of improvisation. I still consider this to be one of the key skills for any youth worker.

This type of youth work soon became referred to as 'off-street work.' The skills that were needed were similar to working with young people on the street but now there were more of them, all gathered in one place. Some of those that we now started to see were some of those we had met nearly two years ago on the streets of Minchinhampton. They recognised both Andy and myself, referring to the night that we had given them all mince pies. They remembered the aggression and told us that some big fights were planned for that night, but because of our improvisation with mince pies, peace prevailed. Now I often wonder, 'What is the worst thing that we have prevented?' Only God can answer that one. The presence of that Golden Thread was more powerful than we could imagine.

It was also during that first month of opening the coffee bar that we decided we needed to sell our house. Zion House, the place that God had led us to. Our debts were far too big to ever be able to pay them off without selling. We needed to sell, but it wouldn't be easy. It wouldn't be quick. We would have to learn patience and would learn to trust God in many new ways. Twenty-one months would pass before a buyer would be found.

With the house on the market and after just two months of opening The Door, I felt that God wanted me to venture into full-time work for him. My building work was drying up and doors were opening that were leading me into youth work as a full-time career. One particular door that opened was an advert in the local newspaper which asked people who had been unemployed for more than six months to consider training in a youth and community course. I wasn't unemployed and should not have been allowed to qualify, but I was allowed to join. Another door opened and led me to work in a County Council youth club working with seven- to twelve-year-olds after school, a kind of 'latchkey kids' club. Another opportunity was offered to me, to work in a local day centre for people with mental health issues. I worked just with young people who were struggling to cope with life. It was a huge learning curve.

It was now January 1992 and I stood up in front of the church, telling them all that I believed, "God is calling me." They understood and they supported me. I was living by faith. No fixed wage. I had signed on to state benefits to have some form of income, but it wasn't enough. Our bank overdraft was a huge £20,000 debt, due to people who hadn't paid me and due to delaying cutting down my building workforce. Working and living by faith, I knew that God would provide all of our needs and it was amazing what he provided. Yes, he used people and obedient servants, but he knew exactly what we needed and when we needed it.

Every so often roughly every fortnight, someone would hand me an envelope. The delivery person would tell me that someone had asked them to pass this on. It may have been another person who had given them the envelope and wished to remain anonymous, but it could have also been that God had spoken directly to them, asking them to give it to us as a blessing. We truly were blessed with what we considered to be an abundance as each envelope contained large sums of money, often hundreds of pounds.

We were only just getting by, managing to survive, money was always tight. If any unexpected expenditure happened, we would never survive. The unexpected inevitably always happens and our unexpected need was related to the car again. It was a generous offer that Rob had given us his car, but it required serious maintenance, full of rust but at least it worked. However, the legal requirement of the annual MOT was due. The trip to the local garage revealed the unsurprising news, the vehicle was no longer road-worthy and the cost of repairs would be excessive. We gave the car back to Rob and he presumably scrapped it.

We had managed to somehow scrape together £300 which we planned to spend on a cheap 'Banger' of a car. We knew that we wouldn't see much for our money, but it was all that we could possibly afford. We decided to take a trip into town and drew the money out of the bank in readiness to make a quick purchase. I safely placed the money in my wallet just as Derek Morris walked up the street. He asked what we were doing and we told him of our situation. "I've got a friend that runs a garage. Don't buy anything until I have spoken to him."

We returned home and later that day Derek phoned, "He has something suitable, just pay him the £300 and the car is yours."

As we drove to the garage, we didn't know what to expect. On arrival, we were shown an Austin Maestro with a price tag of £950. We couldn't believe what we were being offered; for the second time in our lives, we were being blessed with the gift of a car. We continued to live by faith and we were continuously blessed as God provided our needs, which were being channelled through the obedience and generosity of his people.

This car was a real blessing; however, it wasn't long before we needed to replace the exhaust pipe which had almost broken in half and sounded like a tractor. In a short space of time, we would be unable to drive it. We told nobody of this specific need, we had already been given so much, but I did enquire how much a new exhaust pipe would cost. I was told that it would be £76.32 and realised that this was money that we didn't have. Most of what we were being given as gifts was being used to pay off debts and the mortgage, with any left being used for basic foods.

I decided to just pray and ask God to help. I told him that without the car it would be hard to work. I was living in faith and in faith, I knew that God would listen and step in if it truly was a need. So, I asked him to provide the money for the exhaust and then went to bed.

The next morning an envelope was lying on the front door mat. Someone had delivered it in the night. When I opened it and counted how much we had been blessed with, I was amazed to see that it was £76.32 the exact amount that was needed for the exhaust pipe, not a penny more, not a penny less. We hadn't told anyone about this need, but obviously God had and we were so grateful to once again have transport.

The struggles were endless, but God provided and we experienced no end of humbling moments.

As we lived more and more like this, the more we grew in faith. A foundation of faith was being built. This foundation would lead to even greater things.

Forget your own problems

The work at The Door now became more and more intense. It seemed I was on call at all times and found myself drawn into situations that I wasn't properly prepared for. I made several trips to the hospital with young people who had attempted suicide. The phone would ring at 2.00am and it would be a police officer or social worker looking for a young person that had gone missing. I would help those who had been involved in fights, patching them up where I could or taking them to hospital if their injuries were more serious. I would spend numerous hours sitting in Magistrates' Courts supporting young people who had been arrested. I could see another side to these young people and provided character references and reports. For most of them, it was a wake-up call and they never committed any offences again.

One particular young person who was struggling with life was Scott (not real name). He had a quiet disposition about him and had struggled to make many friends at school, although he did have two very close friends and he was gradually growing in confidence. His new-found confidence had now helped him to find work and life was beginning to feel good for him. However, when a person is in a vulnerable state, it doesn't take much for all of the good feelings and confidence to disappear. In Scott's case, it was a major trauma that would upset his state of mind and his fragile emotional balance.

It was around seven in the morning and Scott was making his way to work. He had been fortunate enough to find work close to home, so it wasn't far to travel and Scott enjoyed the early morning walk. The fact that it was mid-November and still dark didn't put him off, as life was looking good. His route took him down a dimly lit footpath next to a park and it was here that a dark shadow of a man approached him.

As the person moved closer and the shadow became clearer, Scott looked at the man's face. He had a desperate look in his eyes and he was close enough to identify the smell of alcohol on his breath. The unknown character stopped and demanded, "Give me your money!" Scott refused. He didn't see the blade of the knife but felt the immediate searing pain as it was thrust into the top of his leg.

Scott started shouting for help, which was enough to panic the assailant and he ran away. It was a short distance to the hospital and Scott made his way there for help, where the police were called.

Scott gave a very accurate description of his attacker, but couldn't believe it when just a few days later he saw him again. He followed his attacker with some friends for safety and then reported his presence to the police.

The man lived near our coffee bar project and we witnessed the police arriving to take him in for questioning, though without any evidence or witnesses, the man denied the attack and was released without charge.

Anger, fear and hate surged out of Scott as he wanted justice and without it, he would seek revenge. He wanted to fight back, to hurt this man, but it wasn't in his quiet meek nature. Instead, each time that he saw the man from a distance, he would 'phase out.' It was as if his mind just switched off, as he couldn't cope with the level of stress that he was now under. He would sit and stare, but never respond to anyone talking to him. It was as if he was a shell, alive, but no life. Each time he would return from one of these episodes he would be angry and scream out, "I want to kill that bloke!"

A doctor confirmed that this is likely to be the mind's way of protecting him from the traumatic stress, it was a form of post-traumatic stress disorder.

The feelings and behaviour continued for months until eventually, Scott decided that he could not live like this any longer. As his friends ran after him to stop him, he found himself at the top of the multi-storey car park. The drop on one side is about seventy feet and in recent years several people have jumped from there, bringing their lives to a tragic end. On the other side, the side where Scott now stood, the drop was about thirty feet. With a crowd in pursuit, he didn't hesitate to jump and plunged to the hard tarmac surface below.

With no more than bruises and shame, more anger came flooding into him. His friends helped him up; all of them showing concern for his state of mind.

It was a short walk back to our coffee bar and the first that we knew about what had just happened, is when Scott came in; he was angry. The anger was directed at himself as he made comments of, "I wish I was dead!"

As he threw himself from the top of the stairs into the basement, he had reached his lowest point and the gravity of the whole situation was acknowledged.

He just sat and talked, he talked so quietly that his voice was barely audible. Now as he talked, he realised that there were people who cared about him. It would take five months from the point of his attack until he returned to work. His 'phasing out' would eventually stop and he would also learn to speak louder than he had ever previously been able to speak. I would meet with him regularly to talk through his feelings, help him set goals that would develop his confidence and teach him how to project and express himself more clearly. Slowly his life returned. Slowly the desire to live was restored. He had talked and I had listened. This formula has helped to save many like Scott over the years, but I do think that he was the first that I had helped in this way.

*****

After just six months of living by faith and dealing with some of the most serious and unexpected issues that you could imagine, I couldn't handle any more. At the time there was a saying that the average life span for a Christian youth worker was about two years. On average, burnout would hit and you could cope no more. I like to think that things have changed since then and that youth workers who are employed in Christian settings are now properly managed, resourced and supported.

It's easy for me to look back now and realise that there was another reason why I was on the edge of burnout. I had worked by faith, but I had also carried out all of my youth work duties and beyond, in my own strength

– that was a mistake!

For now, I felt that God was saying, “You have done enough.” He was calling me back out of working for him, living by faith. Six months after standing up in front of the church and telling everyone that God was ‘calling me,’ now I was telling them, “God is calling me back out.” They had understood when I told them that God had called me, but now many of them struggled to understand why I should be called back from where he had led me.

I believe that we are all like tools in a toolbox. The toolbox is God’s toolbox and we are his tools, to be used as and when he chooses to use us. He chose to use me for six months, so that I may learn and become better prepared for what was to come in the future. He put me back for a rest, although it wouldn’t be a complete rest. I would continue working coffee bar shifts for another three and a half years before he would call me again.

At the end of this six months ‘taster’ calling I looked back feeling as if I had failed, but God showed me where the foundations had been laid for the work that lay ahead. He reminded me of those who were alive or out of prison because I had been there for them and he had also worked a small miracle on my debts, which were now less than when I had stepped out in faith.

Chapter Thirteen

Highs and Lows

My songwriting had continued and during my six months of 'taster calling,' Dave and I decided that we should produce an album. It was recorded in a day in the basement at The Door. A mobile studio arrived and filled the room. Nowadays it can all be done on one computer.

The album was produced on cassette. It was a very low budget and never made any money, as we gave more away than we sold. We called the album 'Poetic Justice,' which was the same name that we called ourselves. This may not have sounded very imaginative, but the lyrics were. They were powerful, they were from God. Each track carried a message and that message would change lives.

*****

It was the summer of 1992 when I first met Kimberley (not real name). She came running into the coffee bar on a sunny Saturday afternoon, with two police officers chasing her. She couldn't understand why the police were allowed in and allowed to confront her. To her, 'The Door' was a safe place, a refuge and a sanctuary, a place to hide and that also included hiding from the police. It didn't take us long to realise that she was a missing person and the police were trying to find her for her own safety. She was also panicking because she had been shoplifting. In those early years, we saw a very high level of shoplifters and we are convinced that this was reduced as a result of some of the work that we have done.

The police took Kimberley away, back to those who had reported her as missing, but for how long?

Over the next few weeks, we saw Kimberley regularly. As we started to build a relationship with her, trust developed. Sadly, that trust would lead to Kimberley being led to temptation and her skill and nature as a thief would get the better of her.

My box of albums was now on display in the coffee bar as I was trying to sell them. The sight of the bright yellow cassette caught her eye and, in a flash, it was in her bag. In her mind she had nothing to lose, she had made plans to run again and this time it would be far enough away that she would not be found.

A week passed and no one saw Kimberley, not even the police came looking this time. Her absence had not been reported. In the same way, the absence of the cassette had gone unnoticed.

As Kimberley walked back into the coffee bar, she looked different as I approached to chat with her.

"Hi Kim, we haven't seen you for a while, how's things with you?"
"Yeah, uh... I've been to Cornwall." This was over two hundred miles away.
"Cornwall? What were you doing in Cornwall?" Were you on holiday?"
"No, I ran away again, needed to get some space to sort my head out."
"And did you? Sort your head out?"
"Yeah, I need to stop nicking stuff and start to behave and I wanna start by giving this back."
She handed me the cassette tape. It was the first that I

knew it was missing.
"Oh, uh... how long have you had that?"
"'bout a week."
"Did you listen to it?"
"Y – e – s," came the long-drawn-out reply.
"What did you think?"

Then came the story. "I sat on top of a cliff overlooking the sea. I had my Walkman (cassette player) with me and popped the tape in. What I heard in the headphones spoke to me. God spoke to me and I gave my life to Jesus. I want to give the tape back to you now and say sorry."

I smiled as I said, "You can keep it or give it to someone else who might need it."

Kimberley never did say why she was sitting on the top of the cliff. She may have just been admiring the view, but the fact that she was running away again could have meant that she was going to run off the cliff. I didn't ask any more, I didn't have to.

*****

Kimberley was not the first to find Jesus through the work that we were doing at 'The Door.' The first fruit came just four months after opening. We had met Joe (not real name) on the first day of opening, though with so many young people on that first day, we never really remembered him. He didn't stand out in the crowd, but to God, he was someone special.

Joe told us that when we met him, he was on the streets of Stroud entertaining himself and his friends by glueing coins to the pavement and then watching unsuspecting members of the public try to pick them up. He was seventeen years old and enjoyed an element of fun in his life. His life had not been entirely happy, as his parents had divorced when he was just fourteen years old.

Joe was also one of the two close friends that Scott had and was almost certainly amongst the crowd that had chased after him, just before he jumped from the multi-storey car park. This may have caused Joe to start thinking more about life and death, the age-old question of, 'What happens after death?'

He would talk to us quite openly about his life, and the things that he had done and explain that he felt as if something was missing.

It was December 31st 1991, New Year's Eve. Joe was getting ready to embark upon a new year, but little did he know that it was also going to be a new life.

Like most towns, Stroud would traditionally see a gathering of revellers that form a crowd around the vicinity of the town clock. Joe was amongst the crowd. As the time approached midnight, the throng of the crowd grew and as usual a few scuffles would break out. Alcohol-fuelled fights were seen as a regular occurrence during this night of the year and police were on standby. Joe was normally a quiet gentle type, but alcohol can transform a person, causing them to react differently.

The crowd rapidly grew restless and out of control. Joe felt a knock on the back of his head. Someone had hit him. He didn't know who it was, it didn't matter, he just turned and immediately punched the first person he saw. As his fist made contact with the unknown person, his brain went into meltdown at the realisation that his target was a policeman. Suddenly his world was spinning as in an instant Joe found himself restrained. In his head, he was questioning, 'How did this happen?' His question of the situation had a repentant nature to it. Now almost as quickly as he had been restrained, he was being released. I like to think that Jesus intervened and said, "Let go, I've paid the price for his wrongdoing, leave him with me and I'll take care of him."

In those early days at The Door, one of our volunteers was allowed to live in the flat upstairs. Joe knew that if he went there, he would find peace and sanctuary. He spent the night sleeping in the Drop-In (something that we wouldn't allow today). As he awoke the next morning he reflected on the events of the previous evening and his life. He had known that something was missing and now he recognised what it was. He had heard the Gospel message and he knew that Jesus had paid the price for him. The price of life over death. He was alone, but God was with him, then as he sat and opened up his heart, God came in and filled it. It was New Year's Day 1992 and Joe was a new creation. We previously had many conversations with him and planted the seeds of truth, God's truth, but it was the Holy Spirit that had brought Joe to the point of realisation and revelation. Everything that he had heard about Jesus was true and real.

Three months later Joe was baptised in a river that runs through a meadow. This place was special, as it was where he had played when he was a child. Now he was a child again, a child of God.

*****

One of the things that attracted me to youth work was

the energy and liveliness that is associated with young people. That energy can help to keep us young. Then occasionally, we meet someone with no energy for life. Lizzie was such a person.

In that first year of opening, she would call in for a drink and a chat, she always had a support worker with her and always talked about her unhappy life. She lived in a children's home, had no family and felt as if everyone was against her. At some point during every conversation, she would talk about killing herself. The support worker would smile and raise an eyebrow as if to say, 'We've heard all of this before.' The cuts on her arms, though, told a different story. Each cut is neatly in line with the one next to it. It was a form of order in a life full of chaos. Each single cut shouted out, "I am being serious! Why won't anyone listen to me?"

I slowly lost count of the number of conversations that I had with Lizzie, but I was always pleased to see her and to listen, but it seemed that she needed more. The last time that I saw Lizzie she was describing how she was going to kill herself. Two days later she was found hanging from her stairs. The rope around her neck had brought an end to her tragic life!

Now in 2015, twenty-three years later, I still question, 'Did I do enough? Did anyone do enough?' Lizzie was the first young person who I had worked with, supported and tried to help, who was now dead! There would be many more.

By the time the project had been running for ten years, I had counted twenty-five young people who had died. Some died in car accidents, others from drug overdoses and some from natural causes. I would come to realise that although these young people were mainly full of energy, they were also very vulnerable, precious and in need of protection. After ten years of counting, I would stop, as I would hear God speak to me saying, "Count the ones that you save, not the ones that you lose." Others have died since, but I don't count any more. Some of their stories will be found further on in this book.

There would be many dark moments, but in that darkness, the Golden Thread of God would be ever-present.

The next two songs that you are about to read were written in 1991. 'What a Mess' was inspired by the state of the whole world, whilst 'What's going on?' was written in about five minutes one evening after returning home and the frustrations of the day were getting to me. This was how God led me to be released from the tension that was building up.

What a Mess!

The progress of the nation,
destroying God's creation,
All around the world,
it's just the same old situation.
We fight for right we fight for peace
and for this generation,
Don't give me deprivation
what we need is revelation, c'mon!

Jus' take a look at the World
an see jus' what it's got,
All work no play school every day, it hasn't got a lot!
This World which we live in is in a bad old way,

All war an fights, famine and plights, look like they're here to stay! Here we go now.

Chorus:
Oh, what a mess! This World which we live in,
Couldn't care less it's a World without love.
Oh, what a mess! This World which we live in,
Couldn't care less it's a World without love!

Let's make this World a better,
place in which to live,
Recycle this, recycle that,
we'll take the things you give.
The people of this World
all think they know the way,
But there are some, you may be one
that could be led astray!

Chorus

Now the programmes on the TV and
the things that we all read,
They change your view of what you do,
they plant an evil seed.
Like Teenage Mutant Heroes,
what a bunch of weirdos,
They smell they're green, they look obscene,
they're nothing like my hero.

Chorus

Well, if you think you've found the answer,
of how to make the World right,
Just think again now who's to blame?
Will you blame anyone you like?
The problem lies in all of us and
it eats you from within,

The problem then is S.I.N. or call it plain old sin!

Chorus

*****

What's Going On?

Feeling tense, feeling angry when I'm feeling low.
Feeling down, feeling fed up
with the whole of the show!
All the bad, all the wrong,
all the guilt and all the shame.
People dying, people lying,
people causing people pain!
After all the violence, a World full of silence.
No one knows and no one tells
in a World of defiance!

Chorus:
What is it? What's going on?
What is it? What's going on?
What is it? What's going on?
What is it? What's going on?

Smoking dope and popping pills
it's just a way of life.
A pocket full of money on a pushing parasite!
Smoking dope and popping pills
it's just a way of life.
A pocket full of money on a pushing parasite!
An alcoholic teenager is more and more the norm.
At the latest victim's funeral
two hundred people mourn.
How many more will have to die before they realise?
They burn their hands when they play with fire when will they realise?

Will they realise?
Chorus

Now this is what I do when I'm feeling low and angry with the system.
I turn to my God, get down on my knees and pray Lord give me wisdom!
I pray Lord give me wisdom!
I praise my Lord that he answers my prayers and fills me with his peace.
Thank you, Lord, for your love, joy and strength and your miracles that never cease!
Your miracles that never cease!
Miracles that never cease!
Chorus

Chapter Fourteen

A time to say "Goodbye"

In 1992 my mum started to come to Minchinhampton Christian Fellowship with us. She enjoyed the vibrancy and the family feeling; the place had an exciting buzz of expectancy. She felt comfortable and of course, she enjoyed watching me, leading worship and leading young people.

Her enthusiasm for church was now growing and enthusiasm is an infectious thing. It didn't take long before Dad was also coming along every so often on a Sunday morning. He also started to visit the local Catholic Church, as this is what he had grown up with. This provided him with the familiarity of what he knew, but something it seemed was missing. At Minchinhampton, he was developing friendships and relationships, as people would genuinely ask after him. He found socialising easy, with a natural charisma about him, the Irish charm that could connect with most people.

My relationship with Dad had now become close. The childhood and teenage years were now long behind us. He had been sober for sixteen years and during this time a deep love for each other had grown.

No matter where I would be working on a Friday afternoon, my dad would finish his work early just so that he could visit me and admire what I was doing. He would pretend to inspect my work on the building that I was working on and I began to look forward to his Friday afternoon visits. I longed for them and on reflection, I now liken this to the prodigal son in The

Bible yearning to see his father again.

Bad health was slowly taking hold of my dad. When he was in his early fifties, he had undergone a heart bypass operation and we knew that angina still affected him. Every so often he would have to stop what he was doing and put a small tablet under his tongue. This had become quite normal and as is often the case, with normality comes a lack of concern. It was just another angina attack; we had seen so many and everything would be ok.

During a Sunday morning service at the Catholic Church, Dad had a very bad angina attack. If you were not used to them, they could look quite scary, but he might as well have been invisible. Nobody noticed or if they did, they just ignored him. He staggered towards the door and eventually one concerned lady asked if he was all right. When he recovered, he left, then later commented during the week that no one had contacted him to enquire about his health. He also said that if he had had an attack at Minchinhampton Christian Fellowship, he would have immediately been given help, prayer too if he wanted it and someone would have checked that he was OK later in the week. He was beginning to notice some differences. He also started to play worship music in his car and even played some on his harmonica.

The more he fellowshipped at Minchinhampton, the more he realised that there is a Jesus who wants a personal relationship with us. He was meeting people who could testify to such a relationship. He was seeing a new way. He had been blinded by religion for his whole life and now he had his eyes opened to relationships. He never asked many questions, as his way of learning was to watch and learn. The way that we act is very powerful and therefore very important. My dad would comment about the comparison of people that he had met at the Catholic Church and those who he now grew closer to. One experience was cold and unwelcoming, whilst the other was warm and friendly, but most of all God was slowly revealing his truth through his people.

None of us realised how badly his health was deteriorating and now at the start of the New Year, he returned to work after a two-week Christmas break. January 1993 was a cold winter and Dad was working outside. He loved to be outside working with his hands and this time he was building a Cotswold dry-stone wall. A week after returning to work he was taken ill and what started as influenza quickly turned into pneumonia. Now with his strength fading rapidly, he was rushed into hospital, where he would be in good hands.

He started to recover slowly and things were looking up. The medical staff would look after him and before long he would be back home... how wrong we were.

On the Sunday before he died, Mum called my brother Chris and asked for a lift to the hospital. Dad had developed a kidney infection and it was a touch-and-go situation. He was in a bad way, though we were not told at this stage quite how serious it was. Therefore, it was just Chris and Mum who went. Later Chris told me that he thought Dad was going to die right there in front of him, but he made a remarkable recovery.

Three days later I went to visit him. He looked tired but seemed to be well. I stayed for an hour or so, chatting about life, family and work. It was an everyday conversation and then out of the blue he says, "I've seen the light."

My ears pricked up, "What do you mean by that Dad? I believe that Jesus is the Light. Are you telling me that you've found Jesus?"

"Yes," he told me. We talked about how he was feeling about that and joked about how long it had taken him to realise what was missing in his life. I had never seen him as peaceful as he was then. He had a beaming smile and was almost glowing with a new-found enthusiasm, but it wasn't to last long. The last thing that I did for him was to go to the hospital shop and buy him two cartons of Ribena blackcurrant drink. Now every time that I see a Ribena carton, I am reminded of that night.

As I travelled home, I pondered over the conversation. My dad had given his life to Jesus. He was now not just my dad, we were both 'Brothers in Christ,' part of God's big family. I had never told him that I loved him, but it wouldn't be long now; now it would be easy.

I arrived home and settled in for the evening. Twenty minutes later the phone rang, Dad had died from a massive heart attack just after I had left. I couldn't believe what I was hearing I had only just left him. It couldn't be true. This must be a mistake.

He was sixty-four years old and none of us had any idea of just how close to death he was. He could have died on that Sunday night when Chris and Mum had been called. God though had other plans; he had kept Dad alive so that he could tell me that he had found Jesus. Now, less than two hours after telling me the great news he was dead!

Jesus told the story of the vineyard workers. He

explained that those who came to work for the last two hours of the day received the same pay as those who had worked all day. Dad had only been a Christian for a few hours, but he would have the same reward as those who had invited Jesus into their lives many years ago.

Doubt can tend to creep in and shortly afterwards I asked God if he could put my mind at rest. I picked up my Bible and was led to Thessalonians 4:13-18, I knew immediately that I had my confirmation of where Dad was. I knew that I would see him again one day, as I read:

Brothers and sisters, we do not want you to be uninformed about those who sleep in death, so that you do not grieve like the rest of mankind, who have no hope. For we believe that Jesus died and rose again and so we believe that God will bring with Jesus those who have fallen asleep in him. According to The Lord's word, we tell you that we who are still alive, who are left until the coming of The Lord, will certainly not precede those who have fallen asleep. For The Lord himself will come down from heaven, with a loud command, with the voice of the archangel and with the trumpet call of God, and the dead in Christ will rise first. After that, we who are still alive and are left will be caught up together with them in the clouds to meet The Lord in the air. And so, we will be with The Lord forever. Therefore encourage one another with these words.

When my dad died, my biggest regret was the fact that I had never told him that I loved him. He did know it, as I knew that he loved me, but sometimes it is important to tell people what they already know. I now encourage anyone who I work with, young and old, to tell their parents that they love them. I am also still learning to do this more myself, none of us will ever get it right, but it is important to work towards it.

Slowly life moves on and we all learn to adjust to our loss. Friday afternoons would never be the same without Dad arriving to see what project I was working on. I missed that immediately and I still miss it now.

Humble pie is hard to swallow

Five months later we eventually found a buyer for our house. They had negotiated us down considerably in price, but at least we could now pay off our debts and start again. It took a few weeks for all of the legal bits and pieces to be done and we were set to move out in August 1993.

We now had to find somewhere to move to, but couldn't find anything. To make matters even worse, we had now become so far behind with our mortgage payments, that the building society told us that we were too high a risk. We would not be offered another mortgage. We therefore had no alternative but to move into rented accommodation; it was as if God was teaching me some new lessons.

I had always looked down on the thought of renting property. My parents had brought me up with the understanding that it is better to have a mortgage and buy a house, rather than live in someone else's and have nothing to show for the money that is spent. Now, moving into rented accommodation was my first lesson in humbling. I had also personally never wanted to buy a house on the new housing estate which had been built near to us. In my head, I would think, 'That is where all of the losers end up!' Little did I know that after eight months of living in rented, I would also end up on the Manor Village housing estate. My opinion has now been well and truly changed.

It was the day of moving into the rented house and I was the last person to leave Zion House, the house that God had led me to build. The rest of the family had left just half an hour before and I had just thrown the last few final items into the back of my clapped-out old pickup (another humbling experience to drive this).

Now I felt angry with God. He had led us to Zion House and we were losing everything or so it felt. As I sat in the pickup, I was shouting out loud with anger, rage was taking over and I didn't care if the neighbours heard me. "GOD, WHY HAS THIS HAPPENED? You tell us in The Bible that if we turn to You, we will have life in ABUNDANCE (John 10:10). **I DON'T CALL THIS ABUNDANT! I'VE LOST EVERYTHING!"**

I kept shouting as I pulled out of the drive and heading down the hill I continued, with the rage building. The journey was only about a two-minute drive and I felt like I was going to explode, but as I arrived at my destination, I felt a calming peace touch me. God spoke into my heart and said, "You do have life in abundance, if you have Jesus in you, He is the abundance, everything else is insignificant. You do have life in ABUNDANCE!"

My view changed instantly as if a download had just been placed straight into my head and my heart. I had been thinking materialistically all of this time, now I had had my eyes opened. I had lost nearly all of my material wealth, which allowed me to have a new outlook and to enable me to value that which cannot be seen more than that which is seen.

The rented house turned out to be a real blessing. It was

an old Cotswold stone cottage and it was a little like being on holiday, although having to go to work each day (at least I still had some work).

Heather now decided that she would approach our building society again. There had been a change of manager and the new person told her that we should never have been told, that we would never be allowed a mortgage again. The Bible tells us to, 'Ask and we shall receive.' She had asked and once again we were able to step back onto the housing ladder and start again.

Now the second stage of the humbling process arrived as we bought the house and moved onto the Manor Village Estate. Although this house was ours (and the building society's) it was so small, a third of the size of Zion House. It would take some getting used to.

We did what we could to improve it and make it ours. We fitted new central heating, landscaped the garden and decorated throughout. We were starting all over again, but this time with three young children.

Decorating the lounge was the last task and as usual, choosing the right colour was a problem. At last, after much debate a colour was picked, but after a first coat came the words, "I don't think I like it." Heather was right of course; it was not as we had expected. Then I had a brainwave, "Let's take the rest of the paint and add it to all of the other paints that we have left over." We added about five other colours, gave it all a very long stir and the colour was perfect. I still keep this picture in my head as God said to me, "You have access to lots of different people. Individually they may not look like much, but blend them in a team and they will be perfect." Who would have thought that choosing the wrong colour paint would teach me so much about teamwork?

It was teamwork that was now causing the work of The Door Youth Project to develop. The project had been running for over two years. At first, we had only taken on a one-year lease to see how it would go, then at the end of the first year, we repeated it. We stepped out even more in faith at the end of our second year, as we had now taken on a three-year lease. This step would take us to a point of five years and at that point, another huge step of faith would be required.

Chapter Fifteen

The Callback

It continued to be a struggle to find building work and in October 1995, I was earning such a small amount of money it wasn't enough to exist. It was worse than the time that we had to sell our table to be able to eat, but this time help came in the form of government funding. We applied for and were awarded Family Income Support. This was a fixed amount of money that would be paid to us each week for six months. (This benefit has since been replaced by the Working Families Tax Credit).

At the same time work at The Door was becoming more difficult. We had survived for just over four years since opening and the work had been carried out entirely by volunteers. These volunteers were all feeling tired and worn out. Now as we met to discuss the future of the project, the management committee were asked, "What is the future? Where are we going? What are we going to do?"

Option one was to stop everything. With volunteers struggling to keep going, myself included in this, it had to be considered, but it wasn't considered for long.

The only other option was to employ a full-time project worker. This person would take the reins and drive the project forward. We would then be able to open more hours and the work would start to become more co-ordinated.

The choices for this role were Andy or me, although Andy was not in a situation where he could stop work and so I was asked. The post would commence at the start of January 1996 and I would still have four months of Family Income Support to help me. With that help, I was able to work at a reduced rate of pay for three months.

I was asked if I was willing to take that step of faith and I accepted in a flash. Then, after that flash came the doubts, the hesitations and the 'What ifs?' Doubt is the enemy's way of chipping away at faith. I have seen it happen in many projects where doubt has crept in, chipped away and eventually blown faith out of the water. Did I have the faith? I had been called before, my 'taster calling.' Looking back now, it was as if God said, "The previous time was your audition, you were good, but you needed a little more time. Now is the time, this is your 'CALL BACK.'"

I asked, "What can I do this time that will help me? How can I be better?"

God reminded me, "Don't do things in your own strength and trust in me. Yes, my Word says that you can do all things, but it doesn't say that you WILL do all things. Whatever your hand finds to do, do it with ALL of your might, but remember to leave room for my JOY. The JOY of the Lord is your STRENGTH. Be filled with my joy and be filled with my STRENGTH."

These words, these scriptures have carried me through not just the six months of my previous audition, but for the last nineteen years. Those years have been years of faith without which we would have nothing.

I stepped into this full-time role with just three months of funding and guess what, in 2015 we still had only three months of funding. There have been times when we have had up to six months, but generally, it is always around three months. We exist like this; we exist in faith. Sometimes when I tell people this, they are surprised. "Why are you surprised?" I ask, "If we had three years' funding, where is the faith in that?" Not that God can't provide three years' funding, he just chooses not to.

As we have grown so too have our financial needs. In the first year we needed less than £6,000 to exist, but now twenty-three years later and with a team of staff that has increased to twenty-five, we need over £400,000 every year to survive. Our needs are now over sixty times more than when we first started, but God still provides all that we need.

So, if my short trial or 'taster calling' was like an audition, here I am now on the 'Main Stage' and I had to make this thing work. I had learnt from my previous experience and this time it would be different, Jesus would be at the centre of everything that I did. I would ask him to show me His way.

My job title was 'Project Co-ordinator'. This rather ambiguous title really means 'General Dogsbody', but I was prepared to do whatever God showed me and led me to do.

Sitting in the upstairs room of the project, the first thing that I noticed was how cold it was. It was January and we had no central heating. There was a small electric heater which Di Rowe had introduced to keep her clients warm, but I couldn't dream of using that. We didn't have money for heating, so I kept my coat and many layers on, but still, I shivered as I sat at my second-hand desk, with my second-hand typewriter.

Along with a small pack of paper and a handful of envelopes, this was the extent of my resources, this was the office. Now I had to source and secure more money. Yes, I had the incentive that I could be out of a job in three months, but the bigger incentive was that the project could be closed in three months. The needs of the project and the young people who we support have always been greater than my own needs and they still are today.

It didn't take long before people started asking the question, "What do you do all day?" This question would just make me work even harder, as they couldn't see what was going on behind the scenes and that foundation stones were being laid.

The coffee bar was now open every day after school and I worked every shift with a volunteer. We now also suddenly had more volunteers, once again highlighting that God does supply all of our needs. The continuity now improved greatly and instead of just opening and being there, we were now far more proactive in engaging young people. A programme of issue-based work was now planned and delivered to educate young people informally and to focus on the specific needs that were highlighted. We did this mainly through fun games and discussion. Young people were learning, but not as they did at school and they had a choice to attend or not.

It wasn't until later when I did my youth work training that I discovered that informal education and voluntary participation were two of the four principles of youth work. I just naturally started to work in this way. I also now know that the other two principles are to provide equality of opportunity and empowerment. These four principles have been woven through everything that I have done in youth work, just like the Golden Thread of God being woven through my life.

I quickly filled my time. Mornings were spent trying to find money and developing projects. As a need became highlighted, I would look at how we could best meet that need. I had drawn up a mission statement which said, "We exist to seek, identify and meet the changing needs of young people." The seeking and identifying part was easy, as I only had to ask young people and observe. The hardest bit then, and still is, is how can we best meet the need. If money was no object, we would never have to ask that question, it would never be a problem, but it is so frustrating when you know what needs to be done and you can't do it because of the cost.

Y.U.P.I.S

The counselling service headed up by Di Rowe was still running and therefore meeting the needs of those with emotional issues. Now a new need was being recognised. Many of the young people that I was building relationships with were struggling to find work. How could I help?

I had employed many people in my building business and it would be these practical skills that I would now fall back on. Looking around the building I could identify endless maintenance tasks or projects that needed doing. Combined with the nagging question from people asking what I did with my time, a new idea was emerging. If I could allow these young people to volunteer with practical jobs around the project, they could include this on a C.V. I thought to myself that it's got to look better than just saying that you are unemployed or doing nothing when looking for work.

It was a two-way incentive, it helped us and it helped

them. The Young Unemployed Persons Incentive Scheme was given birth in 1996; YUPIS for short and it was an immediate success. The first two that participated found work within a month. It was a very random and organic project. If there was someone who needed something to do, I would dream up a project and spend two or three mornings each week working with them. It was very informal, with no timetable and very little planning. I believe that it was this spontaneity and availability that allowed the young people to feel valued and one of the key reasons why it worked.

Bent finger part-two

You will recall that in chapter nine I had a lot of prayer for my bent finger and God had healed the end, allowing it to move. You will also remember that in chapter twelve, in 1992 I was working with a group of primary school children in a local youth club. This was the 'Latch Key Kids' club. These children were all very interested to know about my bent finger and I would always be glad to talk to them about how my injury had happened, but never told them about how God had partially healed it. If I was playing them at pool, for example, one would eventually ask, "Why do you bend your finger like that?" Two such people were Laura and Sam. They were seven or eight years old in 1992 and young people can change considerably in the space of four years. Now, here they were walking into the coffee bar, though they didn't recognise me and I had failed to recognise them. They were both now twelve years old.

We chatted about any old nonsense, anything that came to mind, it was a way of getting to know people if it was their first time at The Door. It wasn't long before one of them suddenly shouted out as if they were welcoming an old friend, "Hey I know you, you're that bloke with the bent finger!"

They told me where we had met and then I remembered them. The conversation then took on a whole new dimension. I had known these two for just six months and it was four years ago, but the memories now came flooding back. The relationship picked up where it had been dropped all of those years ago and God spoke into my heart, "Now you know why I didn't completely heal it. Your finger will be a talking point for many."

I have long lost count of how many conversations I have had about my finger. Sometimes I tell people that God partially healed it and at other times I don't. It's a matter of who I am talking to and the circumstances. One thing that I do know though, I am so privileged to know why God chose not to fully heal me.

That first year of being full-time, the first paid person at The Door, was unbelievably difficult. If difficulty could be measured, this was now much harder than my 'Audition Calling'. Now though, I wasn't trying to do it all in my own strength, God was in it with me, because I had invited him in. I had realised that I couldn't do it without him and this time was going to be different.

The rest of this chapter contains three stories that happened during my first year of paid work. There were many similar stories that I experienced and I am sure that others have experienced similar things in other parts of the country. I wrote these stories down in 1996 and now looking back, I feel that I have learnt from each one and even more so, others have learnt from my experiences.

Carol

I will often say that our greatest outcome is the fact that some young people are alive today who may not otherwise have been. If we hadn't been there to help and support them, some of them could quite simply be dead. This became so much the case at one point that, in answer to the question, "What do you do for a job?" I would simply answer, "I save lives."

The person would then assume, "Oh, you're a doctor," but I would simply say, "No, I am a youth worker."

In 1996 we were constantly helping drunken teenagers, particularly on a Friday evening. It was a common sight to see a young person staggering around the streets and we quickly adopted a policy that said, "If we see you drinking outside our premises you will not be allowed in." Another rule stated that if you came in drunk and started to cause problems, you would be asked to leave. The one exception to these previous two rules was when the person was so badly intoxicated, they became a casualty or they needed somewhere safe to sit and sober up.

The worst incident of alcohol poisoning that I have ever been involved in happened so fast! Carol had taken a large bottle of gin from her parents' drink cabinet. She had passed the bottle around her group of friends, but many of them had declined the drink as they sipped and said that they didn't like it. Now her friends all wanted to come into the coffee bar and Carol had three options. Number one: she could hide the bottle outside somewhere, but there was a risk that others may find it. Number two: she could hide it in her bag, but staff may find it and confiscate it. Number three: just drink it all as fast as possible. She chose number three and poured the best part of a bottle into her stomach as fast as she could.

She walked in and said hello, but I instantly realised that something didn't seem right. She walked to the toilet and I asked Di Rowe to check that she was OK, but by the time Di had arrived at the toilet, Carol had already collapsed. Her legs could no longer support her weight, though she was still conscious. As Di tried to help her up from the floor she reacted violently. In no time at all she had Di's thumb in her mouth and was biting down as hard as she could before she eventually passed out.

We were used to phoning for ambulances or parents to come and collect inebriated teenagers but this was the most serious. Her breathing was shallow; her pulse was weak, she was paralytic and unconscious. She was rushed into the ambulance on a stretcher and left almost immediately with blue lights flashing and sirens blasting.

We had done all that we could to help her, now to find her parents and to inform them. They weren't home but a friend of Carol's then told us that her parents are always at a certain local bar on a Friday night. I ran to the bar and upon making a few enquiries found them and broke the news about their daughter.

Upon arrival at Gloucester Royal Hospital, Carol had the contents of her stomach pumped out. She stayed until she was fit enough to be taken home by her thankful parents.

The headline of the local newspaper later that week read, '13-year-old girl found drunk.' The story read that the police had found her slumped in a shop doorway.

The police had kept our name out of it to protect us. The truth though is that we had quite possibly saved her life.

We took a huge advantage of this incident and did a vast amount of follow-up educational work around the dangers of alcohol. As a result, we did see a massive drop in the number of serious cases. The problems with alcohol would never really go away, but we have never since seen such a severe case of alcohol poisoning.

Lenny

Lenny was twenty-seven years old (yes, I know that is older than 25, the age that we now, in 2015, work up to at The Door) when he accepted Jesus as his Lord and Saviour. For many years prison had been his security, but now whilst on his way to his friend's baptism, God touched him and revealed his truth to him and there was one extra that went through the waters of baptism that day. A happy day, a joyous occasion, but it was to be short-lived.

Lenny was living in a centre for recovering addicts and whilst he was there, he broke the house rules and found himself thrown out to live in a hotel which was full of addicts, where heroin was being used daily. For Lenny, the slippery slope was a fast one, the temptation of the heroin was too great. He quickly lost contact with all Christian friends, apart from the times that he would bump into people on the street and he would explain to them that he had been ill, with a touch of the 'flu.' That was the reason he said why he didn't look too well and why he had lost so much weight. The truth though was a different story!

During February 1997 I met Lenny on one of those occasions on the street. This time he seemed more desperate than usual with an additional problem, the threat of becoming homeless again. He asked me if I could help him, but his needs were far greater than anything that I could help with by myself, so I put him in touch with the local drugs project.

A few weeks later I met him again and this time he was so desperate that he was talking about applying to access treatment for his addiction. We began to work seriously towards this, with mountains of forms to plough through and assessments to attend.

Lenny had also recently committed more crimes to feed his habit and the courts were in the process of dealing with him. It was a race against time; prison or treatment centre.

After taking him to a drug rehabilitation centre in mid-Wales he was accepted with certain conditions. He now had to show that he really did want help by 'cleaning up' and coming off all of the drugs. He also needed to telephone the centre every week and to clear the charges that were still being dealt with in the courts.

Lenny tried hard to clean up and sometimes he would call in to ask me to pray for him. This was usually at a time when he particularly needed a 'fix', but he continued to use it in a small way.

The pressure continued for Lenny and one day following a misunderstanding with his probation worker (parole officer) he looked for comfort in a bag of heroin and forgot to phone the rehab centre. The result was hard to handle, his name was off the waiting list and he had lost his place.

As he telephoned the centre and pleaded with them his world just seemed to fall apart even more than ever before. Several other people also phoned and pleaded on his behalf, but it was no use, rules were rules. Lenny had lost his chance and the Magistrates would be sending him to prison.
During this time of pleading to the rehab, there was also a considerable amount of pleading made in prayer and I knew that God was in control.

With only one week to go before Lenny's court appearance for sentencing, I felt that God was leading me to contact a Christian drug rehab centre in South Wales. It was a Friday and the person on the other end of the line, having listened to the situation, told me that if Lenny could get there on the following Tuesday, they would carry out the necessary assessment. There was no hesitating, we drove down on the following Tuesday and Lenny was offered the chance to start treatment on Friday (the same day that he was due in court for sentencing). Amazingly all of the necessary paperwork and 'red tape' was dealt with in the next two days (it sometimes takes months).

Friday arrived - Lenny's day in court. I had written a letter to the Magistrates explaining how Lenny had been trying to better himself over the months that I had been close to him. Lenny's solicitor also stated that I was willing to take him to the rehab centre straight from the courtroom.

The prosecution stated their case and the Magistrates were considering sending Lenny to prison.

Lenny's solicitor pleaded his case with the Magistrates, whilst the Christians in the courtroom pleaded their case with God. There was compassion in the courtroom and Lenny found himself on his way to the rehab that he needed so much, that he had waited so long for and that God had provided.

At this stage of the story, you may be thinking that this is the happy ending. It quite easily could have been, but we all have free will. The sad end to this story is that Lenny arrives back in town on the following Wednesday. After only four days he had walked out and was heading back to his old ways. The thought that 'You can lead a horse to water, but you can't make it drink' came to mind. Anger rose in me. I had been used. Other people had been used and worse still, God had been used. I repented of my anger and I began to realise that there are lessons to be learnt from every chapter of our lives.

This chapter told me that it is God who sets us free. He wants what is best for us but he allows us to choose what we do, giving us a completely free will. We are free to do whatever we want but sometimes in doing so, we become captives to the things that we choose.

Lenny walked away a free man but he still had the chains of heroin addiction in his heart.

Lenny soon left Stroud and returned to London, which raised the question, "Would any of us ever see him again?"

Our paths did cross again one evening at a filling station in Stroud, as Lenny was back visiting old friends. He told me that he was still trying to clean up and that he was going to do it. He asked me to forgive him for running away and letting me down. I replied by telling him that he shouldn't let himself down and that he should try not to let God down. That was the last time that I ever saw Lenny.

A few months later I had a phone call from his mum; Lenny had been found dead after a heroin overdose. He had cleaned up but temptation had drawn him back, only this time his body couldn't handle what he had previously become accustomed to and his usual comforting fix had killed him. Whilst cleaning out his flat his mum had stumbled across my name and contact details.

Those same doubting questions then hit me between the eyes again, "Did I do enough? Could I have done any more to help him? Should I have let him go to prison?"

The answer is of course that I did my best, the best that I could do to help him. Lenny had been given another chance so many times. We can't live people's lives for them; we can only point them in the right direction and hope that they make the right choices.

Jim

Jim had been touched by God at a huge outreach event in Swindon. The truth of Jesus had dawned on him and he went forward for the altar call; but like so many seeds that are sown, some are choked by the weeds and the thorns. Jim continued in his old ways and found himself in trouble again and in prison.

After his release from prison, he found himself in Stroud and walked into The Door coffee bar one Saturday afternoon. Now living in Gloucester, he was still awaiting trial for an act of aggression he had committed. He spoke to one of the youth workers on duty that day. He shared about his life and the things that he had done, he mentioned the troubles and explained that God was in his life.

I met Jim later that week and he began to tell me about himself, but I felt that some things weren't adding up. The stories were now slightly different to what had been said at the weekend to another member of the team. I began to realise that he may have a problem with truth, with fact and fantasy and knowing right from wrong.

One day when Jim came in, he was crying. He told me that he had just found out that his girlfriend had ended her life by suicide whilst he was in prison. He opened up, telling me that she couldn't live without him, that it was all her fault that he was in prison and that in her distress, she had taken her own life. I listened to him and helped him to calm down, but a few days later he came in extremely distressed again and in tears. It was the day of the funeral and he told us that he wasn't allowed to go. We later found out that his girlfriend was very much alive, she hadn't taken her own life and that the whole story had been a fantasy to help him cope with some of life's problems. He was amazingly convincing with his story and the truth didn't come out for some time, not until after the following sequence of events.

It was the day of the fantasy funeral, but it felt so real to Jim. He was so worked up about it his anxiety was building towards suicidal thoughts of his own.

"I wasn't supposed to go to the funeral, but I went anyway," he sobbed. His eyes were red from the tears, in an obvious state of upset. Continuing his story, he told me that his girlfriend's best friend had later on turned up at his flat with a knife and the intention of killing him. Something was thrown through the window and he escaped out of the door onto the street. Unable to gather his belongings he just ran for his life.

So here he was now, homeless, suicidal and hunted. It was a fantasy, but it was all so real for Jim. It was a fantasy, but we didn't know it at the time. He begged for help and as he talked, I listened. It was at this point that I enlisted the help of one of the counselling team and he took over listening as I went to try to find Jim a bed for the night.

As the rest of the team became aware of Jim's predicament, I knew that they were praying and I felt that those prayers would be answered. One telephone call and I was able to book him into a night-stop accommodation. This was not a hostel it was the home of a young Christian couple. They were expecting their first baby, but nevertheless, they were prepared to take him in for the night and give him breakfast in the morning. There were still a couple of problems, firstly he couldn't arrive until 7.00pm and secondly, he didn't know the way. The answer, I decided was to take him home with me, feed him and then take him to the night stop myself. Everything went according to plan and when I dropped him off, he continued his fantasy with his new-found hosts.

The following morning when I collected him, he looked happier, but there was still obviously a certain amount of anxiety that was bothering him. From experience, I knew that it would be difficult to find him more permanent accommodation and as I phoned the first number on my list I prayed. Again, the prayer was heard and answered as the lady on the other end of the line said "Yes," I have a room and a bed available, "come on up and see me." It was a bed and breakfast just five minutes from our coffee bar and the landlady was able to sort out all of the necessary forms for the Benefits Agency. Prayers had been answered, Jim was no longer homeless and from the love that he had been shown he was beginning to realise some self-worth.

I had given Jim a parcel of food and some clothing. He seemed happy, making plans for his future with thoughts of college and a career. Then three days after moving into the bed and breakfast, he disappeared without a word. His landlady called me a week after he had moved in and told me the news. Where was he? What was he doing? Would we ever see him again? He had gone taking the key to his lodgings but had left the food and clothes that I had given him.

We see people, we help them, and then we never see them again. The pattern was a familiar one and one that we had become used to. It came as no surprise to hear the news and when this type of news comes you ask yourself, "Why did I bother? I might as well just give up." Then I would realise that this is quite a natural reaction and think to myself, "I did do all that I could for him. It's just a case of some you win and some you lose!"

We naturally give up, but God never gives up on his children. Five weeks went past and life continued as a group of young people began to decorate the basement of the coffee bar. This was a regular event which allowed them to put their mark of ownership on the place. It was at this time that Jim reappeared as bold as life. He explained that he had been living in Staffordshire with his dad but was now homeless again and sleeping in a night-stop hostel in Gloucester. The painting project in the basement made good progress and Jim continued to hang around, watching but not participating.

After a few days, I realised why he had been watching. One Wednesday morning I arrived to find Jim sitting on the doorstep. He asked if he could make a private phone call to his mum. He had no money and asked if he could use the phone in the office. I left him for five minutes as I sorted out the painters who were now arriving to work in the basement. Disappointment struck as I returned to the office. Jim looked smug, guilty and afraid. It didn't take me long to realise why he looked this way. I discovered that four pounds was missing from the coffee bar float that had recently been made up and I knew that he was guilty. I confronted him, but he denied it. So, I confronted him again and he admitted taking it and gave it back. The trust that I thought had developed between us was immediately gone. Anger, frustration and disappointment rose inside of me as I suppressed my feelings and remained calm.

"I'm sorry Jim," I explained. "I trusted you and you've blown it. I'm going to have to ask you to leave. You're welcome back at 12 o'clock when the coffee bar opens, but the people who are allowed in before then have to be trusted. I can no longer trust you, I'm sorry."

As he left, the thought struck me that it may be the last time that I see him, as I said to him, "See you later."

It was as if nothing had happened. Later that day he returned asking for favours. Any feelings of guilt and remorse had gone. Looking back, I realise that it was the fantasy world and the confusion of fact and fiction that must have caused this.

Thursday, the next day, I again arrived to find Jim

sitting on the doorstep. We talked for a while, but as the painters arrived to work in the basement, I had to ask him to leave because of the lack of trust. He left quickly, saying that he understood and that he would return later when the coffee bar opened.

He returned later that day nearing closing time and he had with him a new friend – a fresh source of bad influence. He said hello and talked briefly before Jim asked his new friend if he wanted to see downstairs in the basement. I assumed that he was referring to looking at the new designs that were now on the wall and almost finished, but I later found out that wasn't the case.

As closing time approached, I checked the basement was empty of people. Suddenly I was distracted as another young person with a lot of problems came running in. He had just punched his brother and the police were looking for him. He too had a criminal record, was out on police bail and panic was affecting him. It was dealt with in a matter of a few minutes, as incidents like this would frequently blow up. They come and go, but this one distracted me.

It was the following Friday morning that I realised my distraction. I didn't notice that the pay phone was missing from the wall in the coffee bar as I ascended the stairs to enter the office. "Who's been eating chocolate bars and throwing wrappers everywhere," I thought as I discovered the mess. I still didn't realise that a crime had been committed as I settled down to the task of the daily accounts. The takings and the float were missing. They weren't where I had left them and the thought occurred to me that someone was messing around. That thought quickly changed as I discovered that the cash box was missing. The week's takings from a busy summer holiday had gone. That Friday I had intended to bank all of the money, as I was set to go on holiday for two weeks at the start of the next day.

How? What? Who? I was dumbstruck. I paused and switched on to automatic pilot. Another problem... solve it! I ran down the flight of stairs into the coffee bar and flew down the next into the basement where I found the open fire escape. The previous evening, I had been distracted by a minor incident and the result was now major. I walked through the first door, into the short passageway and out into the open, rubbing my eyes with disbelief. As I returned through the passageway I tripped over a black object that was lying on the floor. It was the payphone with screws projecting from its back, indicating that it had been ripped from the wall. Its body was smashed open and the contents gone. The payphone itself was worth about £200 whilst the contents were probably only about £5. This was senseless and the pool table had been given the same treatment, locks ripped off, cash box empty.

I phoned the police and whilst waiting for them to arrive I started to make a list. As I was doing so the horror and disgust of it all hit me. The perpetrators of this crime had sat in the office eating chocolate. Even the hot water urn had been switched on to make a cup of tea, but they hadn't stuck around for one. The automatic pilot in my brain now switched off and everything seemed to hit me at once. It was no longer just another problem to solve, this now felt personal. I felt as if I had been defiled. "Oh Lord! Who could have done such a thing?" I asked and instantly thought of Jim.

I shared my suspicions of Jim with the police, but they

had no evidence and were in no hurry to find him, let alone arrest him.

As the young people started to arrive, they were disgusted – their place, their haven had been burgled. Now it was they who felt violated and their suspicions were the same as mine. "Was it Jim?" They asked. I just shook my head, "I don't know, but strangely you suspect the same person as me."

Later that day I found Jim and his friend waiting for a bus and asked them to come back to my office where I questioned them. "Don't know anything about it," said Jim as he continued to give his alibi. "It wasn't me," said his friend, "I only knick cars, get twenty-five quid for each one." I phoned the police, but they didn't want to question them, so I had no option but to let them go. Soon some witnesses heard them bragging about the burglary and saw them spending a lot of money but still, there was no arrest. There was not enough evidence.

I went on holiday and was consciously aware that Jim knew where I lived. He also knew that I was on holiday and I wondered if I would be coming home to another break-in. I am glad to say that I didn't and when I arrived home everything was as I had left it. I realised that I couldn't go on carrying these concerns, so I handed it all over to God and I knew that he was in control.

Guilt is a difficult thing to live with and almost six weeks after the burglary Jim arrived one morning. He looked different. His hair was cut differently, but not only that he had lost the redness from his face and had normal, healthy-looking flesh tones. His facial muscles seemed more relaxed and at ease. We talked about the break-in. We also talked about the fact that his girlfriend wasn't dead. He admitted that he was messed up and was going through a difficult time back then, but that he had changed.

"You know I didn't ever expect to see you again," I told him. He just nodded and I asked where he was living, "In a Bail Hostel," he told me and he added, "I'm getting my life straightened out." Again, we talked about the break-in, "You know there is no real evidence against you and your mate but I still know that you did it. You know that you did it and God knows that you did it. Can you live with it? I asked him.

"No, I can't," he replied, "I was involved." He then told me how he had opened the fire escape door that evening just at closing time and that he wanted to tell the police everything.

Whilst waiting for the police to come and arrest him, I explained that our God is forgiving and that even though he had to go through the courts and be dealt with by the law of the land, God had already forgiven him on the confession of his sin.

The police came and took him away. He gave a statement and later returned to the coffee bar. His greatest fear was not facing the police though, it was facing the other young people when they came into the coffee bar later that day. At first, they didn't recognise him. He did look different. Then when they realised who he was, there was anger that he had dared to return, but when they heard that he had confessed there was respect – respect for him as a person, for who he really was, for the real Jim.

Jim still had a long way to go to get his life straightened

out, as I suppose in some respect, we all do. We can all learn from the actions of this 16-year-old who made a mistake, but saw the error of his ways and asked for forgiveness. We all need to ask for forgiveness occasionally and find it so difficult to do. I have learnt a lot from the actions of this young man; about temptation, trust, forgiveness, guilt and honesty. He regained my respect, the respect of his peers and most of all respect for himself.

Looking at this story seventeen years on, there are many things that we would now do differently. We would now work much more closely with the police, asking them about Jim's girlfriend, the reported suicide and the threat with the knife. I would not now take a person home with me to feed them; that could be done with food from other sources. We now have a far greater awareness of those distracting tactics and our security processes are far tighter than in those early days. We have learnt much and we keep on learning. We may be a target for temptation, but we don't want to be an easy target.

The most important thing that we can all learn from this is the importance and the power of forgiveness, plus the release that we find through the truth.

Chapter Sixteen

Changing Seasons

Occasionally I will visit other projects. I do this to learn new ideas, but also to help them wherever I can. At times I will ask the question, "Why do you do it like that?" (or something similar). Sometimes I am answered, "We have always done it like that."

No method or project should ever be done just because of tradition. The, 'We have always done it like that' type of attitude can often slow down development. A lot of us though can become set in our ways, but we need to remember that some things have a season and to embrace change can be healthy, even if it is a struggle. This short chapter will look briefly at some of the projects and activities that I ran for a season and then stopped, but firstly I will share a little more of my personal life.

Incredibly when I was running my own business, I never knew if I would be able to pay myself each week. Now, working for God's business, it suddenly felt as if I had security. Some people may say, that to have just three months of funding isn't a great deal of security, but it is when it is wrapped up in faith. I now had a regular wage coming in. Yes, it was less than my wage in the building industry, but it was regular. This level of security made us feel as if it was a good time to move house again. None of our previous houses had been for a long season, as we were never really satisfied. It had always been our desire to live in a red-brick Victorian house. God now led us to the perfect property, once again giving us the desire of our hearts. We have been there ever since for over seventeen years. Looking back to the time when we had to sell Zion House, I had been so angry at God. Now we are overjoyed with where he has led us and what he has provided for us. We were no longer in the dark valley of misery and debt; we had been restored. This house has been far more than just a house, it has been our home.

* * * *

Di Rowe was supporting me in all that I was doing. I had been a builder for so long that I was now struggling to call myself a 'Youth Worker.'

"Have you considered doing some training?" Di asked, "It would help you to adjust and it will be good for you and the project."

I looked at various training options but kept coming up against obstacles. Gloucestershire County Council seemed to be experiencing various problems around funding for training youth workers and there was nothing available. I was about to give up hope when Di showed me an advert in a magazine. It was asking people who were involved in youth and community work to contact them, as they were offering training with a qualification.

Ironically the course was funded by Swindon Borough Council and I attended an interview at their offices. It was at this interview that I found out that the course was better than anything I had previously looked at. All students were enrolled at Brunel University and the study type was distance learning with regular tutorial meetings, residential courses, assignments and assessments. I could cope with this.

It took me the best part of two years to qualify but when I did finish, I was told that the course had now been upgraded to a foundation degree. The road that God had led me on had given me more than I had expected or could ever imagine. Now I was a youth worker by name and qualification and that was my season of training.

*****

In 1995, the year before I went to work at The Door full-time, we entered a float into the Stroud Show Carnival. I had been involved in helping to build a few floats in the past, but they had been designed and built in just a couple of days, with not much thought. These floats for The Door would be different. The carnival would take place every year in July, but our planning started in January. Various young people were involved right at the design and planning stage. Models were sometimes made, but always plenty of sketched-out drawings to develop ideas. Enthusiasm would grow slowly with people discussing the costumes that they would be wearing on the float. Roles were assigned and each float looked remarkable, the result of a real team effort.

The actual build would start in April and every week this group that had now taken ownership of what was planned would meet to carry out their designated tasks. Everyone put in 100% effort and their efforts were rewarded with prizes every year, often winning the prize for the best in the carnival. I still regard these creations as some of the best youth work projects I have ever been involved in.

Each float was also designed with an evangelical purpose; this was not surprising as four out of the five that we built would be based upon one of my songs. I performed each song live, repeating it at least thirty times as the carnival procession weaved its way through the town. We gained a reputation for being the liveliest and loudest float.

At the peak of the Stroud Show Carnival, over 20,000 people would line the streets to watch as this amazing spectacle passed by. We had a team of volunteers who would hand out flyers which explained the message of the song which, combined with the visual image of the float, left a lasting impression.

The young people talked about it all year long, as the fun and memories lasted, which in turn inspired others and each year the team grew with new members.

We did this for five years and each year there was a powerful message. The carnival eventually stopped due to health and safety guidelines. People started to lose interest as insurance costs soared, which was strange because, during all of the years of the carnival, no one had ever been injured. One of our greatest youth work projects had naturally ended. We let go and moved on.

*****

Another thing that we did for five years was to enter runners in the London Marathon. Our first experience of this was in 1996 when a young person approached me and told me that it was his greatest ambition to run in the London Marathon but he didn't know how to get a place. As a charity, we applied and were accepted for a 'Golden Bond', which enabled us to enter five runners each year until the year 2000.

Participation in this event meant two things, yes, we could raise money, but equally important was the fact that we could enable young people to fulfil their dreams. Over the five years, we would see at least two young people each year presented with a London Marathon medal.

We decided to make a weekend residential trip out of the event, contacted the Methodist Church in Bethnal Green and used this for overnight accommodation. For some of the young people that we took as supporters, it was their first time in London and it was an experience for some that they would never forget.

As the years went on it became more difficult to raise sponsorship and to find the willing runners. We had enabled twenty-five different people to have the experience of their lives and we had all enjoyed five great weekends in London, but the season came to an end.

*****

My role as a youth worker was to assess the needs of young people and to try to meet those needs. In 1996 Linda was fifteen years old and had a baby. She would regularly visit the coffee bar and tell us that whenever she visited the local mother and baby groups, all of the other mums would look down at her. She was struggling to find somewhere that she could feel comfortable and accepted.

We had only identified this one person as having this need but thought that there may be others. Teenage pregnancy was not as common as it is now, which is the reason why the older parents shunned her.

We decided to do something just to help this one young mother. Toddlers of Teens Support (TOTS) was launched and was headed up by Rachel Coysh, who later set up a thriving project called 'Tiddlywinks' in the town centre.

TOTS never attracted large numbers, but we never really anticipated that it would. However, those who did come along found the support and friendship that they were seeking. It was a toddler group, but all of the parents were under the age of twenty-five.

This was again another five-year project, which came to a natural end as more teenagers were having babies and they all found strength in numbers. They could now attend a main playgroup and not feel ostracised. Society it seemed no longer discriminated against them or judged them. We had played our part for a season, but now this too had ended.

*****

During the late nineties, I had the privilege to be invited to work in an inclusion unit within a local secondary school. This project was very forward-thinking and aimed to keep students who were struggling in certain lessons within the school, rather than excluding them. My role was highly pastoral and I know that I was instrumental as part of a team that helped those young people stay in school and also achieve.

One young person whom I helped very closely one day told me that without the support that he was being given, he felt that he would end up in prison or worse still die very young. Both of his parents were heroin addicts and I offered him some of the support that was missing in his life.

It was this young man who made me start to realise that there are many others that we have supported who may not have been alive without that extra encouragement, understanding and support. I too had learnt through working in the inclusion unit, but this season also came to an end.

*****

Each of the projects in this chapter came to an end. They were all like my babies. What would happen beyond them? What would replace them? Would God continue to weave his Golden Thread in my life? It is easy to avoid change and stop moving forward as fear reaches out and holds us back. The Bible tells us that "God has not given us a spirit of fear, but of power, love and a sound mind." (2 Timothy 1:7) This knowledge has allowed me to move forward, to embrace change, to take a chance and to continue on this walk of faith.

Chapter Seventeen

Move on Up

At the age of forty years, I had been the Project Co-ordinator at The Door for four years and therefore gone way past the then-regarded average life span of a Christian youth worker. The project and my work now gained more recognition from other youth workers. Some of these started to ask when I would be moving on. I would often hear the comment, "You need to move on with your career." Perhaps if the project hadn't been moving, I may have then moved on, but the project was far from stagnant.

With the counselling service growing in popularity, it highlighted the need for a separate and private entrance. Until now, anyone who was visiting us for counselling had to walk through a potentially crowded coffee bar. This was rather daunting for some, so money was raised to install a new shop front and carry out a complete refit. This did require closing for a couple of months, but the youth work didn't stop. By now there was a growing population of unemployed young people who were keen to have something to do and to help by putting their mark on the place. They would also have more chance of finding paid work if they were busy doing something positive with their time. They were helping us, but we were also helping them.

This was not the easy-to-manage established church youth group that had helped us to set up nine years earlier. This group were unpredictable and often potentially volatile. On the whole, though they performed well and took pride in their achievements.

When we re-opened, they had an all-important sense of belonging.

If a person feels like they belong, the chances are they will behave and they are also more likely to eventually believe. If these three-mile stones are reversed to believe, behave and belong it would be an almost certain recipe for anarchy. I have sadly seen some projects that have operated like this; they never survive and are very quickly closed down.

The building now looked even more the part, but there was still uncertainty about the future, as we were still paying rent.

We were now about to take another huge leap of faith. Our journey had started with a step of faith when we first opened. Another step had been taken when it was decided to start employing people in year five. Every day had been a walk of faith and the place that it had now led us to was beyond what we ever could have imagined.

The decision was made to try to buy the building we were operating from. There was so much more that we could be doing to make better use of all of the space but we didn't want to spend any more money on a building which we didn't own. I contacted the landlord and was amazed that he agreed to sell. Not only did he agree, but he was only asking for £60,000.

Reality starts to hit with the thought of, '£60,000 - Where would we find that kind of money?' We decided to launch an appeal and called it the 'Squeal Appeal.' The idea was that we asked people to empty their Piggy Banks, asking them for small contributions to make their 'Piggy squeal' with joy.

It was me who squealed when shortly after the appeal launch, £30,000 dropped through the letterbox one morning. It was in the form of an anonymous banker's draft and to this day we still have no idea of who donated it. What we do know is that God had provided it and said, "I have given you half, now all that you have to do is find the rest!"

We found it from a variety of different sources and by the end of our tenth year we had taken the leap of faith and landed with both feet on the ground. Now we could develop the rest of the building.

It wasn't long before news of what we were doing with unemployed young people had spread and we were being asked to join a much bigger training project. The Gloucestershire Newstart Network approached us and we soon became a partner training provider. Our delivery of training soon became more structured, with a timetable of who should be here, when they were with us and what they should be doing.

Some chose to do music, whilst others would learn the skills of woodwork or help out in the office. Whatever subjects were chosen, it was me who would deliver it. If anyone now asked what I did all day, I would often give a look that said, "Do you really want to know?" I had been full-time for four years and it was time to find more help, although that did also mean that I would have to find even more money. Over the years we have grown, slowly, systematically and strategically. We now (2015) employ over twenty paid staff, but the growth started with the introduction of the Newstart Network training programme.

Lindy was the first person who signed up to take part in this new and much-needed programme. She would come in and help out, mainly with admin tasks, but she would struggle with everything that she was given.

No matter what task she was being asked to do, she would always say that she couldn't do it. These were some of the simplest of tasks and even when she hadn't really tried, she would still say that she couldn't do it. She had absolutely no self-belief. At times I would need her to sign a form as evidence that she had been with us and without even thinking about what she was being asked, she would answer, "I can't do it." Her mind had become programmed with this response and she had conditioned her thinking to believe this.

I became frustrated with her lack of belief in herself and one day questioned her, "Why do you always think that you can't do something?"

She replied instantly, "A teacher at school told me that I was a failure. I was in the school hall during lunchtime. It was packed with people and he told me, in front of everyone else. He said, 'Lindy you're a failure, you fail at everything you do and it is likely that you will always be a failure.' That's why I am the way I am, he told me that I would be!"

My response came immediately, "I don't believe that you will always be a failure or indeed that you are a failure." Then thinking on my feet or perhaps it was God prompting what to say I asked, "If you could talk to this teacher and confront him now, would you like to?"

There was no hesitation as her answer came, "Yes!"

Where would this lead? Was I building her up to a false hope? Doubt started to creep in as I made the phone call to the school. The teacher in question had since been promoted to the position of deputy head and I was put through instantly.

I explained the situation and who I had with me. He remembered the incident immediately and knew me from school assemblies. "Come and see me tomorrow lunchtime, I would like to talk to Lindy."

The next day we arrived as planned and were shown to the deputy head's office. My mind was now flashing back to the times that I had been in a school office and it brought with it memories of fear and trepidation.

The smile on the teacher's face soon alleviated all fears. A smile is such a powerful tool. His attitude was humbling and merciful, as he began to explain his actions.

"When I left school," he said, "I had nothing. No qualifications. I had failed everything and was a failure. It wasn't until I joined the Navy that I started to make anything of my life. I was afraid that you would end up the same as me. How I communicated that to you was wrong and I am sorry. I am sorry that my actions have actually had the opposite effect than I had intended. Please accept this explanation and my apology."

It was a short meeting, but in that brief time hope came into Lindy's life. The look of worry and fear was replaced with a smile and a feeling of happiness, followed by release.

We returned to the office and I suggested that she write something that expressed how she was feeling now. She responded without question or doubt, picking up a pen and paper, and turning her hand to poetry. Her first poem portrayed a beautiful release from the pain that had been deep within. Over the following weeks, one poem after another flowed out and before long, she had written a whole book. She was no longer a failure - she had succeeded at something in her life.

As is often the case it can take a long time to fully undo the damage in a person's life. The visit to the school was just the start and it would be another two years before Lindy would have the confidence to move forward into work.

That day did eventually come and it was such a joyful day, at last, she believed in herself. She had confidence, was overflowing with happiness and was certainly not a failure. She stayed in her job for two years before I was asked to give her a reference for another job. She was progressing, independent, standing on her own two feet. The two years that were invested into her life had provided a good foundation for her future.

Empowerment and trust

I have met several youth workers who struggle to empower young people. Often there is a lack of trust and a doubt that a young person will do something good enough, unable to meet the worker's high standards and fail. It is important not to set young people up to fail but to trust them with the tasks that they have been empowered into, supervise them from a distance and intervene appropriately when the need arises.

We now empower young people in a variety of different ways, with some responsibility for decision-making and supporting others.

In the year 2000, I found myself having to confront two young people who had broken the trust that they had been given. They were working as a pair behind the coffee bar, serving customers and taking their money. It wasn't long before we suspected that they were stealing from the cash register. Takings were suddenly down and our observations told us that about five pounds was being taken daily. We watched. We gathered evidence. We confronted. They denied it.

I never directly accused them. I used phrases such as, "We have been closely watching and we are concerned that you may be at risk." After a long conversation, with loving reassurance in every word that I used, they both opened up and admitted that they had indeed been stealing.

Their reluctance to admit to the crime was due to their consideration of the consequences. They thought that they would be thrown out, banned, never to return again or even worse, we might report them to the police and they would be arrested!

What happened was the complete opposite. They were forgiven and allowed to continue working behind the bar and handling money. Trust was reinstated. I would regularly ask them how they were coping with the temptations and it didn't take long before they told me that, before my intervention, they had both also started to steal from local shops. Now they had both stopped shoplifting and thanked me for the understanding, non-judgemental and forgiving support that they had been given.

The powerful combination of trust, empowerment and forgiveness enabled them to understand right and wrong and also to become valuable in their own right. That value led to them both becoming employed in local shops. The second chance and the power of forgiveness had transformed them.

The power of forgiveness

In that same year 2000, I was talking to a good friend of mine, Roger Spiers. We both had a desire to set up and run a Christian Union type of group in a local school during lunchtimes. Archway School was chosen, as their recent inspection had highlighted that there was a need. A group of Christian teachers would meet weekly to pray about the 'spiritual needs' of the school and the students that they supported and we were invited to join this group.

We could see that there was a huge need, but was there also a want? If we provided something, would anyone bother to come? To answer this question, we were permitted to survey the whole school. This was the first large-scale survey that we had ever carried out and the results were most interesting.

The majority of young people had questions such as, 'Who made God? Why does God allow suffering? What does God look like?'

These are questions that we have been asked again and again over the years. We never really expect these questions to end, but the survey also asked two most important questions, 'Would you like the opportunity to chat about your questions? Would you attend a lunch-time group called 4U2 CHAT?'

At least half said that they would like to chat about their questions regarding God and his existence. This reinforced that there is a whole generation of young people who are hungry for the truth. Only about fifty though had said that they would want to attend a lunchtime group to discuss some of the issues. It was enough though and we launched '4U2 CHAT' which attracted on average about fifteen young people. This may not sound like a huge quantity from a school of almost 1,500 but the quality of what we were providing was high.

Our programme looked at various issues and where God fitted into each of them. Relationships, peer pressure, anger, bullying; we had a different focus each week.

It was the week where we would look at bullying and having been a bully at school, I mentioned to Roger that I would like to explain a little about the reasons behind bullying and what may lead a person to bully someone. He agreed that it would make sense to do that, but that we would also need to balance it with someone who was a victim of bullying. It made sense and so he asked his friend Martin to come and join us.

I spoke first and talked about my home situation, that my life felt out of control and that bullying was a form of taking control. I told them about my pain and suffering, about my self-harming and my mixed-up emotions that had almost caused me to take my own life. It was powerful and they could see that the bully is so very often a victim themselves. I also told them that, as a reformed bully now looking back, I realised that I didn't have many real friends whilst at school. What I had was some people who associated with me so that they didn't become victimised, but they weren't real friends. Percy was my only real friend and even when I had shot an arrow into his face, he was still my friend.

When I finished speaking, I knew that their minds had been opened, but I wasn't prepared for what was about to happen.

Martin stood to speak, "I was bullied at school," he said as he began to share his story. He continued with, "I was a victim of bullying, I was one of Brendan's victims!"

I looked at him in horror. I didn't recognise him. I couldn't remember him from school. How many more were there like him?

He talked about the fear, pain and oppression that he had lived with daily. It sounded similar to my own life. He couldn't control those who were bullying him and I couldn't control what was happening at home. The similarities were uncanny, but I had been one of his perpetrators and just one of many it would seem.

He told the group that the pressure and emotional stress had become so bad, that he too had considered taking his own life. WHACK! A reality check hit me! What had I done? How many others were like Martin?

Before the meeting, we had been chatting and I found out that he was married with two children. This wouldn't have been the case if he had taken his own life. My empathy was growing for this man then he said something that was like a lightning bolt. He explained what had saved his life.

He said, "I realised that the only power that I had over those who oppressed me was the power of forgiveness. I learnt to forgive the bullies. They continued to bully me and I continued to forgive. Forgiveness won. They stopped. There is power in forgiveness and I forgive Brendan." Needless to say, at the end of this, I was welling up with tears.

It has taken me a long time to accept Martin's forgiveness. The shame of what I had done to this man was a struggle. He would have to tell me on many more occasions that he had forgiven me before it would eventually sink in. I knew that God had forgiven me, but then that's easy for God, he's almighty and powerful and dishes out forgiveness all of the time. Martin was just a man, but he had learnt the most amazing power that is available to us... the power of forgiveness.

This lunchtime meeting was the most powerful that we ever had with this group.

The story somehow found itself out in the public domain. It was a human-interest story and we were soon being contacted by newspapers, radio and TV. We both appeared on the local BBC TV news and I participated in several phone-in programmes organised by BBC 5 Live. However, not one of the media sources would mention the forgiveness angle. They mentioned that we were both Christians and used sensational headlines but the power of forgiveness was carefully omitted.

Interestingly the last newspaper that picked up on the story was the local Stroud News and Journal. When they asked for an interview, we agreed on the condition that the whole story was told. They reported on the power of forgiveness and over 20,000 local Stroud people read the story.

I had bullied Martin in 1975 and 25 years later we had come face-to-face. Martin is now the pastor of Stroud Christian Fellowship and in 2014 this is the church that I now attend. Martin is my Pastor, but more than that, he is my friend and there truly is power in forgiveness.

Chapter Eighteen

Darkness Descends

Much of this chapter contains stories about some of the dark and oppressive situations that I have had to face. It contains the story of the darkest, most difficult and depressing situation that I have ever had to face as a youth worker.

As I look at these stories, I can't help reflecting that God has always been in these dark places with me. His light shone into the darkness, to show me the way through. A well-known poem can sum all of this up:

Footprints

One night I dreamed I was walking
along the beach with The Lord.
Many scenes from my life flashed across the sky.
In each scene, I noticed footprints in the sand.
Sometimes there were two sets of footprints.
The other times there was one set of footprints.
This bothered me because I noticed
that during the low periods of my life,
when I was suffering from
anguish, sorrow or defeat,
I could see only one set of footprints.

So, I said to The Lord,
"You promised me, Lord,
that if I followed you,
You would walk with me always.
But I have noticed that during
the most trying periods of my life,

there has only been one
set of footprints in the sand.
Why, when I needed you most,
you have not been there for me?"

The Lord replied,
"The times when you have
seen only one set of footprints,
is when I carried you!"
Mary Stevenson

Inspired by this poem, I wrote a rap version and called it 'Mystified'.

Mystified

God moves in a mysterious way... Mystified!

Chorus:
I am mystified by the way you walk,
I am mystified by the way you talk,
I am mystified by the things you do
I am mystified by your love so true.

Sleeping in my bed, a dream inside my head,
A dream I do not really understand.
I see my feet go walking and you beside me talking,
Two pairs of footprints walking in the sand.

Walking in the sand, walking hand in hand,
Walking in the sands of time.
Walking hand in hand in the sands of time,
Listening to the voice with the words that rhyme.

Chorus

The footprints in the sand see them side by side,

The footprints in the sand they will never die.
Joined together in love, with a love that is above.
Joined to live and not to die in a love to mystify

When the going gets tough,
I know that you are there,
When the going gets tough,
I know you're there to care.
When the going gets tough,
feel you holding my hand,
When the going gets tough,
see your feet in the sand.

In the struggles of life, the toil and strife,
When I'm feeling like there's no one there to care.
I reach out for your hand and I look into the sand,
I'm all alone, there's just my footprints there,
And I despair, where've you gone
Lord, where've you gone?
Where've you gone Lord where've you gone?

Chorus

I pray to my God, I cry to my Lord
Don't desert me Father, you gave me your word.
You left us your spirit to carry us through.
The bad times, the sad times, I know that you are true.

When I cry to you Lord, I cry from the heart,
You answer me saying you will never depart.
I know that you are always by my side,
I know that you are watching over me.
I know that you are always by my side,
With a love I know is gonna set me free.

Chorus

In your troubles and your struggles,
when times are hard to hack,
Just look a little closer, you'll see you're on my back.
When all you see is one set of footprints in the sand,
The love of God will carry you
and help you understand!

I am mystified... I am mystified... I am mystified...

You may be reading this and thinking, 'What do you mean by saying 'his light shined into the darkness?'' The answer to that is simply that prayer has underpinned everything that I have done. The twenty-four-year existence of The Door Youth Project, my eighteen years of working for the project full-time, and the growth and success, are all the product of prayer. In essence, prayer is the battery that generates the power for the light to shine!

It was during the late 90s that we were out on the streets of Stroud, chatting to young people in the parks and other popular areas where they would gather. Some of the conversations focused on the good news of the Gospel and for that reason, we had a group of people back at the project who were praying for us. The arrangement was that they would pray until 10.00pm. We would then be finished and back with them.

The evening went well, it was the summer and we met loads of young people, what's more, we had some fantastic conversations. We were seed planting and they were searching for answers about life.

I was teamed up with Andy as a pair and Tony was one of those who we talked to. He had an emptiness in him and was searching for something to fill it. He would hear the Gospel message on this Friday evening, but little did we know that he would be found dead from a drug overdose on the following Wednesday.

We moved from one group to another. It was like Gospel networking. As the evening drew near to an end the small groups were now gathering as one bigger group. They were all showing signs of great interest in the conversations that were taking place.

The church clock struck 10.00pm and although we knew that the prayer cover would now be lifted, we continued. This group were so interested, so keen, so hungry. Then as the clock finished striking there was an immediate and noticeable change.

It became instantly darker as if a switch had been thrown! The temperature dropped and a chill was in the air, even though it was summer. The crowd now transformed and the conversation became aggressive and attacking. We knew that our prayer cover had gone, and the protection that it had provided was no more, it was time to leave.

Leaving our spiritual home

From 1986, the year of our salvation, until 2001 we had been members of Minchinhampton Christian Fellowship. We had learnt a great deal and been blessed more times than we could recall through this group of friends.

The Door Youth Project was born out of this group. It was like our spiritual home, with the members being one huge, loving, caring family.

The leadership of this church was abruptly changed as if overnight the three leaders retired or stepped down and were replaced by a new chosen three. This new regime of unprepared leadership brought about more changes and their lack of preparation resulted in mistakes being made. These mistakes caused unhappiness and eventually, people left. We were some of these people.

A lesson to be learnt here is that anyone, in any form of leadership should make plans for the continuation of the work, project or church. If the three new leaders had been properly apprenticed and empowered into their roles, there could have been a completely different outcome.

We were now spiritually homeless. It would be two and a half years of wandering and drifting, searching for the right church. People would tell us, “If you find the perfect church, don’t join it as it wouldn’t be perfect anymore.”

They are of course right, as you will never find the perfect church. We did however in January 2004 drift into Stroud Christian Fellowship. This is the church that Martin led and it was now two years since our reunion at the 4U2 CHAT lunchtime session.

Less than a month after our first visit, someone gave me a piece of paper on which they had written a word from God. It said that it was time that we stopped drifting and put down an anchor. I had never met this person before and he certainly didn’t know our situation, but the word was so right. Nine years on we are still there and still putting down anchors, I also now realise that you need to put down more than one.

It was during our period of drifting that we would face some of the darkest periods. It is interesting to look back at how darkness creeps in when no anchor is holding us. This first story came to light in 2005, but I do believe that a lot of the damage may have been caused during my drifting years.

Stress is an unseen killer and around the time of Easter 2005, I was feeling the stress. These Easter holidays were a particularly difficult time as several young people were drinking alcohol during the daytime and arriving in need of help. I had called for ambulances on numerous occasions, but we were now seeing a huge increase in drunken teenagers.

My stress started to manifest itself as physical chest pains, combined with shortness of breath and dizziness. It was a struggle to even walk up the stairs. Various appointments and tests later led to a diagnosis of angina. Angina? I couldn't believe it. This is what had killed my dad.

I would now have to take medication for the rest of my life. As the gravity and the reality of the situation took hold of me, so too did the depressive feelings. The darkness started to take hold, covering my life like a black velvet shroud, heavy and oppressive.

As I talked with other people who had been diagnosed or knew someone with angina, my burden seemed to lift and hope slowly returned. Then with the aid of medication, so did my health. The light was returning and pushing the darkness out.

The darkest hour

Three years earlier in 2002, I had to cope with the most difficult emotional experience that I have ever had to cope with and it happened when we had no anchor in a local church. I would be constantly assessing the needs and asking the question of what next?

The need to expand our training provision was high and the shop next door had become available. Should we grab it? Should we take another step of faith? Yes, of course.

This new space would provide a new shop selling fair-trade goods, which would allow us to teach retail skills. There would also be a small creative art space and a woodwork room in the basement. These workshops would also be able to produce items that could be sold to generate an income.

The project also allowed more young people the chance to learn from participating in the building work that was required to refurbish the property. A mixture of decorating, carpentry and plumbing tasks were carried out by a small group who worked tirelessly on an almost daily basis. I taught, they learnt, the building was transformed and so were they. It was as we were working on this and watching the double transformation of the building and the people, that it was decided to call the shop 'Tranzform,' based on the book of Romans chapter 12 verse, which says, 'We are being transformed by the renewing of our minds.'

This new project was injecting new hope and new light into the darkness by removing some of the barriers that prevent young people from moving forward.

The shop was almost complete and the sign overhead was installed on the day that I went on holiday. I received a phone call as I was about to embark on the ferry that the job had been done and the shop would now open when I returned, but another phone call would change everything.

It was the first weekend in August 2002. I had returned from holiday on Saturday and wanted to make the most of what remained of the weekend. So, on Sunday afternoon I was just setting out for a walk on the canal towpath with Heather when my mobile phone rang. I thought to myself, 'I'm still on holiday, should I answer it?'

I almost wish that I hadn't answered, but I would have received the news at some point anyway and however or whenever this type of news comes it's never good.

The voice at the end of the line told me that it was Jo Barber. I knew her as a reporter for the Citizen (local newspaper). "Hi Jo, how can I help?"

"I just wondered if you have a comment about the young person who died this weekend."

"I don't know what you're talking about, I've been on holiday? Who are you talking about?"

"Jade Blundell, she was stabbed to death by her boyfriend." She went on talking, but it didn't register.

I did not comment, as the shock wave hit and rippled through me. Jade had been one of the main members of the small group that had helped to get the shop ready. During the process of working as part of this team, she started to realise that she had such a high level of creativity and she had expressed this in various forms of art including music, photography, poetry and rap. She was like a budding flower, just blossoming before having her petals violently ripped off and her beauty destroyed.

Her opportunities had gone, and her potential would

never be reached as her life had been taken. Not an illness, not an overdose, not a suicide or an accident, her life was stolen, crushed in anger!

An argument over money had been building all day with her boyfriend. Upon returning to her boyfriend's house, the rage was at a climax. The Ghurkha knife was used as an ornament over the fireplace, but now it was put to its intended use and the knife penetrated her soft delicate flesh fourteen times before he stopped.

I was honoured to be asked to speak at Jade's funeral. Fighting back the constant stream of tears and squeezing the words out between the sobs, this was emotionally the hardest thing that I have ever had to do.

This was a dark place. We were there for Jade's parents, supporting them however we could, but nothing would ever replace their loss.

The 'Tranzform' shop still opened and we dedicated it in memory of Jade. A stained-glass window was also made to sit above the entrance to the coffee bar. This was based on a photograph of a daisy, which was one of the last pictures that Jade took. It has a jade and pink (her nickname was Pinky) border. Although The Door project has now moved, the window is still there above the entrance to a Pizzeria.

Thirteen years on, I can still find myself crying for Jade. She was seventeen years old when she died, but the memories of her still live on in my head.

This is probably as bad as it can get.

Fred Chance, an old youth worker friend of mine, once

said to me, “Never lose sight of the reason why you do what you do.”

He is so right, yet it is so easy to become sidetracked, distracted and bogged down with things.

I do what I do for various reasons, but one of the reasons is to prevent any more young people like Jade from dying.

The shop struggled to survive, as very few people would walk past and hardly any would go out of their way to find us. The location just wasn’t right. So after just two years the shop was closed and the space was more appropriately used as an art room. This art space would now help young people who were struggling with life. Mental health issues had been identified as being on the increase in young people. The new project was named HOPE in Art and launched in 2004.

This project would run for a further eight years before we relocated the whole project to the High Street, giving us a chance to open a proper charity shop still called ‘Tranzform’ and still dedicated to Jade. Her memory lives on. The move would also expand and rebrand all of our training under the name of HOPE Training. Though, for now, we were making the most of what we had.

The power of love...

Our training service was now receiving enquiries from many different sources; social workers, teachers, doctors, parents and of course the young people themselves.

Neil arrived to have a look around and to see what we could do for him. He was accompanied by his social worker, who asked if we could help him. The social worker explained that Neil came with a kind of health warning. He could be gentle, loving and friendly one moment, but suddenly change. When the change happened, he had been known to threaten staff and throw things through windows. He was labelled as 'potentially violent.'

As the social worker talked, Neil just sat, listened and smiled. His cheeky, grinning smile said one thing, but his eyes were pleading, looking, hoping. I could hear his thoughts crying out, 'Please help me.' He was desperate, as he had been in care since he was three years old. His mother was an addict and couldn't cope. Now at the age of sixteen, he was asking for help.

We of course took him and he quickly demonstrated his creativity through photography, film-making, art and woodwork. It was so easy to like him. What was the social worker concerned about? Then we found out.

The subject of art involves using a variety of different tools and it happened that Neil was using a hammer for a task that he was struggling with. His frustration rapidly grew and the art teacher didn't see the moment when the hammer changed from being a tool and became a weapon. She was first aware of the change and the frustration as she was being threatened. He had switched so quickly.

Aggression and bad language now spewed out of Neil; hammer raised high and threatening to break the art tutor's jaw. It was real and he meant it. This was what we were warned about.

Joan the art tutor was a caring and wise person. She remained calm and talked to him calmly; at the same time, she was praying. This was real - no doubt about it.

If Joan had shown fear, Neil would have won. If she defended herself aggressively, he would have become more aggressive. Instead, she just showed him love, calmness and acceptance. It worked, Neil calmed down and we never did see that side of him again.

After this incident, I met with Joan and she told me that she didn't think that she was cut out for this kind of work. I had to explain to her what she had done and the difference that she had made. It is so easy for self-doubt to creep in following this type of incident, but God carried her through and the fear left her.

After two months the social worker asked what we had done to Neil. He was puzzled, "Neil is so different, how have you done what no one else could do?" He was genuinely inquisitive and I thought back through the previous two months before finally answering.

"I think the main thing is that we have loved him. Loved him for who he was, regardless of his history and baggage. That's probably the main difference."

He agreed and said that Neil had rarely known any love in his life, but now Neil was being transformed by the power of love. Yes, he was learning all-important new skills, which would help him to find work or further training, but his attitude had to change. This change could only happen with love.

After he had been with us for just three months, he was moved from his children's home, where he had grown up. Now he was able to live with foster parents, his first real home.

After a year the transformation was complete and Neil no longer needed our help. He progressed from us onto a college course where he would qualify in media technology.

Neil is a typical example of a young person who was trapped in life unable to move forward, with fear of the future, and without hope. The strap line of The Door Youth Project is, 'Unlocking Potential... Opening Opportunity' and for Neil we did just that. We say that we work with ALL young people that come to us and we do give ALL young people a chance in life, but sometimes we have to make the painful decision to stop working with someone.

Notice the danger signs

At fifteen years old Mark was already over six feet tall and built like an 'All Star' basketball player. His imposing size could instil fear in many who encountered him, but it didn't deter me from giving him a chance and teaching him woodwork.

It was not long though before danger signals were flashing across my mind; something was different about Mark. His posture and body language were odd, but his reaction to slight humour was aggressive. He was constantly on edge, and unpredictable, but was he untameable? Discernment kicked in and alarm bells rang in my head after just two weeks of trying to support Mark, I had to accept that occasionally the risk was just too high. He was working with sharp tools and these could easily become weapons.

Giving up on Mark was one of the hardest decisions I have ever made, but I now know that I was right. Just a few weeks later, someone shouted across the road to Mark. It was a light-hearted humorous comment but Mark took it to heart.

He promptly crossed the road, pulled a screwdriver out of his pocket and casually stabbed the other young person in the neck. Thankfully his victim survived, but Mark went to prison for his actions.

Doubt started to creep into my mind. Could I have prevented this? Could I have educated him and transformed his mind? Thoughts that led me to feel that I had failed Mark, 'Why did I give up so easily?'

The answer is of course that experience, wisdom and discernment enabled me to make the right judgment call. Mark was given a chance and the risk was assessed. Both of these things are essential, but when the risk is assessed as too dangerous, we need to take appropriate action.

Without trying to over-dramatise the situation, the screwdriver could have been in my neck and I could have been dead. With that thought in my mind, I know that I made the right judgment call.

What's the point?

The three years of my life from 2002 to 2005 had seen many dark episodes. Jade had been murdered, Neil threatened a teacher with a hammer, Mark had stabbed someone with a screwdriver, I was diagnosed with angina, our shop opened and closed again, plus we were looking for a new church home. The escalation of stress does often go unnoticed and even though I still stood on that word in The Bible that says, "The joy of the Lord is my strength," there is a limit to how much stress the mind can take.

The point at which stress turns into depression is unknown, but it can and does happen. I had considered ending my life when I was just fourteen years old and again when I was at the age of thirty. Now at the age of forty-five, the same thoughts returned. Thoughts of, 'What is the point in carrying on?' My mind was already making plans of how to end everything. There was no one definable incident that led me to this place and I can't explain how I arrived at it again, but it was real.

Then, in the darkness, the depths of despair, the depression, I noticed something different, something that I had never seen in the previous episodes. I was not alone.

I started to realise that others who were close to me also suffered from what some now referred to as the 'Black Dog.' One of my friends who didn't know my situation told me that the great man Winston Churchill also suffered from it, but he fought back.

My good friend Di Rowe heard about how I was feeling; no one else knew apart from Heather. I had learnt to wear a mask, to put on my shell and not allow anyone in. Heather did know though and understood how I was feeling, perhaps from experiences of her own.

As a visionary person, I will often describe my feelings and situation in picture form. I explained to Di that I felt as if I was standing on the edge of a cliff, looking down and considering when I should jump. Not '*if*' I should jump, the decision had already been made and it was only a matter of time.

I can't remember the details of the conversations, but as I met with Di every week, the picture gradually developed further. The first change was my mindset. I was still standing on the edge of the cliff looking out to sea, but the thought of jumping had already left me. Is this what had happened to Kim all those years ago when she listened to my music looking out to sea, contemplating the drop below her?

My mind changed almost instantly, but it would be a few more weeks before the picture in my mind would change. Gradually each week I moved further from the cliff edge. I was still looking out to sea, but now admiring the magnificence and splendour of the vista, God's creation.

As the weeks passed, I imagined a fence in my picture and I was now leaning against it, but again looking out to sea. Di asked me which side of the fence I was on. I told her that I was on the sea side, the dangerous side of the fence, though I was leaning against it, relaxed and peaceful. She asked me if I would like to be on the other side of the fence, where it would be safer. I told her, "No, I am happy here, where there is a little risk and a bit of danger but I have the reassurance of the fence."

Since then, I have also allowed my mind to realise that there is a gate in the fence and that if the storm blows in, I can easily pass through the gate and head for cover.

I know that some of this imaginative thinking may sound a little odd to some people, but this ability to picture things such as this has not only saved my life, it has also made me the visionary person that I am today.

Interestingly, we called our coffee bar project 'The

Door' because Jesus said, "I am The Door, if anyone enters through Me, he shall be saved" (John 10:9). Some versions of The Bible translate this to, "I am the gate..." I am now so thankful for my imaginary fence and especially the gate, but of course for Di who helped me to see this.

*****

Even through these dark years God's Golden Thread was weaving and bringing a glimmer of light and hope. In 2002 we launched the 'Undiscovered Youth Talent Contest.' The aim of this was to build young people up, by providing them an opportunity with direction and guidance, growing their confidence and motivation through performance art. For some, the whole experience of the audition was more than they could cope with, but we would always be constructive with feedback, building them up and encouraging.

Fifteen years on and this contest has seen an endless stream of talent. The story of one young person can sum up what this project has achieved. He came to us for his first-ever audition but was so nervous that he had to turn away from us when he sang. His voice was amazing, but he lacked the confidence for the big stage of the final with over four hundred people present. We did, however, work with him throughout the year and he took on board what he was being taught. Then when he auditioned again a year later, he had improved so much that he went straight through to the final and we continued to watch him develop and win prizes for the next three years.

We have seen many winners move on into the music and entertainment industry as a career; Nathan Sykes (The Wanted), Mary-Jess Leaverland (world-renowned classical artist), Harry Jones (team Danny The Voice UK), Kieran Powell (entertained Olympians & Royal Family). The list goes on and on and the standard that we have seen has been extremely high, but it is those who have been trained through our studio sessions that touch my heart. I can see where they have come from, how they have struggled and what they have overcome.

Karen had struggled to be accepted by those around her. Family arguments and health issues had made her life difficult but now, through her music, she was a force to be reckoned with. Instead of shouting and arguing with people, she could pour her emotions into song. Gradually a powerful change took place as she realised how much people truly valued and admired her.

Christine struggled with a speech impediment which would knock her confidence but she still wanted to sing. At nineteen years old she had struggled with more emotional trauma than many of us face in a lifetime, but she was determined to overcome.

I introduced Christine to vocal shaping exercises that not only improved her vocal ability in singing, it also developed her ability to talk without any impediment.

Both Christine and Karen have stories of their own to tell, and I look forward to one day reading theirs.

Alison also came to us and gained from singing, but there will be more about her in the next chapter.

*****

A final glimmer of hope that I want to share with you

in this mainly dark chapter happened in 2004. We would occasionally be asked if we would take a student on placement from Redcliffe Bible College. These students were preparing for missionary work all over the world, and it is amazing to think that we now have people who have learnt and gained from their experiences with us in all corners of the globe.

Meok was Korean and spoke very little English. She was with us for a two-week block placement, and it was a real struggle. Sign language and gestures can help so much, but it is not enough.

On her last day, I felt that I had failed to communicate with her properly. We really could have done with an interpreter, but then, something amazing happened. She arrived with two gifts, the first of which was a picture that she had drawn and, on the back, she had written, 'Brendan, you are a Pioneer for God, you will drive forward and others will follow you.' Although I already knew this, we all need to hear words of affirmation every so often. What a great gift.

Then she presented me with a small black book, so small that it could fit into the palm of my hand. It was a Korean Promise Bible. Every page was covered in verses from The Bible. On one page, it was written in English and on the opposite page in Korean. Now I was able to use this to communicate. I would find a verse that related to what I wanted to tell her and point to it. She could then read it in her own language. We used the Word of God to communicate, relate and understand. That was the last day that I ever saw Meok; she had come to us to learn, but I had learnt so much just on that last day. Just when I thought that I had failed her, God intervened and showed me something different.

Chapter Nineteen

Prodigy

Alison's Story

I take great peace in knowing that we have positively touched the lives of so many young people. Some have just been brief encounters, though still worthwhile. Others have been for many years, where deep relationships have developed with very deep roots. Alison is one of those stories.

I first met Alison when she was just fourteen years old and she quickly became a regular at our daily drop-in sessions. At times she would be waiting on the doorstep before opening time. Her school was a half an hour bus journey away and if she was staying to the end of the school day, she shouldn't be on the doorstep at opening time.

I soon started to question her presence at such an early time and she began to talk about how difficult school had been for her. Everything was a struggle, teachers, lessons, learning, other students; she didn't enjoy school. For Alison, as is often the case of those who struggle in school, instead of support there was ridicule and at times even physical bullying.

Alison was no exception, she often felt ridiculed by both teachers and students. Her reaction to this was anger, uncontrolled and often physically aggressive.

When she was fifteen years old, she asked if she could do some singing in our small music studio. The courage that this must have taken was huge and we really cannot grasp how much of a challenge that must have been for Alison. She had very little confidence, and low self-esteem and was completely de-motivated.

However, we had been building a relationship of trust with her for almost a year. She knew that we would not judge her or criticise her ability.

When a negative seed of doubt and condemnation has been poured into a person for many years, it's not surprising that you start to believe it is all true. She was so nervous the first time that she sang that I stood outside the room and listened. After just a short time of singing she started to condemn herself, "That's rubbish," she said, "Who am I kidding? I can't sing!"

I couldn't believe what I was hearing. Her voice wasn't perfect but she did have very good quality with great potential. She just didn't believe it.

I questioned her, "Who has told you that you can't sing?" Then she looked at me as if to say, 'How do you know people have told me that?'

Her answer was quickly blurted out, "EVERYONE! Everyone that I know tells me that I'm rubbish and shouldn't bother!"

"Well, I'm telling you that they're all wrong. You can sing; furthermore, you sing really well. If people are telling you anything different to what I am saying, they are either jealous or deaf."

I now had her attention and she was listening carefully to what I was saying. I wondered if this was the first time that she had ever heard any positive words as I continued, "Trust me, if I tell you something, it is true. I will tell you where you are good and where you need to improve, but I will always be honest with you and never lie. You need to know the truth and the truth is that you have a gift, that gift is your voice. You can sing. Now start to believe it!" I have since talked to many other young people like this for them to start to believe in themselves and to undo the damage that others had inflicted upon them.

Alison was on the verge of giving up but the straight-talking, positive encouragement impacted her as reality hit her. She never said it, but in her head, she was thinking, 'He's right; I can sing and I'll prove it. I'll show them all.'

Singing was only the start of building confidence and self-belief for Alison. When she sang, she would lose herself in another world. This was her escape from the struggles that were going on in her life, but when the singing ended the other problems were still there.

She soon entered our 'Undiscovered Youth Talent Contest' and stepping out onto the stage was perhaps one of the hardest challenges that she had ever faced. With an expectant audience and a judging panel of seven experts from the entertainment industry, she was determined to show everyone how good she was. Now as she sang the emotion was powerfully strong, as it reflected the pain in her life.

Her school life came to an end and she left with no qualifications feeling as if she had failed, but relieved to be free of the oppression that had crushed her spirit and caused her so much anguish.

By the time Alison was seventeen years old, I had

known her for three years. I had supported her through endless upsets and she had developed a deep level of trust with me. She would come to me on countless occasions in tears. There was a small child inside of her, but she struggled to cope with the emotional stresses that were in her life. She wanted to be an adult, a woman, but the child always dominated. Tears always came. Over and over, I would listen to one problem after another. Then eventually, one day when the trust was fully established, I told her, "I don't know what to say... I think you just need to grow up!"

I would not recommend saying this to just anyone, but I knew that it was right for Alison, for that moment and so did she.

She looked at me and the tears stopped almost immediately. I could hear the cogs of her brain as she thought once again, 'He's right; I can deal with this. I'll prove it. I'll show them all.'

Soon after this, I had a dream; it was one of the clearest dreams that I have ever had. In it, different young people were coming into the coffee bar, dragging suitcases and bags behind them. I recognised the faces of every one of them. Some were entering the building opening up their bags and pouring out the contents. What was coming out was a mess, but they were unloading. Then in my dream, Alison arrived. She was hugging her case, unable or unwilling to let go. She had a look of fear on her face that said, 'Don't touch my case, I need my baggage, I can't open it.'

In my dream, Jesus spoke and said, "I am the key that opens the case, come to me and I will carry your burden."

I told Alison about the dream and she listened with interest. Soon afterwards she asked if she could have a mentor (we had launched our mentoring service in 2006). This was another turning point in her life and would now lead to her getting help to access a college course with the right level of support, it would inspire her to find a part-time job in a shop. Things were looking up, but still, something was missing.

*****

In 2008 a national campaign was launched to bring HOPE to the nation. Churches across the country became united in HOPE 08.

In Stroud, The Door was the only project that was associated with this cause. We decided to provide a nightclub-themed church setting and called it Club HOPE. In total five events were planned throughout the year. Each event was a two-hour session, but with two hours of technical setting up and an hour of stripping down at the end of the evening, even with an army of volunteers, it was very hard work.

During each event, a prayer team supported what was happening and lives were being touched. Alison went to every Club HOPE event that we ran, she was being touched by God and the seeds of the Gospel were being planted.

There was an almost tangible presence - a power in the air, the Holy Spirit was here. Every event had a different focus and the fourth one was a Drum 'n' Bass night.

The first three events had attracted mainly young people who were already attending a local church and some who were already Christians, plus a handful of young people from The Door. Now at this event, we would see many that we had not previously talked to.

As the evening started there was a clear division of regulars and newcomers, the churched and the un-churched. Slowly the divide closed and God gave me a picture. I saw a long suspension bridge with Christian young people on one side and unbelievers on the other side. The two groups started to cross the bridge and they met in the middle. God said to me, "You have built this bridge, but you have to cross it and meet in the middle. Never expect anyone to cross from the zone of unbelief into my Church, without meeting them on that journey."

We cannot have an attitude of simply, 'Here we are, come on in if you want to join us.' We do need to meet people where they are at!

Halfway through the evening a group of young people who had been working on a social action project called 'The Noise' were to give a cheque presentation, to the work of The Door Youth Project.

As the camera started snapping, remarkably the group of un-churched young people joined the group for the photograph. The divide had closed and they were all now united as one group. I believe that barriers were broken down and seeds were planted on that evening, not to mention that since then some of those who were present have accepted Jesus into their lives.

*****

Maybe Alison had made her way into the middle of the bridge that evening. Although, as far as I am aware, no one crossed right over that bridge in any of the Club HOPE events. No one invited Jesus into their lives, but seeds were sown and bridges were built.

For the following two years, I was asked to put the Club HOPE band back together, to provide a time of worship at the end of 'The Noise' weekend in Stroud. During this event, groups of young people spent the weekend working within the local community, painting walls, digging gardens, litter picking, giving away balloons and generally having great fun together.

The event took place in May and we provided a Club HOPE style of worship for 2009 and 2010. At each of these events, we saw at least two young people invite Jesus into their lives. Alison made that step in 2010, she was now twenty years old and I had known her for six years. She had been on a journey, but she had crossed that bridge, been met in the middle and now arrived.

As the music played, she experienced a new feeling, a new sensation, it was an overwhelming feeling of knowing that she was loved. She had cried out to God and He had responded. She immediately felt different – changed. The suitcase had been unlocked. She had accepted Jesus as the key to the burdens and already the load that she had been carrying was being removed. Rejection had been replaced by acceptance. Her repentance and His response had set her free!

It is important to realise that the step of acceptance is only the first step and every step is followed by another, which is why we refer to it as a 'walk of faith.'

If we look closely every walk of faith has the odd milestone placed along it. Significant steps that when taken will lead us onto the next exciting part of our journey.

*****

Heather joined the team at The Door in 2004 as the administrator. However as the project grew, so too did the administration tasks. It was decided that we should take another step of faith and employ an apprentice to help with the increasing level of work and Alison applied.

Each of the applicants had been interviewed initially by the college, with three being shortlisted for us to meet. It was exciting to have a choice, but before the interview date, the other two dropped out leaving Alison as the only choice – God's choice!

We interviewed her and she started work with us in November 2011. She was passionate about giving back to the project which had supported and helped her, but she wasn't interested in administrative tasks, and paperwork was an obvious struggle, as the school had also been. The reason why, soon became known. It had taken twenty-one years of her life, but now she was told that she was dyslexic and she began to understand why she had struggled at school. Now she understood why she hadn't learnt and why she had been misunderstood.

She did complete her business administration apprenticeship, but it was obvious throughout that she would rather be directly supporting and helping young people. She had a heart to become a youth worker and as I have often said before, God will always give us the desire of our heart.

We never felt that it would be right to take Alison on as a youth worker without her first gaining more experience in a wider setting. She was disappointed to hear that, but as her apprenticeship with us ended, another opportunity arose.

We worked very closely with many other organisations and PSALMS was one of them. This organisation provides a variety of youth and children's projects across the district and they were now looking for a new intake of Interns.

Alison was accepted and started with PSALMS in September 2012 and also started on the Centre for Youth Ministries Engage course. I would see her every so often and I could see that she was growing, growing in ability, maturity and in spirit.

Within six months she came back to The Door and joined our team of sessional youth workers and was showing a natural talent to be able to empathise with those in need.

During her teenage years, she had been tempted into shoplifting, sought solace in alcohol and even had a few run-ins with the local police. All of this was part of her life experience and all of it was providing her with a knowledge base, equipping her for the work that she was now doing.

Alison is now a major part of the team at The Door and I feel so privileged to have walked with her on her journey, to see her overcome, to witness her maturing and blossoming, but most of all to see her giving back and taking the project on with the next generation.

Rosie

I first met Rosie when she was 11 years old. She seemed

mature in her attitude for her age and I constantly asked her if she was really age 14.

She was just 12 years old when she came with me on a walk. After walking several miles, we sat for a rest on a fallen tree and started to talk about her hopes for the future.

"I think my mum would like it if I became a teacher," she said.
"Is that because your mum is a teacher?" I asked cynically.
"Probably, but I don't think it's for me."
"What is for you?"
"I want to be a youth worker." She said it with such conviction.

I had often heard other young people say that they would like to be a youth worker. Usually, this is because they see the youth worker having fun, playing games and generally socialising. They fail to see the struggles associated with the role and the associated paperwork, planning, preparation, reporting, etc.

Rosie was different even at this young age she knew what was involved and what she wanted!

As The Door developed, so did Rosie mature as a person. She was keen to volunteer, helping wherever she could, learning whenever she could, and participating in everything that was going on.

Rosie was another who had attended every Club HOPE event that we had delivered and a spark had been planted in her heart. As she grew, that spark grew into a flame and she too invited Jesus into her life when she was about 15 years old.

There is an expression that I love, 'People don't care about how much you know until they know how much you care.' When I hear this expression, I often think of Rosie as she continued to volunteer in such a caring and genuine manner.

It's not surprising then that when she had completed her A levels at the age of 18, she started a university degree in... Yes, you guessed it, youth work. She had come a long way since the day we sat on the fallen tree, but Rosie's focus and determination, combined with the influence of a team of great youth work role models, will guarantee that she will become a superb youth worker.

Gill

I have appeared on numerous radio programmes and one occasion I was asked if I could be interviewed at The Door. It was with Richard Atkins from BBC Radio Gloucestershire and he asked if we could also include a young person's comment.

We stood outside in the open air; it was one of Richard's techniques for creating an atmosphere. I can't remember any of the questions that Richard asked, but I clearly remember what Gill said – "Before I came to The Door, I didn't really feel valued, not by friends or teachers, not even by my family. Then I came here and realised that these people cared about me and valued me."

Richard immediately placed the microphone by my mouth and asked what I thought of that comment. I couldn't speak properly and I cried on the radio as I choked the words out, "I never knew that we had had such an effect on Gill's life."

Gill was another who volunteered with us and was a valued member of the team when we launched a weekly detached youth work session on the streets and in the parks of Stroud. She had learnt enough about youth work to encourage her to step out on her journey in a youth work career.

Gill now works as a youth support worker for the Targeted Support Team. She is now helping others to believe in themselves and to feel valued.

When you throw a rock into a pond the ripples radiate outwards. We impacted the lives of Alison, Rosie and Gill, but the ripples of our impact are continuing. What's more, they will never stop, as these three will also be blessed with prodigy of their own.

Chapter Twenty

A time to build up

As is the case with anyone's life, many of the stories overlap, intertwine and run parallel to others. Our lives are a continuous, ever-expanding, ever-increasing tapestry of new challenges, decisions and excitement. In fact, every day is a new day and an opportunity to change.

At times I will hear a person say, "I just want it to stay the way that it is." Those who dwell in the past will also be heard to say, "If only we could get back to the way it used to be."

My life has moved on. The Door Youth Project has moved on and the time will come when I will move on to whatever is the next chapter in my life. First though, let's try to bring the journey so far right up to date, to a conclusion that will hopefully inspire others.

The book of Ecclesiastes talks about, 'a season for everything... a time to build up and a time to tear down.' Looking back over the last twenty-four years, there have been definite times when this has been the case for The Door Youth Project.

Our Toddlers of Teens Support group was in place for a season. During those years it had served a purpose, but we recognised that we had reached a place where it was no longer needed.

The counselling service that was set up by Di Rowe continued for twelve years until 2003 and was provided purely by volunteers. These volunteers were in training with Teens in Crisis (another Christian organisation) and were working towards a qualification in counselling. Teens in Crisis were specialists in counselling and were gaining contracts to provide a counselling service in various schools. With these contracts came the necessity to employ paid staff and these volunteers were offered these emerging opportunities.

The need for young people who were not in school, to be able to access a free and confidential counselling service still existed and we could still provide the space for this. It was therefore decided that we should enter into a formal partnership agreement with Teens in Crisis, so in 2003, we made that step.

For two years we continued as we had previously. Teens in Crisis delivered counselling from our property, we charged them for room hire as we always had and nothing else developed. Then after two years, we both asked the question, “Is this really a partnership? Is it worth continuing?”

The formal partnership as it was ended, however nothing changed. We continued to provide space to deliver counselling and we continued to charge them for the use of that space.

We both learnt something about true partnership through this process. Now, whenever I am considering a partnership, I consider what both we and the other parties can bring to the table. I now feel that a true partnership should result in the combined sum of resources being greater than its natural sum. In other words, if each organisation brings one skill, service or resource to the mix, the natural sum is two. However, in a true partnership, the combined force is greater than the natural and one plus one becomes three or more. That's synergy.

Interestingly as the TIC partnership came to an end in 2005, I felt that God was saying, "Now is the time to rebuild." This was confirmed as I prayed and was led to the book of Haggai chapter 1 verses 3-6 which read:

"Then the word of The LORD came through the prophet Haggai: 'Is it a time for you yourselves to be living in your panelled houses, whilst this house remains a ruin?"'

Now this is what the LORD Almighty says: "Give careful thought to your ways. You have planted much but harvested little. You eat but never have enough. You drink but never have your fill. You put on clothes but are not warm. You earn wages, only to put them in a purse with holes in it."

The way forward needed to see us increase capacity, capability and sustainability. We needed to assess the needs, identify how we could meet those needs and determine how we were best suited to deliver what was required.

Having severed the TIC partnership, we quickly identified that there was an increasing demand for emotional needs support of a different kind, as most of the issues that we were seeing were not as deep and severe. They didn't require counselling.

Mentoring was becoming a buzzword. It had a growing popularity amongst young people as it was now regarded as 'cool' to have a mentor (it was also helpful). So, in 2006 we launched 'The Light at The Door' mentoring service for young people.

Nine years on this service has expanded to include the parents and carers of young people and now provides: school-based mentoring, peer mentors, family support, parenting programmes and of course continues to provide one-to-one mentoring for young people.

The Light at The Door is now regarded as one of the leading family support services within Gloucestershire. The service has come such a long way since the decision to rebuild.

A year later in 2007, it was becoming increasingly apparent that we were running out of space. I quickly lost count of the number of times someone jokingly said, "We need a bigger building."

26 Gloucester Street was our birthplace, with years of memories, my memories. The emotional attachment was massive and God knew that, but He also wanted us to move.

Now I realise that when emotional attachment gets in the way of where God wants us to go, He will often show us an easier, more achievable step towards where He wants us to go and what He wants us to do. This was certainly the case with how we moved from our outgrown building to where we are now.

A large building which was just across the road from our project had stood vacant for some time. It seemed the answer to our space issue, as we would be able to stay where we were and expand into this. It seemed like the perfect answer.

Sitting at my favourite place on the local common, I prayed about the situation. I was led to various verses in The Bible to inspire me and I believed that God wanted me to call for volunteers to walk around the building opposite. If we were to claim this building, we had to do it like Joshua walking around Jericho. We would walk around for seven days and on the seventh day, we would walk around seven times. The number seven was very significant in what God had shown me and I sent out a request for seven volunteers to be at the property at 7.00am for seven days, starting on the 7th of July (7th month) 2007.

This is what I felt God was leading me to do and if less than seven people would turn up, I would feel that I had to cancel this whole thing. The seven people would be the confirmation that this is what was needed to be done.

On the morning of 7th July, I drove the car into Stroud with Heather by my side. As I arrived, I counted, 1 – 2 – 3 – 4 – 5. "Yes, with the two of us, that's seven."

Each day the seven of us met at 7.00am and walked around the building in silence as we prayed.

On the seventh day, we met and started to walk and pray in silence. There was a powerful presence with us. God was with us. I had confirmation of this presence as a man in his 30s, called 'Timmy' approached me.

Timmy always wanted to talk and I had a concern that he would distract from what we were building here. As he approached, I felt God tell me to put my hand up as if to stop him. I never touched Timmy, but as I put my hand up, it was as if he was physically pushed back. The power of God truly was working in what we were doing.

By the time we had completed seven laps, a few people were watching from afar, as Bill produced a Ram's Horn Trumpet (Shofar Horn) and blew loudly. The gathering audience may have thought that we were a bunch of weird religious 'nutters.' I doubt whether any knew what we were doing, but none of them asked.

How would we have answered them anyway? Did any of us really know what we were doing? The simple answer is we were being obedient to what God had told us to do!

We thought that this was the building to meet our needs, but it was more like the building to meet God's needs. He needed to motivate us, to stir us up to think beyond where we were at. This wasn't the building that he wanted us to go to but it was what we could see and relate to, so God used it.

In faith, we negotiated a price for the building, but following a structural survey we realised that it was in such a bad state of repair, we would have to spend too much money on it. This is not to say that we did not have faith that God could provide this money but we have to be good stewards of what we are given and suddenly this didn't feel right.

The thought seed though had been planted, God had stirred us up and we would find something else!

God had given us the push that we needed and now we launched an appeal. Calling it the 'PUSH The Door Appeal,' we asked people to get behind the project and become PUSH Partners.

These PUSH Partners would commit to donating a regular amount of money, which could be used to pay a mortgage on a new building, if we had enough.

We looked at three more buildings, each one with potential. The first of these was again not quite right, as it was considered to be in the wrong location. We had asked young people in a survey where they would like The Door situated and we were listening to them. Were we listening to God though?

The next property was huge, more than we would need, which would mean that we could rent some of the space out. We made an offer which was not refused. The building was owned by a large corporation and they told us that they would be happy for us to have it at the offer price. Then nothing else happened until we heard that they had sold it to someone else, without telling us.

The next building was in a great location, but not big enough. Once again, we found ourselves in a situation of potentially buying a building and spending money on it, for it to not be worth what we had paid in total. We were reminded that we need to be good stewards of money and even more so when it has been donated by others.

There is an expression that I have used on many occasions, 'When one door closes another one opens.' Nearly three years had passed since the 'Joshua walk' around the original building. Now with the world in economic crisis and the country being declared as in recession, youth services amongst others were being cut. The 'Connexions' service had been situated at the top of the High Street for many years, supporting young people and helping them to move forward in life. Now though, as a result of the cuts, they had closed.

God had led me to this building or at least a small part of it, many years ago when we were looking for workshop space in 2002. On that occasion, I had just missed out on the chance for this space, which was about 25% of the whole building. Now though it was the other 75% that was available, with a high street location, a more visible presence and a chance to set up a shop to raise part of our income. This property would take almost a year of negotiations and to work through the legal requirements.

The owner didn't want to sell and so we were back in the situation that we had faced when we first started all of those years ago in 1991. We were paying rent, but God had told us to rebuild, so here we were starting over again.

In 2007 we had stepped out in obedience with the Joshua walk. This was followed by almost five years of what now seems like wandering in the wilderness.

A seed has to be planted and propagated before it grows and in February 2012, we were given the keys to our new building.

In faith, I had advertised an open evening on 5th February at 7.00 pm and was given the keys at 5.00pm, just two hours before the event.

I ran around this amazing new space putting notices up to explain what we were going to do with the building. It took me just ten minutes and at the end of it, I felt God say, 'This isn't going to be big enough.' Now after just two years of being there, we are beginning to say, "We need more space."

Our plan for the first year in this new building was to just settle in and consolidate, but God had other plans. In that first year, we saw the number of young people that we engaged with increase from 700 to over 1,000. Our training, mentoring and family support services all increased in capacity, with increased service level agreements. Staffing levels had to be increased to meet the rising demand and inevitably so did expenditure, as our turnover rose from around £200k to over £300k.

We had rebuilt. At times it had been painful, tedious and frustrating, but we had done it. We had remained hopeful, faithful and prayerful. It is the power of prayer and the support of others praying, that had brought us to this place. It is that same power that leads us and drives us on now, as we know that, God will supply all of our needs.

Chapter Twenty-One

Reaching Out With More HOPE

I have previously mentioned that 2008 was the year of HOPE 08 and we provided an opportunity for young people to attend Club HOPE. Not surprisingly this year was also a year with more difficult struggles.

Our mentoring service for young people was now in its second year and some of the issues that we were now dealing with were some of the most serious. Now six years on we still see situations of the most serious nature, but this next story sums up all that we do and the difference that we have made.

Annie Watkins was now heading up our mentoring service for young people and she found herself supporting three who had established a suicide pact. They had all agreed between them that if one died, the other two would take their own lives. To make matters worse and to increase the risk of death, they were playing very dangerous games such as 'chicken' with trains. We nicknamed them the 'Railway Children' and over time Annie helped each of them to see the danger of what they were doing, to value their lives and to move forward. Each of them found something positive to focus on and work towards. Before Annie had intervened, these three were desperate and depressed, but having someone to talk things over with had saved them. Others have taken their own lives since, others who perhaps had no one they could turn to for help, no one who would listen to them.

At about the same time in 2008, groups of young people in Bridgend in South Wales were taking their own lives, as they too had agreed to their own suicide pacts. The difference between Stroud and Bridgend was that in Stroud, these three young people found help through The Door Youth Project. We were there for them. It would most likely have been more like the sad stories that we heard coming from Bridgend if we hadn't helped.

I know that I say it over and over, but I'll say it again, "There are young people alive today who may not otherwise have been so. This is one of the greatest outcomes that we can achieve."

More health issues

2008 was also the year that I was diagnosed with Polycystic Kidney Disease. This hereditary disease can cause raised blood pressure, reduced kidney function, risk of stroke and could even result in the eventual need for a kidney transplant.

As the news of this latest health issue started to sink in, I questioned my ability and my worth. As I prayed about this, God spoke to me once again through his Word and a picture.

First, I saw a picture of an apple in a bowl. It had been sitting there for so long that the bottom had started to rot under its weight.

Then I opened my Bible and started to read Leviticus chapter 3. It was talking about 'fellowship offerings' and mentioned kidneys four times.

I felt that God was saying, "Your kidneys may be rotten, as is half of this apple, but the rest is useful. You are useful. You may not be as fit as you used to be, but

I want you and I need you to be wholly available to me."

I still had a use, and a value and my self-worth quickly returned.

Preparations for the future

I can often liken myself to 'Eeyore', the depressive donkey in Winnie the Pooh. For brief moments, I may find myself in extremely low places, with the thoughts of, 'nobody loves me' in my mind.

Then I feel as if God reaches down and picks me up. He carries me when times are difficult, just like that 'Footprints' poem (previously mentioned in chapter 18).

If 2008 was designated as the year of 'HOPE,' what hope was there for The Door and the future of the project? I went to the Trustees and explained that the project was vulnerable because I was vulnerable.

It was decided that it was time that I had a deputy, someone who could take on some of the ever-increasing workload and eventually take on the succession when I have gone. This step was considered essential if it was to continue beyond my lifetime.

We placed an advertisement for this new post in the Christian Youth Work Magazine and in September 2008 I received a phone call from Barrie Voyce.

Barrie was still in his final year of a Centre for Youth Ministry BA course in youth work and theology. He explained that he would not be available for nine months, but would it still be worthwhile if he applied?

I told him that I would be willing to wait for the right person, the person that God wants for us. Whilst most of the other students on Barrie's course were seeking work in church settings, Barrie had felt that God was leading him to a different challenge, the challenge of supporting un-churched young people.

The next month, in October, Barrie came to visit. Whilst I was showing him around, he asked how long we had funding for. This, for some people, maybe a difficult question to answer, as the real question could be considered to be, "Do you have enough to pay me? How secure is my job?"

I told him that nothing is ever guaranteed, that we could usually see about three months ahead, but that we had faith that God provides all of our needs. Later Barrie told me that it was this honesty and faith that had convinced him that this was where God wanted him to be.

In December 2008, Barrie returned with his wife and two children. Would they want to move from Nottingham to a new town, a new job, a new step of faith?

Both Helen and Barrie agreed that they felt God was drawing them to Stroud and on 1st July 2009 Barrie started work with us. At first, he found rented accommodation, but when he announced that he was buying a house in Stroud, I had two thoughts. The first was, 'Good he is here to stay.' The second was, 'Now we need even more faith, that we can keep paying him so that he can pay his mortgage.'

It is these often nagging second thoughts that can stir up fear and prevent the step of faith ever being taken, but when we rise above them, it is then that we see amazing things happen.

Over the years that Barrie has been with us, he has moved from leading one department to the next. Firstly, heading up the youth work team and the Drop-In, then the Mentoring and Family Support, now he is managing and developing the HOPE Training Department. He has learnt the intricacies of each department, to the extent that he became the Director of all Operations.

Like me, he has great vision and passion for young people and their families. He is my successor and will eventually lead the whole organisation forward into new and unchartered territory. The thought of that is rather frightening, for both him and myself, but I also realise that it is necessary.

I have seen too many projects die with the death of the founder. I want to see God's legacy continue to survive, I want to watch it from a distance and smile as I see it grow. I want to see others continue to nurture the seeds that I have planted, but most of all... I want to know what God has planned next for my life. I want to continue to step out in faith and to walk in faith, walking into the next chapter of my life... whatever that may be.

Chapter Twenty-Two

Climb every mountain

I started my story with my reflective thoughts from childhood and mentioned The Sound of Music. One of my favourite songs from that musical is 'Climb Every Mountain.'

Something that I haven't mentioned yet is my love for mountains. I didn't climb a mountain until I was 37 years old, which is when I was invited to North Wales for a weekend of walking. That first mountain was 'Tryfan.'

A year later I was taking part in the National Three Peaks Challenge, climbing the tallest mountains in Wales, England and Scotland, all within 24 hours. I am pleased to say that I managed all three in 23 hours and 20 minutes. What an experience.

My love for mountains continued to grow and so too did the level of challenge that I would push myself to achieve. I was 41 years old in 2001 and for many years I had wanted to climb Mount Kilimanjaro, Africa's tallest mountain and the tallest free-standing mountain in the world. I had wanted to do this in my 40th year but the house that we were living in was in a mess. I had to finish building the new extension and fit the kitchen before I could go. We all need some form of motivation and incentive in life and Kilimanjaro was mine.

The year following 'Kili' I rose to another challenge. The 15 Peaks challenge involves climbing the 15 Welsh mountains, all of which are over 3,000 feet above sea level. I did this in three days, unlike some who do it in a breathtaking 24 hours.

I had developed a real passion for mountains, or so I thought. I now say that I enjoy being on top of a mountain, but the climb up is often a hard, difficult struggle. Although the pain of the climb is worth it when greeted by the pleasure of being on top of the mountain, the feeling of success outweighs the pain and the freedom of the top of the world is breathtaking.

I don't wish to bore you with stories about mountains, but needless to say, I have now climbed many.

My favourite mountain to climb with people who have never been up a mountain is Sugar Loaf in the Brecon Beacons. I have been there on many occasions with small groups of young people and after a long hard walk, when we are in sight of the summit I stop and sit. I give them the choice to continue to the summit or to give up, taking the easier exit route off the mountain. Not once has anyone ever said that we should give up.

Before starting to walk again (and they are very keen to reach the top) I ask them all to look back at this time, that if they ever feel like giving up with the huge mountains (tasks) that life throws at us, remember that the end is in sight.

I have had to remind myself of this on many occasions and have been supported by the people that I have around me. They have encouraged me in life, just as we encourage each other to press on towards the goal of that mountain summit.

I have so many people to thank for supporting me on my journey through life, but most of all I thank God, for continuing to weave his Golden Thread and I ask with great expectation, "What next?" I don't expect to 'climb every mountain' but I do know that He will show me which one is next.

This book is my story, but it is not my whole story. I have had to make decisions about what to put in and what to take out. I hope that it has given you a 'flavour' of who I am and most of all has inspired you to climb every mountain that God gives you in life.

When you are writing your own life story it is hard to know where to end. After all, the story of my life is still being written. Every day a new chapter is being played out. One of my most recent chapters was an eight-day stay in hospital. My angina had suddenly changed and I found myself waking up with pains in my chest and arms. I knew what it was and suspected what the outcome would be. The medical team put me back together again, fitting three small devices called 'stents' into my arteries, the shock was soon over and normal life restored.

It was just after this time that God placed a picture of a balloon in my mind. The balloon was fully inflated and I asked God why I was seeing this. He said, "This balloon is like your confidence, fully inflated and this is how people see you." Then he said, "But it only takes one small pin prick and it is burst, your resilience is thin and weak. People don't see this; they only see your confidence."

This book may have been a revelation to some people. This last statement may have been especially revealing to some, as I lowered my guard and allowed people to see me for who I am and what I am. My experiences in life have taught me that honesty, integrity, truth and respect are the four virtues that will bring us success.

Richard Branson is well-known for quoting this, but long before Mr. Branson made this profound statement Jesus said, "I am the truth and the truth will set you free." (John 14:6 & John 16:13).

We all have a story. Stories are powerful. So, I urge you to write yours. Be truthful with your words and honest to yourself, you deserve it.

Start small… dream big… believe!

The next instalment...

I'm Still Valued

I have to be honest: when Brendan Conboy spoke about a sequel to his autobiography, I did think: surely the sequel to a biography is an obituary … I did not realise at the time how close to an obituary his story would be. However, as the book makes clear, this volume is a continuation of Conboy's story, largely picking up where the first part left off. The nine years since that earlier book have certainly been a roller-coaster for the author. A "Timeline of Events" highlights two major threads through those years: health issues and creative writing.

He has found, developed and used his gift for writing verse, producing books of poetry, as well as science fiction, children's books and Bible study. Conboy also tells how he began this work with little conviction he actually could be a writer. He admits his imperfections and his story is certainly challenging rather than entertaining. But it is this which is the book's great strength. Brendan is no con-boy. He's the real deal.

Martin Leckebusch – Hymn Writer

Read on for the next instalment...

Beyond broken

Dedication

To God, the Author of Life, my life,
my protector, provider and deliverer.

You have given me the tools and skills to write.
This book exists because of you.

You picked up all my pieces.
Put me back together
You are the defender of my heart
(Rita Springer)

Thanks

To Heather my wife,
life-long companion and friend.
She is my lieutenant on the battlefield,
the soother of my wounds,
my carer when I need to recover,
my aid to understand,
when my brain needs clarity.
She is patient, loving and kind and
helped me immensely to remember
much of the detail of this book.
Her input has enabled me to
tell this story with integrity.
She is more precious than rubies and greatly
VALUED.

Thanks also to my good friend Jason Parker, for his patience in searching for errors in my writing and for helping to make this book what it is today.

I'm Still Valued

I used to climb up mountains.
Be the first up to the top
I used to ride a bicycle
But crashing made me stop
When I worked on building sites
I was a beautiful sight
I used to have more energy
When young and oh-so-free
For sixty hours I worked each week
I could manage on six hours sleep
I used to lead the greatest team
Now I'm lonely in my dreams
My brain still thinks the way it did
My body says, "You are not a kid."
I've lost so much of who I was
A broken man now because
My health has just deteriorated
Left me feeling so deflated
I often wonder what to do
I know that I am still valued
Forgetting what has gone before
I know that I'm so capable
I am valued and can do more
As long as I do live and breathe
God still calls me for His need

Life is complicated

My life is complicated and no book will ever allow you to fully understand the things that I have experienced. The last decade has been a battle, an onslaught of one major event after another. These are usually health events that would make some people give up on life. I haven't given up because I am convinced that God still values me and wants to use me. I know that my life has been complicated and readers may like to have some chronological order. This is why I have produced a timeline. I hope that you find it helpful and you can use it as a spoiler for the stories to come.

Timeline of events

2008 – Diagnosed with Polycystic Kidney Disease and heart disease (angina) in the same year.
2012 – Decided to work a two-year exit plan from my position as charity CEO. My mental health deteriorated (depression and anxiety).
2014 – (Feb) Hospital - Surgery for three cardio stents.
(Jun/Jul) Wrote my first book, The Golden Thread.
(Nov) Leave The Door charity and start charity consultancy work.
2015 – (Sept) **The Golden Thread (book) published**.
2016 – (Feb) Added to kidney transplant waiting list.
(Aug) Surgery to commence dialysis – **life-threatening complications**.
(Sep) Dialysis commenced.
(Oct) Joined The Shaggy Dog Raconteurs (band) as their drummer.
2017 – (Jul) 1st Transplant call.
2018 – (Jan) 1st Potential living donor.
(Feb) 2nd Transplant call.

(Mar) Clinically depressed and suicidal.

(May) 2nd Potential living donor.

(Jul) God told me that **I'm still valued.**

2019 – (Jan) 3rd Transplant call.

(Feb) 4th Transplant call.

(Feb) 5th Transplant call – Surgery for transplant – **life-threatening complications**.

(Jan) **Issues (book) published**.

(Feb) **My Foundation for Life (book) published.**

2020 – (Mar) Lockdown

(Jun) – Accident – **life-threatening complications**.

(Nov) **Rhyme Time (book) published**.

(Oct) **Invasion of the Mimics (book) published**.

2021 – (Mar) **Land of Make Believe (book) published.**

(May) Diagnosed with severe Sleep Apnoea.

(May) Hospital - Surgery for three more cardio stents.

(Jul) **One God Many Names (book) published**.

(Aug) **The book of Psalms in Rhyme (book) published**.

2022 – (Mar) Hospital - surgery shoulder replacement (following accident).

(Jun) **Legacy of the Mimics (book) published**.

(Jul) Left The Shaggy Dog Raconteurs (band).

(Aug) **Popcorn Poetry (book) published**.

(Nov) 1st Book Blest Christian Book Festival

(Dec) Back in the hospital with unstable angina.

2023 – (Jan) Heart surgery – Triple bypass – **life-threatening complications**.

(Mar) Chronic kidney infection - Hospital

(Apr) **Half Man Half Poet (book) published**.

Chapter One

Let's get started

Without any doubt, this book has been the most difficult and painful that I have ever written. I started the first draft in February 2022 and eventually, after six rewrites, it went to be edited in October 2023, that's 20 months in total. In my first book, 'The Golden Thread', I talked about some of the amazing, inspirational and motivational stories that have happened during my life thus far. I also mentioned many of the immense struggles and tangible fears, but also how God came into my life in a transformational way. That book ended at the time when I left The Door Youth Project in 2014.

This book is my continuing story, with some slight overlap with the previous one. In this book, I will take you on a different journey of pain and discovery. My physical health has deteriorated in lots of different ways. Some of those underlying issues were anticipated and inevitable, whilst other conditions I've been wrestling with just seemed to come out of nowhere.

The last nine years have been an almost constant battle. I have manoeuvred through life's many combat zones and all of its setbacks. Although there have been times when I felt like giving up, I have fought back, remained positive and become a 'warrior.'

I always say that it is better to be a warrior than a worrier. I don't think adding anxiety into the mix has ever solved a problem. I want to go kicking and screaming into my grave. I want to keep on fighting to the end and hopefully encourage others to do the same. I wouldn't want anyone to give up. I want to try and help everyone to uncover a deeper understanding of what it means to be valued.

Well, that is what I would 'like' to think anyway, but let's be honest here... does anyone really think like that when push comes to shove? There have been times when I have cried with despair and screamed with turmoil. I have walked through the darkest valleys and wanted my life to end. I have experienced a few highs but also encountered lows, which have been present more often. I have faced an unrealistic amount of trauma and on many occasions questioned God as to why all of this has happened. I have learnt much and I have changed, although I am still far from perfect.

If you can relate to some of what I say... If you have health struggles and feel like giving up, remember this - You are still valued by God and He still wants to use you.

There have been times when I found myself in a hospital and questioned God, 'Why I am here?' Shortly afterwards, a conversation is usually started with a nurse or another patient about being a Christian. God can and will use you in the strangest of places if you are willing and available to be used. How often do you say, "Here I am Lord wholly available"?

If you think God has given up on you, think again. It is much more likely that it is you who has given up on God. It's easy to feel devalued, discarded and rejected. When we feel this way, we tend to treat God the same, we ignore Him, try things our way and blame God when it all goes wrong. In our devalued state, we devalue the power of God. In our confused minds, we doubt that God cares. In our feelings of rejection, it is so easy to just give up and reject all that you have believed.

When my first granddaughter was born, I said that I

wanted to be at her wedding when she was married. She is now 12 years old and I still want that. I figure she will not marry for at least 10 years. In the last 10 years, I have brushed with death at least four times, so in reality, the odds are stacked against me. As I think about those odds, I am reminded that in God, *'all things are possible' (Matthew 19:26).*

This may be the last book that I ever write, although I very much hope not. As long as I can type, I will fight and carry on regardless. As long as I can hear God telling me what to write, I will publish books and share His message with the world.

I do hope that this book and my story will help you realise that God still wants to use you. The question is, do you want to be used by God? Do you want to be part of what He is doing? Do you want to fight, overcome and witness the breakthrough in your own life?

I'm Still Valued

During the time that it has taken to write this book, I have experienced three major visits to the hospital *(see timeline at the start)*. I remember not wanting to give up, with an, 'I've started so I'll finish' attitude, but it has taken a lot of effort. I even wrote some of it whilst in one of my hospital beds. I always grapple with how much to put in and how much to leave out. I decided to keep the chapters intentionally short but hopefully with enough information. My endeavours are mainly in the hope that you might be prompted to think about your own lives and your own problems which you may be facing in your own situations.

This is my continuing life story. The story has already unfolded and I feel it is only right to commit it to paper *(or Kindle if that is your thing).*

For many months before even starting to write this book I was putting off writing it. I delayed by using an assortment of very good and genuine excuses to myself, I now understand why I hesitated on this project.

The title, 'I'm Still Valued', is what I honestly felt God wanted me to call this book, but there lies the problem. Do I believe this? Am I really still valued? Can I write this book with the honesty that it requires and needs? I feel that I have to if I want to maintain my integrity. However, in doing so, I will reveal my insecurities, talk about my fears and reveal my weaknesses. I will scrutinise myself and could easily pass a sentence of self-condemnation. The question rattles around in my head again; with all that I have wrong, physically, mentally and spiritually, how can God still value me? These are the thoughts that haunt me.

Am I alone in feeling this way? Do you ever question your worth, your purpose and your value? Of course, you do *(if you're honest).* Do you believe that God can and will still use you, even in your brokenness? Maybe you feel that you are simply too old and you want to be left to wait out your last days in heaven's waiting room. Perhaps you have been hurt by someone and you feel your confidence has gone, never to return. Do you compare yourself to others, and then condemn yourself as being inadequate and not good enough? This is called, 'Imposter Syndrome' and it is a lie. I now believe that even if you have one foot in the grave, God can still use you. I am an example of this and I hope that you will be encouraged by the stories that I now share with you.

*****

During a recent church meeting, we were asked to discuss

John 14:9 when Jesus said, **"Because I live, you will live also."** We were asked the question, what does this statement mean to us? During the conversation, I realised that for me to live like Jesus, means to make a difference, change lives and have a purpose that leaves a positive impact. We can all do this in different ways, to various degrees and levels. We just have to make ourselves available to be used.

As mentioned, since I published my first book, my health has deteriorated, but I have also published thirteen more books including this one. In fact, I have been far more creative in the last nine years, than before my health issues. It would be so easy to say, "I am creative despite my health conditions", though I never say that. What I do say is that "I am even more creative, 'BECAUSE' of my physical limitations."

So, if you are wallowing in self-pity, self-condemnation and biding your time in 'heaven's waiting room', just STOP. You have a purpose and it is BECAUSE of your limitations and weaknesses that God can still use you. YOU ARE STILL VALUED. Do you believe that?

As I begin to share my continuing journey of this thing that we call life, I hope and pray that you will start to realise that, although bad things happen, good can come from them, if we allow it. I know that this story, in parts, will be difficult to convey. Maybe that is why I have been delaying writing it. Now though, I am reminded of another Bible verse.

'All things work together for the good
of those that are in Jesus Christ'
Romans 8:28

I am aware that some Christians often throw this verse

around in a glib and trite fashion, but it is scripture, therefore, it must be true. Yet, we often fail to see the good or potential in a catastrophic event. Why should we? It is never easy to see the positive side of a negative situation. We easily blame God, in our limited human nature. The problem is, that we look at situations and judge things with our 'human lens', whereas, we need to learn to see things through God's lens. When you start to do that, then you will know that 'you are still valued.' I will keep reminding you of this throughout this book.

*****

I briefly mentioned earlier that you may have been hurt by someone and you feel your confidence has gone, never to return. Why is it that some people have an innate ability to crush the dreams and potential of others? They make throwaway comments that damage a person's self-belief, confidence and emotional well-being. These people are rarely, actively aggressive and do not necessarily, intentionally set out to cause harm. They are subtle and passive in their aggression, gently eroding, wearing away and grinding down. We call such people, 'Toxic, Corrosive and Poisonous.' Do these labels make us feel better? No, of course not.

Have you encountered such people? Have you been a victim of such emotional abuse? Have you witnessed others subjected to this type of damaging treatment? It happens in families, throughout society, at your place of work and yes, even in the church.

I want to tell my story of how I encountered this, but in doing so, I realise that there is a potential to become like one of these people. So, I will be honest and speak with integrity, whilst purposefully avoiding mentioning any names of offenders, places or organisations.

I know that this kind of abusive behaviour is all around us and that people are afraid to speak out about it, especially in the Church and Christian organisations. However, it is only when someone speaks out that other victims can start to feel less isolated. They too may be encouraged to open up and share the pain that they have been through, or indeed are still going through.

The title of this book is, 'I'm Still Valued' and the truth is, we have always been valued by our Father God. Age, health, education, history, family, etc make no difference whatsoever. Disabilities, inabilities, capabilities and competence are still no barrier. You have always been valued by God.

This is my story of how God revealed this to me. This is the true story of God's continuing Golden Thread in my life, the hurdles that I have faced and continue to face and how God told me, I'm Still Valued.

Consider this...

1. Think about what Jesus said, "Because I live, you will live also." What does this statement mean to you?

2. How can you make yourself available to be used by God?

3. Has anyone ever spoken negative words over you, telling you that you are no good at something and that you should give up?

   How did you feel?

   What did you do?

Chapter Two

Tough Decision

I'm sure you've all heard the phrase '*When one door closes, another opens,*' because it's fairly common. However, during the process of change, an element of stress is usually hovering around. None of us enjoys being uncomfortable, least of all enduring any level of pain, for any great length of time. Yet despite this, it's surprising how much we can withstand. The kind of trauma that I am referring to in this chapter is emotional and mental pain. As a founder of The Door Youth Project, having worked tirelessly to develop it, the wrench of leaving was immense; far more than I could ever have imagined. To simply say that it was emotional, would be an understatement. My feelings were mixed with sorrow and joy.

I knew that if I remained as the Chief Executive Officer at The Door, I would eventually become a liability. I had been diagnosed with chronic kidney failure. I had known since 2008 about my Polycystic Kidney Disease and watched with concern as my kidney function dropped gradually. I knew that, in the future, to stay alive, I would require dialysis. By September 2012, just four years after diagnosis, my kidney function had already dropped to just above 30%. I was then in stage 3b kidney failure and by the time I stepped down from The Door Youth Project, in November 2014, I was already at 21% *(stage 4).*

At this point, I had better explain something. Kidney failure has five different stages, with stage five also being referred to as '*End-Stage.*' Each phase brings with it a new set of symptoms or increasing severity of the existing ones. At stage 3b I mainly had high blood pressure, which was controlled by medication, but the realist in me knew that the next step was only round the corner.

Now, if you are thinking that this is going to be a story of miraculous healing and that my kidney function will be restored, then you are in for a disappointing read. I did receive an abundance of prayer, but still, my kidney function declined. I know that God could physically heal me if it was His will, but He didn't. However, even though we may not experience physical healing, healing can still come in many forms. We worship 'Jehovah Rapha' – God who heals. I do say that I have received healing, it is an inner healing and I will explain how later.

I wanted to do the best thing for The Door Youth Project, so in 2012, decided to work on a two-year exit strategy. I informed the Chair of the Trustees and a few of the senior management team. The Chair didn't want to accept it. He couldn't understand. Why should he? He saw a fit, healthy, competent and rising leader. He asked me to reconsider and to give it a year before making a final decision, to which I agreed, although the senior management team already knew what my answer would be. I did it in this way, partly for my own mind, which would have to come to terms with the decision. In 2012 I had been there for 22 years and my mum, who had the same kidney disease as me, had only recently died. I was, therefore, dealing with grief on multiple levels. I also did it for the sake of the organisation. Part of my role included all of the fundraising and income generation, so I would work diligently, with enthusiasm to train a young apprentice as a Fundraiser, whilst hoping there was a good amount of funding by the time I left. Little did I know at the time, that the apprentice, would be a kind of life-saver to me during those final two years. As I worked alongside him, teaching him, I still felt valued.

Consider this...

1. What major changes have you struggled with in your life?

2. How did they make you feel?

3. Have you made any regrettable decisions as a result of change?

Chapter Three

Not the man I used to be?

During those last two years at The Door, it was more than my physical health that eroded, my mental well-being also deteriorated, though, as the Chief Executive, I had to visually keep it together. I believed at the time, that as the leader, the person at the top, I had to stay strong and try not to show any signs of weakness. I thought that, if I admitted I was struggling with depression and anxiety, it would be a mistake. Implementation of change in any organisation is a delicate process and the bigger the change, the more sensitive preparations and procedures need to be. As I look back now, I wonder if I lacked some wisdom. Did I fail to understand how this huge change might impact others? During these last two years, there was a noticeable shift in the atmosphere. Where there was once peace, there was now tension, uncertainty and anxiety. It was noticeable in me and in others.

I was struggling and because of that, failed to acknowledge others may be feeling the same or even worse. During that last year, some of the staff would question me about why I wanted to leave, and this only made the struggle harder, as I didn't '*want*' to leave, I had to leave, and I felt as if I didn't really have a choice. I tried to explain about my deteriorating health conditions, though I am sure some of them thought that I was being melodramatic.

Others, it seemed, were more impatient and frustrations started to show in their behaviour and words. At times it felt as if they couldn't wait to be rid of me. I may have been completely wrong in my feelings, as self-doubt and imposter syndrome started to take hold. I felt like a washed-up, unwanted, good-for-nothing, 'has-been'.

I looked for God's strength to carry me. I remembered The Bible verse, *'The joy of the Lord is my strength' (Nehemiah 8:10b),* but struggled to find any joy in what I was doing. Then my young apprentice would ask a question, I would explain and he would learn; I felt useful again. I drew strength from those moments of joy and wondered, is this joy from The Lord?

During those last two years as the CEO, I had so many questions and doubts. Was I doing the right thing? What did my future hold? Would anyone ever want me to work for them? I felt worthless, lost and confused. I had a fear of not being good enough and I knew that that fear could lead me to a place of not being able to live with myself; I had been there before.

Three curses

Where do those negative feelings come from? They don't just happen overnight; they slowly build as the seeds of doubt are planted in your mind. The words that are spoken over us can give birth to a decline in self-worth and without awareness you are no longer the person that you used to be.

A single, offhand, throwaway remark can cause so much damage. I would even go as far as to say, it can leave you cursed. I will quickly add that I have now learned not to accept these types of comments. I do seriously regard them as a curse and I now know that a curse can have no hold on you if you reject it.

I have struggled with my decision to share these stories but I also feel, that to leave out this part of my journey of pain, would be incomplete. It is also the foundation of the grief and pain that would come.

The first curse was placed on me in September 2012. I was reflectively thinking about my future and what God would have me do next and during a conversation with a friend, I mentioned that I might write a book. My mum had inspired me to think this, as when she died, we found the start of a story about her life. Although she never finished it, it was enough to plant a seed, the thought of, *'I could do that.'*

So, I vocalised my thoughts and the conversation went like this. "I'm thinking of becoming an author."

The response somewhat surprised me, "You couldn't possibly be an author", I respected this person's opinion so I asked, "Oh, why not?"

"Because authors write 3,600 words in an hour and you could never do that."

It was said with such authority, confidence and knowledge that I just accepted it. "You're right, I could never do that." I thought that my crippled finger would always slow me down, but I now know that no disability should EVER stop anyone from following a dream. This one throwaway comment would delay my writing like a curse. God was speaking to me, leading me, but a massive barrier had just been built and it would hold me back for years.

Almost two years later, in the summer of 2014, I pushed that barrier out of the way and I wrote my first book, my biographical story called, 'The Golden Thread'. It was published over a year later after a Kickstarter funding campaign. It felt good to have a book published and even better knowing that other people had helped to make it possible, they believed in me. I have learnt a great deal more about publishing since that first book.

I also knew that my story could impact the lives of many and to share it was a way of glorifying God. Incidentally, that book is still being read all over the world and I often hear from someone whose life was changed through reading it. Back then though, in 2015, I still struggled to consider myself an author, with the comment still echoing in my mind, *"You could never be an author."*

In agreement, I found myself thinking, "Yeah, it's a one-off, a fluke, anyone can write ONE book. It doesn't make you an author." – imposter Syndrome continued to take hold.

That then was that decision made, I'm not an author and it's time to move on. Yet, God is patient and He had other plans, it would take another three years before I knew exactly what He would require of me, but I'll tell you about that later.

*****

I can't remember the exact time the second curse was placed on me, but it was in 2014 *(my final year).* I developed The Door Youth Project after being employed as the first paid worker in 1996. Over eighteen years, I raised the profile of the organisation, raised awareness of the community and proven my skills in marketing, communication and public relations – skills that God has given me.

Now that I have set the scene and the background, try to imagine how I felt to hear someone say, "The Door needs to find someone to help with marketing, as they're not very good at it." They were right, as any organisation, no matter who they are, could do with some extra help when it comes to marketing and communications. The way that it was said though was cold and blunt, it felt personal.

Ouch! I felt that and it hurt. The wound went deep and more imposter syndrome seeds were planted. "Maybe they are right", I thought.

"People will forget what you said,
people will forget what you did,
but people will never forget
how you made them feel."
Maya Angelou

Six years later, I decided to wipe away that thought and doubt. So, in 2020, I studied for a level 5 advanced diploma in digital marketing. I passed every assignment with distinction and completed the whole course in a few short months, it should have taken two years.

The person who had made the original comment had not been aware of the mental damage caused by one single, flippant remark, but the curse had been lifted. Although they were none the wiser, I felt a small victory and knew that the skills that God had given me had made this possible and I am now professionally providing this service for others.

*****

The third big attack on my abilities was aimed at my skill as a youth worker, so it cut to the core of what God had called me to do. As the time for my departure from The Door approached, I received an enquiry from a local Parish Council, they were seeking professional advice on how to inject new life into their failing youth club in the village.

During a meeting with the councillors, one of them voiced his opinion. "Ideally, we would like Brendan to come along and sort us out."

I felt honoured that they would specifically want me, as this was the youth club that I had grown up in. At the age of 16 years old, I was the Chair of the junior committee, so it meant a great deal to me.

Before I had a chance to answer, someone interjected, "You don't want Brendan, he's been out of frontline youth work for five years." They implied that I was a 'has-been.' I felt small and crushed.

It was a lie, but a convincing lie. For a moment, it even convinced me. Then, I started to think about the comment. I had not worked in general youth work for three years, but during all of that time, I had always been involved in some form of youth specialism. Once again, I felt belittled and worthless, my self-belief diminished and imposter syndrome cast a shadow over my life again.

This curse was broken within a few months when the same Parish Councillor contacted me. He had heard that I was leaving The Door and was planning to help small charities as a freelance consultant. The local village youth club became one of my first clients and with a year-long contract, I was able to inject new life, and new funding and save it from closure. For me, it lifted my soul and gave me a new sense of belonging, and a purpose; it made me feel valued again.

Ironically, it was a secular organisation that now filled me with worth. As for my ability to work with young people, I ran four different youth clubs and the young people loved it – they loved me – God was still using and leading me – another curse had been broken.

This village and the youth club were the first of many to benefit from my consultancy, but it was symbiotic, as I also started to realise just how much knowledge I had and I wanted to share every ounce of that knowledge.

I'll end this section with a short story about how I introduced the youth club and the young people to transformational youth work and in particular, restorative justice.

In readiness to reopen the centre, a group of volunteers had been decorating and clearing out decades' worth of accumulated junk. A skip had been filled and now sat on the tarmac driveway. Job well done.

That evening, a group of bored teenagers were hanging around outside the club, they felt that it was their space, even though it had been closed for a year. They pulled wooden boards from the skip and made makeshift skateboard ramps, then they found the old tins of paint. After a little honest tomfoolery, Chris (not his real name) threw a can of paint into the air. On impact with the tarmac, it exploded like a giant red paint bomb.

The CCTV system replayed all of this and the management team insisted that the Police be involved. I agreed, although they also wanted Chris banned and charged. It took a lot for me to convince them to try a new way. I was pleased to see the local police officer arrive. I had known PC Lizzie Brown *(not her real name),* for many years and I knew that she would be an advocate of restorative justice. I knew that she was a Christian, so for me, it was a bonus. The Council listened to her and allowed us to deal with the issue however we felt best.

We let it be known to a few young people that we knew it

was Chris and that we wanted to chat with him. It didn't take long, as Chris turned up at the centre shortly afterwards. He was petrified, afraid that he was going to be arrested. Word had also spread about police involvement. He genuinely apologised and asked what he could do to make things right. Whilst we were chatting, his friend filled a bucket with water and grabbed a brush from the kitchen. Chris turned from me and started to scrub with desperation, but the water was cold and the paint was gloss. It had dried in two days.

I boiled kettles of hot water and poured them on as he scrubbed and his friends all gathered in a circle, watching but not helping. Then Alex piped up and said that his dad had a jet washer that we could use. He ran home and returned five minutes later. Eventually, a whole team of young people came to help Chris and the paint was all removed.

PC Lizzie did visit Chris's home and chatted with his parents. I was present as extra support for Chris and that was the end of the situation. A few weeks later, Chris came to see me and thanked me. He told me that it was the wake-up call that he needed, that he had been doing a lot of silly things and that it could have been a lot worse. Restorative justice had worked. I'm not sure what happened to Chris after that, but hopefully, nothing that involved breaking the law. For me, the whole incident confirmed that I was still a great youth worker and that I was still valued.

Consider this...

1. Do you notice shifts in the atmosphere?

   What does this look like?

2. When have you been challenged about a decision made?

   How did you feel?

   What did you learn?

3. What Bible verse can you stand on for comfort and strength?

Chapter Four

More pain

In February 2014, whilst still working at The Door, I felt under immense pressure with increasing anxiety. The uncertainty of where the money was coming from, the demands of managing staff in a growing organisation, together with the challenges of working with young people with their problems. The personal burdens regarding the future; my future and that of the project were all stacking up.

The mental strain developed into physical symptoms. I was waking up in the morning with serious chest pain. Six years earlier, in the same year that I was diagnosed with kidney disease, I was also told that I had angina *(narrowing of the arteries)*. It had been stable until now, but due to the unpredictable nature of change, my condition was becoming unstable. As a result, I was rushed to the hospital and fitted with my first three coronary stents. Not for one moment did I even consider this health issue was stress related, but I do now. On reflection, I can see that for this reason alone, leaving the project was the right decision.

On 3rd November 2014, I eventually left The Door Youth Project. People would ask me if I missed being there and I would always say, "No." I had given myself two years to mentally prepare and at first, everything felt fine. I had the new challenge of a failing youth centre to focus on, which I believe God provided for me.

If I missed anything, it was the young people and staff whom I had built close relationships with. I didn't miss the stress, the struggles and the daily grind *(some weeks I had worked 60 to 70 hours).* I didn't miss the monitoring, budgets or fundraising and I certainly didn't miss the responsibility.

To be honest, it was a relief to be free. Don't get me wrong, I had an enjoyable time at The Door, it was such a fun place to work and so rewarding to see the positive changes in so many young people. I hold on tight to the good years and try to forget the cost and the toll that some periods had on my life.

To make matters worse, *(but again without going into too much detail)*, soon after leaving The Door, we *(my wife Heather and I),* withdrew from all church life and local churches. We rarely ventured out as we struggled to be in the company of any other people.

This only left me feeling let down, alone, broken, angry and bitter. The Door and the church had been my life and support network until those last two years of confusion and pain. I didn't realise it at the time but I was grieving. I tried to deny my loss but my feelings morphed into anger and bitterness which festered into the most painful of wounds. We did have a few close Christian friends who understood and tried to help, but healing could not be forced, it takes time. The pain was growing into agony and I was spiritually dying, like the walking wounded. Although the scars were invisible, at times the symptoms of mental illness were very visible.

Occasionally someone would ask what church I go to. I would respond with the rather cynical answer, "The worldwide church of broken Christians – it's the biggest church in the world."

At the time that is how it felt and how my feelings

manifested. I would meet other Christians *(mainly online)* who had been hurt by fellow Christians – friendly fire. I wandered that barren place of the outcast for almost a year, with the bitterness propagating within. Then, a close Christian friend guided us toward a small group of Christians who met weekly in a home. The group was led by a local Christian and everyone in the group accepted us warmly and in love. Only one person in the group knew me and my history and she was glad to see me there. It was just what I needed for a short season and the comfort of peer support started me on a journey of restoration.

In my darkest moments of frustration, God would pour poetry into me. He had given me the gift of rhyme in my first year of inviting Him into my life. I sensed a strong connection to Him as He spoke the words into my heart.

The poems were a form of release, but they also indicated to me that I was still in pain... like this one for example.

Let it Drop

Why do I keep letting people under my skin?
Not recognising, that in doing so, they win?
Why do I allow the scoffers so much credit?
When I know that deep down inside,
I need to just forget it?
You see it's so easy to say
"forgive and forget."
Yet oh!
The pain and the hurt won't let go.
Constant reminders,
memories and flashbacks.
Cutting like a knife,
slash, slash, slash hack.
Can't let go, won't let go, don't know.

How to? What's true? Do you?
Do you?
You and your lies, they get under my skin!
You and your lies, I let them win!
Why, oh why, oh why, oh why?
It doesn't have to be like this.
I cry, I cry, I cry, I cry?
And you just take the - please stop.
Please make it stop!
Please, please, will you please just
let it drop?

Consider this...

1. After change, how did God provide for you?

   Did you even notice?

2. What changes have happened in your life that you had no control over?

3. Have you ever felt worthless and devalued by others, especially those who you regard as friends?

4. Where can you find the right help?

   Who can you share your struggles with?

5. Can you think about your own creative skills and start to use them in a therapeutic way? – Try writing poetry.

Chapter Five

Moving on

A year after leaving The Door, my time at the now thriving local youth centre was coming to an end. I had no intention of staying longer than the year, even though the young people and the staff asked me not to leave. I had managed to hide my health issues, it was easier then, but in the end, I had to explain. "I have kidney failure and I need to leave because I don't want to become a liability. I could soon require dialysis and at some point, will need a transplant. I've done what I came here to do."

At that time in my life, specifically in September 2015, the words 'dialysis' and 'transplant' were only words. The same remote, 2nd hand concept, just as they seem to anyone who has never encountered what they actually are. However, I would have a far greater understanding during the year to come.

By February 2016, my kidney function had fallen to 15% and I was now in '*end-stage*' kidney failure. It sounded final like the end was nigh, but... there was still an epic journey to travel. In that same month, I was assessed as suitable for a transplant and my name was added to the waiting list. That list contained at least another 5,000 other people in the UK. This thought was daunting and I tried hard to imagine what 5,000 people would look like. All that I could think was, *'Well, that is a lot.'* I started to ponder, more and more. What if they all needed a transplant more than me? They surely had more worth and value than me. Even when my health was deteriorating and my life was at risk, I downplayed it and did not consider myself worthy of another person's kidney. God did though.

My symptoms were now more obvious, so, I did pray that a suitable donor would be found soon. I guess in God's eyes, *'soon'* could be years. Turns out it was. Little did I know that I would have to wait another three years before I would receive a transplant. The waiting game began, so I took one day at a time, never knowing when I might receive the call, with much of my life on hold. I'll explain more about this later.

Looking back, I now realise that this is where my feeling that God had abandoned me started. I didn't vocalise it, because I hadn't thought about it, but I did feel alone, looking towards an unknown future. It would take me over two years before I finally voiced my feelings, two years before I was so broken and God would speak into my darkness.

I never stopped praying but I did give up on asking others to pray for me. For years I had received prayer for my kidney disease and I gradually came to a place of acceptance. I know that nothing is impossible for God, so that means it is well within His abilities to heal me but for whatever reason, He chose not to.

I think the final turning point of waiting for that healing came one evening when I attended a Christian event. A well-known speaker with a healing ministry would be preaching. Before going, I prayed and asked God to give the speaker or someone else a word of knowledge about someone with kidney problems. After the sermon, the preacher had several words of knowledge for other people. He prayed for people with various pains and conditions but he never once asked if there was anyone present in need of prayer for a kidney problem and nobody else had a word.

The evening was coming to a close and I was at a place of acceptance and just about to leave. At that point, two ladies who were known to me and knew of my illness asked if I would like to receive prayer. It tried to explain that I didn't want any prayer and that I was okay. The conversation lasted several minutes as they tried to convince me, whilst all the time I declined their prayer. Then the unbelievable happened, they prayed anyway.

I sat there, stunned at first, unable to say anything to stop them. As they continued to pray my feeling of shock turned into disgust and I was fuming with anger. When they had both finished their onslaught, I looked at them both and told them, "I didn't ask for prayer, I asked you not to do that. Now I feel as if I have been spiritually raped."

I learned a lot that evening about listening to what people tell you, to respect their wishes and who they are. I grasped never to force your own agenda onto anyone. I hope that the two well-meaning ladies also learnt the same.

*****

For work, I scraped by with a little bit of charity consulting work, but it wasn't enough to live off. Heather wasn't working and so we survived using our savings, *(or rather a small inheritance that we had been given).* We had hoped that it would help us during our retirement, but we needed it now.

We can often fail to notice the small steps that God provides for us, which can lead us to something bigger. One such step for me was to start working with a local infant bereavement charity. I spent several months helping them to develop and find the funding that they needed to expand. Eventually, I helped them to recruit someone to replace me. Once again, I didn't want to become a liability. When it was time to hand over and leave, the Chair of the Trustees thanked me. It was a sincere, heartfelt thank you. She went further and explained that I had saved her charity from closure. I had shown them what they could do and given them hope.

They had also given me something.

It was during one of the fund applications that the funding source asked for a short video about the charity. I made that film using my phone and a very basic editing program. Little did I know that this was the start of a whole new level of creativity that was going to grow out of my adversity. This one, very basic film, would lead me to create hundreds of films under the banner of Message Movies.

In The Bible, we read that the Apostle Paul was a tent maker and he made tents to provide an income to support his ministry. Film production and digital marketing are now my equivalent to Paul's tent-making. It brings in some money, although not much and it also allows me time and space for my creative ministry.

A different kind of hospital

We knew we had to find a church that we could feel comfortable in. It would not be easy, because I was so well-known among the local churches. We considered going further afield, to a place where no one knew anything about us, but that was not the answer.

So, in June 2016, we walked into the Five Valleys Christian Fellowship. We were made to feel extremely welcome. It was a warm, genuine reception, with no questions asked. It is so important to welcome people in the best way for them. This takes discernment by the Holy Spirit, sensitivity and acceptance through grace and love. We were searching and were allowed the space to investigate, without any perceived threats. We were also listened to which was just what we needed.

Five Valleys Christian Fellowship did all this and nobody seemed shocked to see us. Nobody questioned our motives for being there and there were so many friendly faces.

We were spiritually injured, victims of Christian friendly fire, the walking wounded and we had just walked into a hospital. We had taken the first step on the road to recovery, but the journey would be long. We are still on it and we always will be.

Although we were new to the church and hadn't really committed to it, we were invited to attend their summer camp. It was a small gathering at the Lenchwood Christian Centre and we went along with our motorhome. It was here that we started to get to know people more. I was invited to play in the worship team and to share a short testimony. For the first time in nearly two years, I began to feel valued again *(in a Christian context).*

"For where two or three are gathered together in my name, there am I in the midst of them."
Matt. 18:19–20

Even though it was just a small gathering, the Holy Spirit turned up and ministered to us all. It was a powerful presence. During the third evening, I was playing with the band, the meeting had progressed into a time of ministry as many were stepping forward for prayer.

I sensed the Holy Spirit nudging me, convicting me to ask for prayer myself. I ignored the nudge but I started to feel warmer as the Holy Spirit continued to touch me. I still didn't move, I carried on playing whilst something was welling up inside of me. My heartbeat was fast. It was uncomfortable, almost painful like something was trying to burst out.

Let me pause this story for a moment while I add some background scenery.

I had recently read RT Kendal's book entitled, 'Total Forgiveness' *(which I highly recommend).* I discovered what forgiveness actually is and crucially, what unforgiveness really looks like. A valuable lesson or insight had been revealed to me. For example, I realised that simply holding a grudge against a person over something can rot and fester inside of us. If not dealt with, this can grow into feelings of resentment, so you can become angry, which then can present itself as hostile thoughts towards them. Although the incident itself may have been quite minor, it manifests in bitterness and can build into what seems like a crime against humanity to you!

It can get very personal indeed. You can also start to feel that same animosity towards others, who appear friendly towards the original perpetrator. Although they had nothing whatsoever to do with what happened, they became guilty simply by association. It's usually those friends who you perceive to have absolutely no problem with your nemesis. It's especially annoying if you've shared deeply personal thoughts with them, highlighting your concerns. You can even start blaming them because it can appear like they actively encourage your enemy's behaviour. It seems as if these trusted friends just don't understand how you've arrived at these conclusions and why it has become so important to you. It's very easy to retreat from those relationships as well because it's like they have dismissed you, ignoring the situation entirely. It's almost as if they don't even believe you anymore and now, they're batting for the other side entirely!

You can see how these situations can get completely out of hand. The hurting individual can lose most of their perspective. Ultimately unforgiveness doesn't stop growing as it begins to destroy you.

I was now so overwhelmed with this manifestation of bitterness and a battle was taking place within my heart. It was spiritual, but the spiritual state had become a physical one.

So, back to the events unfolding at camp.

I left the stage with tears trickling down my cheeks. The unburdening had already emerged, although there was much more to come. I briefly explained to people around me that I needed prayer for unforgiveness, so two people prayed for me. Then the taps opened. Tears poured down my face and I don't exaggerate when I say, I was soaked. I released the names of those whom I had harboured resentment against. One by one, I named them quietly so that no one else could hear.

The release was instantaneous. My chest stopped banging and I cooled down. The power of unforgiveness had held me in captivity for nearly two years, yet the power of forgiveness gave me unbridled freedom right where I stood.

Forgiveness, however, for human beings, is an ongoing process. Our mind can continue to hold us back as we don't forget, so I still find that I have to continue to forgive. This may sound odd to some people. Surely if God sets you free, you are set free? Yes, that is true, I was set free from the bitterness of unforgiveness and I don't want that to creep back in again. That is why I continue to forgive.

I often wonder what kind of mess I would be in now if I hadn't been brought to that place of forgiveness. It was like the end of a battle and as usual, God's timing was perfect, as I prepared for my next battle. This one would be physical.

Consider this…

1. Are you holding on to unforgiveness?

   Has it developed into bitterness?

   Are you ready to forgive? Find someone to pray with you.

2. Have you considered volunteering your valuable skills to an organisation in need?

3. As we find hope, we can see fear diminish – Where do you find the hope that you need?

4. Make a list of the ways that you do or can help others – including even the smallest things.

5. When you have helped others, how did it make you feel?

6. Where can you find fellowship and support with like-minded Christians?

Chapter Six

I will survive (dialysis)

The church camp ended on Friday 11th August 2016 and just four days later on the 15th, I was in the hospital for surgery. It was *'elective'* surgery, meaning that I had chosen this and that I knew that it was coming. Really? I didn't choose renal failure. I didn't choose dialysis, but it was a necessary means to stay alive. I certainly didn't choose any of the impediments that my body would experience, least of all a complication that could end my life.

When I told a close friend that I was thinking of writing this book, I mentioned that I wasn't sure about talking about the sordid details relating to my medical conditions. He scoffed at me saying, "You have to put it all in and make it real, don't sanitise it." So, this is real, it's what happened. It was horrible, but God was walking through it with me.

My kidney function remained at 15% for 6 months and so toxins had begun to build up in my body. I now had several, noticeable *(to me, but invisible to most),* daily symptoms. I had an almost constant headache, together with nausea and increasing fatigue. My urine output reduced, causing my body to retain fluid and I started to vomit on occasions. I knew that I needed dialysis if I was going to survive and I was given a choice of HD or PD.

The most common form of dialysis is HD – Haemodialysis. This method involves surgery to create a fistula in your arm, which is simply an easy entry point. You then go to the hospital three times every week to be piped up to a machine. Blood is pumped out of you via the fistula, cleaned by the machine and then pumped back into your body. I didn't like the sound of so many trips to the hospital and nearly half of your week destroyed, so I opted for PD instead.

Peritoneal dialysis has its own negative issues that I was not really aware of, but I would soon find out. This next part is all sciencey, so please bear with me. The peritoneum is a membrane that lines the inside of your abdomen and pelvis *(parietal layer)*. It also covers many of your organs inside *(visceral layer)*. The space in between these layers is called your peritoneal cavity. For PD the cavity is filled with a glucose solution, which is a thick solution. Through the process of osmosis *(remember school science)* the thinner solution or fluids that are held in your body can pass into the thicker solution. Then at the appropriate time, the waste fluid is drained off and replaced with a new glucose solution. PD patients have another choice, manual draining or using a machine. At first, you have to use the manual method and drain the fluid off at least three times each day. That, to me, was too much of the day wasted, so I would opt for the machine, but first, a catheter *(a flexible pipe)* needed to be inserted into my abdomen.

So, here I was in this elective surgery.

The whole procedure was considered quick and simple. It was scheduled as day surgery, so I would be home and in my own bed that night – or so I thought.

The surgery went according to plan and I was back on the day ward just after lunch. I managed to force down a slice of toast and then they asked me to drink a litre of water. I needed to be able to pee before they would allow me to leave to go home. I couldn't go, so I drank some more and then even more.

Although the human bladder does have a potentially large capacity and can stretch, just like a balloon, there comes a point of bursting. Unable to pee, I reached that point and was in agony. The nurses decided to scan my bladder, but the day ward didn't have a scanner. I waited in excruciating pain for well over an hour whilst they searched the hospital for a scanner.

I kept screaming at them to find a scanner, I told them that I thought I was about to burst. The pain was unbelievable. I also knew enough about human anatomy to deduce that the ONLY way my bladder would empty and the pain subside, was to insert a urinary tract catheter. Although I had never before experienced this procedure, I sensed that it would not be pleasant, but something needed to be done quickly.

Have you ever heard the expression, *'Sometimes we need to go through more pain to find relief'?* In this case, this statement was very true, though I was not aware of the extent of pain and suffering my body was about to undergo.

When we reach a certain pain threshold or a certain state of desperation, any dignity is cast aside and we just let the medical team do what they have to. I know that the two nurses were gentle as they thrust the pipe into my penis, but the pain was torture and I screamed loud. I could hear the other patients make concerned comments. It seemed to last forever. As it broke through the sphincter muscle, I felt immediate relief and urine began to flow. Within a few minutes, 3.3 litres filled the container at the end of the plastic tube. I felt relieved, that I had been relieved. The current threat had been averted or so we thought. The bladder problem was simply an early sign of something even more sinister that was happening in my body.

Heather came to collect me and I was discharged around 6.00 pm, with the catheter still in place and a bag strapped to my leg. She pushed me down to the car in a wheelchair, but as I stood to move into the car, I told her that I didn't feel very well.

I deteriorated more during the half-hour journey and decided to go straight to bed. By 7.00 pm my head was in a bowl and black vomit poured out of me. I have heard many people joke that, no matter what you have eaten, vomit always looks like you have eaten carrots. This didn't, it was just like coffee grounds and it kept coming, there was so much of it; far more than any stomach could hold. It was frightening.

Heather called for an ambulance and I found myself back in the hospital by 8.00 pm. The accident and emergency department was busy and no one was telling me much. Slowly the coffee grounds stopped and turned into a thick, black, sticky liquid. It tasted disgusting.

A doctor arrived to insert a nasal gastric tube *(NG tube).* The tube was forced up my nose, down my throat and into my stomach. I was given some water to swallow, to make to tube go down easier, but it was so difficult. With the tube in place, they attached a syringe and gradually sucked liquid from my stomach. The tube was then attached to a clear plastic bag and slowly the offending black liquid was syphoned into the bag. That tube would remain in place for the next three days.

A CT scan was deemed necessary to determine the cause of the problem. Was there a blockage? As I lay on the bed of the scanner, I threw up even more black liquid. This was the point that fear hit me and I asked the nurse,

"What is that stuff?"

She simply said, "That is what is inside of you. You are very ill."

Talk about stating the obvious, but just the tone and calmness of her voice were enough to settle my nerves.

It would be another three days and I would spend time in two different wards before I would finally find myself in a side room of the renal ward. That was when I was told that I had experienced a paralytic ileus. All that they told me was that it was a very serious condition, so I consulted Google and found out, that it was a condition where the motor activity of the bowel was impaired; it went into spasm. The black vomit was the contents of my bowel being forced backwards. Google also told me that it is serious and if prolonged and untreated will result in death.

So, August 2016 was the first time that I had such a close brush with death. I thanked God that I was still alive and asked Him to forgive me for being so afraid. It was very scary, remember I had a tube in my abdomen, one up my willie and another up my nose and my insides pouring out of my mouth. How would you react?

I had faced death and beat it, but I had no concept, that I would face more deeply miserable and terrifying trauma again and again during the next seven years and that hospital would become like a second home.

Consider this...

1. As you have become older, there may be things that you can no longer do. Try to focus on the

positive things and make a list of what you can do, be sure to include all the new things that you are going to try.

2. Try to reflect on the fact that there is always someone in a much worse state than you are and keep smiling.

3. If you know someone with serious health issues and struggles, what can you do to help them?

Chapter Seven

Will I survive (dialysis)?

I called the previous chapter, *'I Will Survive'* as I had conquered death. Why then, do I suddenly switch the words in that title to, *'Will I Survive?'*

After one event we move on to the next. That is life. I now had to grasp the reality of peritoneal dialysis and at first, it was overwhelming, with so much to take in. By the way, the word *'overwhelming'* is an under-exaggeration and at first, I wondered if I would cope. Had I made the right decision?

Hygiene was the most important and the first thing that I had to learn, before even starting dialysis. Remember, the tube that exited my abdomen was in my Peritoneum and poor hygiene could result in Peritonitis, a very serious infection that, if untreated, could kill.

The initial problem is the amount of information that you have to learn. I believe that this hurdle is one of the reasons why most people opt for haemodialysis, which is mainly done for you by a nurse. PD is self-administered, which is why I chose it. I wondered if I would ever grasp all that I needed to learn, then one day, another PD patient, who was about a month ahead of me assured me. "You'll get there, it's hard at first, but it suddenly all makes sense."

He was right and a month later I started dialysis and made the same reassuring remarks to people just learning. At the start, I attended the hospital three times each week and that just robs you of life.

Another thing to get used to was the enormous mountain of boxes that were delivered every month to my home. These heavy boxes were full of fluid and equipment, enough to fill a pallet. Every month Heather tirelessly carried all of the boxes upstairs into a bedroom which was now a designated store room. The sheer sight of the boxes was daunting and a constant reminder of my condition. Of course, having a tube coming out of your abdomen and a belly full of fluid was also a reminder, but the colossal mountain triggered a negative feeling – DEPRESSION.

You may be thinking that I regret opting for PD and should have chosen HD. Don't get me wrong, I did make the right choice and the best choice for me, but renal failure is hard, whatever choices you make. You may also be wondering why I'm making such a big deal about starting dialysis and that maybe I have exaggerated the title of this chapter – *'Will I Survive?'*

All of the previously mentioned issues were pretty lame in comparison to this next problem that I now experienced – *'Drain Pain.'*

When I used to make wine, I would syphon off the good clear wine and leave the dregs, the sediment in the bottom of the jar. You never wanted to suck up that sediment, that would be bad. When I had a fish tank and I had to clean it out, it was the opposite. I wanted to suck away at the bottom of the tank to syphon off the dregs instead. I actually found it quite therapeutic. The final visual image that I will give you is that of drinking a milkshake through a straw. Who can resist sucking up that last little drop? Despite making that rude sound at the bottom, it really is worth it.

Peritoneal dialysis is very similar to these three examples. When I started to fill my abdomen with fluid, then at the appropriate time, transfer it back out of my body, I was surprised by the pain. At first, I had to use the manual method whilst my body became used to it. This method relies on syphoning the fluid, so it is relatively gentle, that is until that tube starts to suck on the bottom. The tube lies low, deep within your pelvic region and as you would expect, there are numerous nerve endings throughout the lining. Just like that milkshake straw, the tube sucks to remove every last drop and as it sucks on a nerve end pain shoots through your body. I know that I am carrying two litres of fluid and that it has to come out, but the pain often started at the point of 1.5 litres, with another half a litre left to suck out. The pain increases as the fluid reduces.

At times the pain shoots sideways or straight up through my body, depending on which nerve has been aggravated. These pains are severe, however, by far the most painful and the most frequent are the times that the sucking tube makes contact in the lower pelvic region, where the nerve endings are also attached to my penis. I can only describe the pain as electrical charges to the end of my penis.

On a scale of ten with ten being the highest, these pains were bearable at about three to five and they would last up to 15 minutes. In the same way that sucking the last of a milkshake is worth it, I now told myself the same, *'It is worth it, it is worth it, it's better than being dead.'* This was a kind of mantra that I would repeat in my head, as I tried to remain positive.

Thirst also became another problem, as anyone who is on any form of dialysis knows, I was on a strict fluid restriction. Normal, healthy people are all told to drink plenty of fluids and I was used to drinking many litres of water every day. Keep your kidneys flushed, it's good for them, is the standard advice. So, a fluid restriction on any level is hard. My restriction was reasonable at 2 litres each day because I was still able to urinate a litre. I would suck on ice cubes and make my own ice lollies as a form of comfort to quench my thirst, but there was nothing that I could do to ease the drain pain.

After just two weeks on the manual drain, three times every day and finding it totally absorbing and time-consuming, I switched to the automatic option. This would release my days as I was connected to a machine every night for an eight-hour cycle. It would fill me and empty me as I slept, but first, the process started with the usual scrub-up, connect up and drain down. Instead of syphoning and using gravity, the machine pumped and it was aggressive.

My penis pain was unbearable and I would often be in tears with such excruciating torture. The pain now measured a maximum of 10 *(top of the scale)* and would last more than 15 minutes. I couldn't hold back the tears and the screams. I questioned if it was really worth it. Is it really worth making that rude and uncouth noise just for a few more drops of milkshake? Was it worth the agonising suffering, just to prolong life? What sort of life was this?

I developed a pain scale where I multiplied the pain level by the number of minutes of suffering. The resulting score was monitored on a spreadsheet and I created graphs. Some of the scores were over 200. It may sound like a crazy thing to do, but the nurses were impressed and it gave me some form of being in control, although I was far from it.

I knew that one of my nurses was a Christian and although it was against all of the rules, I asked her to pray for me. She did and after that, things did start to improve slightly and slowly. You could argue that my body was just adjusting and becoming accustomed to the process, as it does, but I was so thankful for my prayer prescription.

I could already feel the physical pain starting to impact my mental health and I hadn't even been on dialysis for two months. I knew that mentally I could crash very quickly, so had to think of something fast. I needed to find a distraction, something creative and something that would make me feel valued.

Consider this...

1. What are you currently going through that seems overwhelming?

2. Who can you turn to for help?

   There is always someone.

3. How are you coping mentally?

   Be honest with yourself and care about yourself.

Chapter Eight

Dog fight or flight?

Just to remind you, I left The Door Youth Project on 3rd November 2014. I felt washed up, rejected and devalued. Then, exactly two years later on 3rd November 2016, I played my first gig with a band. This is that story and how I once again felt useful, wanted and valued.

*****

Some time ago at church, at the start of a new year, we were encouraged to seek God for one single word for the year. The word that came to my mind was tenacious and I had to look it up to see what it meant. This is what I read.

- Tending to keep a firm hold of something; clinging or adhering closely.

- Not readily relinquishing a position, principle, or course of action; determined.

- Persisting in existence; not easily dispelled.

I learnt to fight at an early age, it's in my nature not to give up, tenacious truly is my word. At first, when I was young, I used my fists. I ran toward trouble and never flew away from it. Later in life when I found Jesus or did He find me? I'm never quite sure about that, after all, I was lost and needed finding. Anyway, when my relationship with Jesus started, I found a new weapon to fight with – words. I realised the power contained in words and how just a few strung together in a sentence can change lives, either positively or negatively.

In 1839, novelist and playwright Edward Bulwer-Lytton wrote the words, '*The pen is mightier than the sword.*' I had seen proof of this in the rap songs that I had written and recorded. I had witnessed the transforming power of songs and music in the young people that I had worked with and supported – music had transformed their lives. Now, as I started dialysis, I needed to fight a new fight. It would take a powerful weapon to keep me from falling into the pit of despair.

It had been four years since I had stopped performing as a rapper and this had created another void, an emptiness that needed to be filled. I had been asked to play the percussion at church meetings a few times, but it wasn't enough. The combination of musical emptiness and kidney failure was already impacting my mental health, I sensed a deep loss. I would even describe it as grieving just the same as a bereavement.

All that could be done regarding my kidney failure was already being done, I could do no more. That's when I fought back with what I could, with what I knew. This time it wasn't words, it was music. I decided that it was never too late for anything. That is when I realised that if I'm still breathing, then someone somewhere will still value me. I just have to find out who and where they are.

Something inside of me urged me to search the internet and I typed – 'Find a band.' I found a website called, 'Join my band' and immediately posted a request, maybe it was more like a plea. I said something like, "Frustrated drummer seeks like-minded musicians to play Irish music or similar in the Stroud area." Apart from being half-Irish, I'm not sure why I limited my chances like that. I had never played Irish music but felt that I could give it a go. I thought perhaps I could play in a ceilidh band or find a session gathering that I might join. I believe if we take a small step of faith, God will give us even more than we anticipated and He will always provide what we need.

I needed acceptance, reassurance and friendship. I just wanted to play music, but what we want and what we need can at times be different. In this case, my needs and wants were met by an almost immediate response to my plea. Messages pinged back and forth between myself and Andy. He explained that he was the bass player in a reasonably new band called, 'The Shaggy Dog Raconteurs.' I didn't even know what a raconteur is so I looked it up and discovered that it's a storyteller. I thought to myself, 'I'm a storyteller.' Andy explained that the band tells shaggy dog stories in their lyrics.

I asked what sort of music it was. "Well, it's not Irish, it's Americana. I think you'll like it. I'll send you some songs we've recorded." Andy seemed very keen to get me on board and that is when the beast of imposter syndrome attacked again.

"Who am I trying to kid? They'll see right through me? I'm not a proper drummer, I just hit a box *(Cajon)* with my hands. What have I done?" My mind flooded with doubt. "Have I made a mistake?"

As I thought about the process that had brought me to this point, I realised that God had directed me and given me the courage to post my plea, only now it didn't feel like courage, it was more like stupidity. "They won't like me. I won't like them. They'll see through me. They'll think I'm a fraud. A drummer isn't a proper musician."

That last thought resonated in my head and only amplified the imposter syndrome. As I listened to the songs that Andy had sent, I found that I liked them, but that only increased the negativity toward myself. It felt as if I was on a rollercoaster that was heading for a brick wall; that would end with a crash.

"I couldn't play in a band? I had a rubber tube stuck in my gut and they're bound to notice. Why am I doing this?" I was trying to talk myself out of it, but every time I chatted with Andy, he seemed hopeful. By now we were chatting by phone and it made such a difference, we connected on a new level and he invited me to audition on Saturday 29th October, 2016. Before I thought too much and tried to convince myself to say no, I just blurted out, "OK."

Armed with directions and the three or four songs that I had listened to and played along with, I turned up at Matt's house *(or Kennel as it was referred to).* I prayed all the way there and by the time I arrived, new-found confidence filled me. As I set up, I chatted with Bill (Billdog), Matt (Matlee) and Andy (Bass-it Hound) and I felt amongst friends.

We played the few songs that I knew, then moved on with some new material (for me) and they liked what I could do. So much so that they asked me there and then if I would like to play with them in a few days at an open mic in a pub. Talk about being thrown into the deep end, I expected to go home and then receive a call saying that I failed. Again, I responded without a thought, "Yes, I'd love to."

Then, as I was packing my kit away, I thought that I needed to be completely open and honest with them. "I think I need to tell you that I've just recently started dialysis. I have a tube in my gut that comes out through my belly. I need to go home every night and attach myself to a machine."

When I finished saying my piece, they all said words like, 'That doesn't matter, you can still play can't you.' I would later realise that they each had their own struggles, as we all do and that music and the band were the therapy that they all needed. It continued to be that way for the next six years. We had all gone through tough times and have been there to support each other. During my time with the band, I received my kidney transplant, was involved in a serious accident that put me on life support and had a shoulder replacement, but they never gave up on me.

At that first open mic, we sounded great and it was such a buzz. When chatting afterwards, I commented about their dog names and asked if I could have one. I could tell from their reaction that they thought, 'Wow, he's really into this.'

"Yes, what did you have in mind?" One of them asked, I think it was Andy.

"Yellow Dog", I said and went on to explain that my surname means 'Son of Yellow Dog.' I continued with the story that 'Yellow Dog' was an Irish Celtic chieftain and that I am a direct descendant of him. They were clearly impressed and welcomed me to 'the pack.'

I feel that it's important to point out that none of these three would call themselves 'Christians.' However, I do believe God led me to them to meet my needs and wants. They accepted me and made me feel valued as they gave me a chance and with their support, I have become a more rounded character. I have developed more confidence; playing on stage in pubs, clubs and festivals will do that. Over the years with 'The Dogs' the lineup changed, Andy left, and Duncan and Jason joined. I am so thankful for their help, support and understanding.

This chapter is called Dog Fight or Flight for good reason and I have already mentioned that I am a fighter. Over the next two and a half years on dialysis, my fight would be taken to a new level. My resilience would be tested and pushed to the limit and I would receive a new title – 'Warrior.'

I discovered this title one day when I stumbled across the Kidney Care UK Facebook group page. All the other sufferers of kidney disease referred to each other in this way and by talking with some of them, I too joined the tribe of warriors. I battled alongside them, feeling their pain, suffering and loss. I had found another source of support. However, since I received my transplant, I have not been in the group much. I needed a break.

The problem with any support group for life-limiting health issues is although there is support, there has to be a balance. You also have to give out in return and I came to a place where I had nothing left to give, dialysis does that. You are also faced with the constant reminder that this disease kills, and you eventually die from it. In the group, I heard of people dying on more or less a weekly basis, so I stepped out for self-preservation.

I have no doubt that, in the future, I will need to return, but for now, I have friends that support and that includes The Shaggy Dog Raconteurs.

At the start of 2020, as a band, we were out on the road at least every other weekend and the momentum was growing. Then the Covid pandemic hit and venues were closed across the country. We stayed creative by recording in our own homes and creating music by file sharing via the internet, but we would never hit the peak of where we were pre-pandemic. Outdoor gigs became the new way, but after two years, my body felt weary. In May 2022, I was struggling with angina again and required three more cardio stents. I started to feel like I was letting the band down.

Just two months later, in July, we played at Chalfest, a 5,000-capacity festival and it took it out of me. Sadly, that was the last time that I played with The Shaggy Dog Raconteurs, at a debrief afterwards I stepped down. It was a tough decision and I do miss playing with my friends. True friendship never dies and I am still in contact with all of the band and still help and support them in other creative ways. When I announced my departure from the band, I felt God was leading me and once again telling me that 'I'm still valued.'

Playing with The Shaggy Dog Raconteurs

Consider this…

1. Are you a worrier or a warrior?

   Do you fight or flight?

2. I am tenacious – What one positive word can you hold onto for yourself?

3. What have you lost?

   What part of your life are you grieving for?

4. Have you found a support group that values you yet?

5. Have you started a new activity yet?

6. What new purpose and identity can you seek for your own life?

Chapter Nine

The waiting game

Any expectant parents who have had to wait longer than the usual nine months of pregnancy will tell you that every day over the predicted delivery date is an anxious day. After two weeks of being overdue, the anxiety has intensified and the risk to the unborn child increases. Thankfully, medical intervention is available to bring the struggle to an end. A date is set, procedures are carried out and the waiting game ends. It's a common scenario that we can relate to as many of us have experienced it or know someone that has.

Imagine a prisoner who is waiting on death row in the USA. They have been there for years. They may be completely innocent, having been wrongly convicted and so they have a right to an appeal, called the *'Direct Appeal.'*

Some prisoners will be granted an opportunity for two more appeals, the State Post-Conviction and Federal Habeas Corpus. Finally, there is a last chance for reprieve if the State Governor chooses to grant Executive Clemency.

This process takes years and it is a waiting game, with an unknown end date and a meeting with death. Each new appeal brings with it fresh hope. Each prisoner clings to that hope, as hope extinguishes fear, fear of the inevitable – death.

The expectant parents and the death row prisoner are two different scenarios. Both have been thrown into a waiting game. Which one do you think most resembles the waiting game? The agony of prolonged anxiety, biding your time whilst your life is on hold? During this constant state of anticipation, in reality, you're actually 'hoping' that someone else, *(with a compatible kidney),* dies.

Just stop and process that for a minute or two.

If surviving until a suitable transplant becomes available is a long and painful process, holding on to the chance of finding the alternative, *(a living donor)*, is a much longer affair and is extremely unlikely to be a positive one.

The parents know what they are going to get and when they are going to get it, but it still seems to take forever. The prisoner knows the likely outcome but in contrast, they long for it to be delayed. Waiting for a transplant is something akin to that of the experience of that prisoner. Every night I was a prisoner in my own bedroom, attached to a machine. Days come and go and you wait with an expectant state of readiness, in preparation for when the phone would ring.

At this juncture, travel is restricted to within a limited distance from your transplant centre. In my case that was Oxford. You never know when the waiting game will end. It could be two days or an unknown number of years. It could end well or you might die. Try to imagine what that might feel like. I know that you would find this very difficult because I couldn't envisage anything until I had to play the game for real, this horrible game – the waiting game.

In a similar way that the prisoner has a chance of an appeal and is lifted by hope, the phone rings. A nurse tells me that they may have a kidney. A surge of hope rushes through me and tears fill my eyes as a flood of emotion overwhelms my brain. For me, during my three-year sentence in the waiting game, the phone rang five times. That is the equivalent of five appeal hearings.

I was added to the transplant waiting list in February 2016, along with the other 5,000 people. That is when my unknown wait started, my jail sentence, my waiting game. I waited 17 months before that first call, every day praying, every day hopeful. Then, on 17th July 2017, I thought that it was finally all over. The nurse first told me who she was and where she was calling from. She asked me to confirm my name and date of birth, all the usual routine identity checks. My heart instantly tried to leap from my chest as she told me that they may have a possible kidney match. Then it sank, dropped like a stone as she explained, "You are second on the list, that means you are on standby. There's no need to do anything, but please don't eat or drink. We will call you later if you need to come to the hospital."

As soon as she hung up, confusion hit me. No one had even mentioned that the protocol was to always have another potential recipient. On that day I learned that for every deceased donor, four people on the waiting list are called, two for each kidney. A new waiting game started for me, one that I thought would be over soon, one that was even more intense. It lasted over 14 hours and I was starving. Friends had been contacted and people were praying, but the phone didn't ring. I couldn't wait any longer, so decided to call them back and was given an apology. They forgot to call me. They left me hanging on all day and forgot to stand me down. I learnt some hard lessons that day, though the whole experience did give me a short-lived hope.

I tried to convince myself that the waiting could be over soon because they had at least started to call me, but it didn't work like that. I suppose it's a little bit like waiting for your lottery numbers to come up, the odds are massively stacked against you. It would be another 13 months and four more calls before this current season of misery would end. For all I knew at that moment in time, it could have been much longer.

You may be thinking that I am exaggerating my emotional feelings with that call, so let me explain a little more about where my mind was before they phoned. As I approached the first anniversary of being on the waiting list and playing the game, I had also been on dialysis for six months. My mind was in a very dark place. I was having thoughts such as, 'Life isn't worth living.'

Every night as I prepared to attach to my machine, the darkness closed in on me. Even now, writing this memory triggers the feelings, they were so powerful and overwhelming. Tears would often roll down my face as I scrubbed up, but I managed to hide them from Heather. At one stage I remember being overcome with a sense of grief at the thought that someone would have to die so that I could live.

It's very easy and also possibly cynical to read this now and say, "That is what Jesus did for you." I know that, of course, I do. I knew it then, but in that darkness that engulfs and consumes you, it's easy to lose sight of that glimmer of light. That is why some people take their own lives. They are so consumed with torment, that they see only one way out. I know this. I mentioned in my book *'The Golden Thread,'* that I was first suicidal at the age of 14.

As I alluded to earlier, the darkest time for me during this season came one night as the thoughts around the raw facts of the transplant process were rammed home. Someone has to die! The thought changed into, 'What if one of my children had to die? What if they were to be *my* deceased donor?'

This thought was becoming very active as it started to infect my mind every night. It was a devastating reflection that I just couldn't shake off. I dreaded going to bed because I knew that the monster of debilitating anxiety would attack. It would take me about half an hour to get ready for bed, attach to my machine and go through the physical drain pain. I was usually in bed by the time Heather came up and managed to wipe away my tears, compose myself temporarily and disguise my true feelings.

As soon as the lights went out, the monster crawled around in my stomach. Physical pain caused by anxiety is a real thing and I pulled my knees up and curled up into a ball. In the darkness, I cried myself to sleep. I did it silently so as not to raise Heather's attention. Hiding my true feelings *(or at least I thought I was),* only made the problem worse and I would grab my head with my hands.

My nails often dug deep into my scalp. It was a physical pain to mask the emotional pain. I knew enough to know that this was a mild form of self-harm and could ultimately end in suicide. Some mornings when I woke, I noticed the dried blood under my fingernails and I scrubbed up in haste, before disconnecting from my machine. I was free again.

My life had been saved that day because I phoned the Samaritans and talked. What's great was the simple fact that the person on the end of the phone listened. I learned something that day, talking about a problem can save your life.

I knew that I had to be honest with Heather, so eventually

I told her how it was. I maybe didn't share all the details, but enough for her to realise that I needed help. I confided with one of my nurses and she said, "I'm not surprised to hear this, but please understand that you have done well. Most people hit this wall much earlier. You have managed over a year without any support for your mental health. We have a clinical psychologist as part of our team. Would you like to see her?"

A fresh hope surged through me. She understood. I had shared my feelings and no longer felt alone. Help was available and offered to me. In the space of three months from March to May 2018, I attended four sessions and things did slightly improve, although it may have also been the anti-depressants that I had been prescribed.

When you play this waiting game, resilience gets thinner and it doesn't take much to drop you back into the pit of despair. That first phone call lifted my hopes high, only to be dropped back into the pile of 5,000 other people who were also playing the same game. It was no surprise to find myself back in the battle with that beast that is anxiety. I had won the previous battle but was losing the war and two months after that first call, I sat in the chair opposite the clinical psychologist in an even worse state.

I remember around the same time speaking to my renal consultant and I said I don't know how much more of this I can take. His bedside manner was not the best and he offered me the option of coming off of dialysis and letting the disease kill me. He explained that they could make my end comfortable. It shocked me and I reacted by saying, "I don't want to die." As I look back now, I believe his abrupt manner brought me to a turning point. Instead of helping me to end my life, I was referred back to the psychologist for three more sessions.

During this time, I also began to channel some of my anguish into poetry and I'll share a couple here. I hope you like them and I hope they help you to understand my state of mind.

Anxiety

Anxiety came again last night!
I thought he had gone forever.
I was wrong,
thought I was free,
and thought that I was better.

Anxiety just waits,
waiting to strike.
Patient until the dark of night.
I first hear his breathing, snorting,
powerful and loud.
Followed quickly by the rush
of the crowd.
Rushing, crushing,
consuming, controlling.
Too late,
I have gone,
Anxiety has won.
He has won,
though the battle has just begun.

I fight.
Naturally, I fight.
Fight or flight?
I always chose fight.
Wrestling with all of my might.

The blows come hard.
He attacks my head.
He wants me dead.

My desperate whimpers,
a pitiful sound.
Need to find the solid ground.
Tossing and turning.
Hot then cold.
Soaking, sweating.
Time to be bold.
Two hours of struggle
have left me weak.
Have I reached my defeat?
I find something to help me sleep.
I awake again to another day.
Anxiety has gone,
thank God I pray.

What I want for Christmas

What I want for Christmas,
what I really would adore.
I want the same as last year and the year before.
It's not just what I want, It's what I really need.
But for anyone to have this,
someone needs to bleed.
I'm not alone in waiting,
5,000 want the same.
Just waiting and a waiting,
it's called "the waiting game".
It really is the greatest gift,
that anyone could give.
Your sacrifice is more than nice,
you give a chance to live.
So what is this gift so precious?
What then can it be?
If you can please spare one,

I need a new kidney.
If you would like to leave this gift,
after you have gone.
Just register now,
tell your family,
but please don't wait too long.
For some, if they don't have this gift,
the pain will make them cry.
And all that they can do,
is watch the time go by.
They wait and then they die.
What I want for Christmas,
is a kidney transplant, that's what.
I think if I don't have one soon,
I might just lose the plot.

Consider this...

1. We all have giants; it doesn't matter if yours are bigger or smaller than mine.

   The thing to learn from this chapter is that I didn't face my giants alone. If I had, I would not have survived.

2. Who do you talk to and share your burdens?

3. Do you find it useful to share your struggles?

4. It doesn't have to be poetry, but write down how you are struggling and feeling.

   Share it with someone that you trust.

Chapter Ten

Don't Give Up Hope

As I start to write this chapter, I have just tested positive for Covid-19. I am trying to write in between some very bad shivers but it isn't easy. With my immune system suppressed, it could develop into something quite serious. I am currently waiting for medication to help fight it off and people are praying for me all around the world.

The warrior in me says, 'Don't give up, fight this', so I write. Even with this new health complication, I am still valued and I can continue to share my story. Before I continue, please know that whatever your situation, whatever ailments you are battling, God can and will still use you. You are still valued.

*****

Six months after my first transplant call and almost two years of the waiting game, another glimmer of hope came my way. In January 2018, a friend offered to be tested as a potential living donor. This is a huge ask of anyone and I did try to talk them out of it. Nevertheless, they insisted and we visited the transplant centre together. I didn't know how to respond to such a generous offer. When the conclusion of the tests came back as unsuitable, I didn't know whether to sigh with relief *(for them AND my potential guilt towards them)* or, cry for the hope that had once again been ripped away from me. The waiting game truly is an emotional roller coaster and you wonder every day if you will jump off; before crashing into the wall at the end.

Another well-meaning friend approached me just four

months later to be considered as a living donor. We went through the same procedure of tests and interviews, only to be told yet again that they were not suitable. I simply cannot describe the emotions that I felt after these two events. The thought of these two people being prepared to undergo life-threatening major surgery and give a physical part of themselves, takes a lot of courage, compassion and love.

God loves the world so much that He gave us His one and only Son and as Christians, we are all called to be like Jesus. These two potential living donors were both Christian friends and they were demonstrating their selflessness and willingness to help me in my moment of need. I look back to this time and question, what price are we prepared to pay to help a fellow human being?

After yet another letdown, I needed to find another weapon for this battle – all warriors need weapons. In the same way that I had sought out The Shaggy Dog Raconteurs, I now discovered Longfield Care. I had known where they were based for decades, as they ran a hospice just up the road from me. However, like many other misinformed people, I thought that a hospice was where you go to die.

As I searched their website, I was re-educated and found out that the majority of their patients don't die *(well not for a long time anyway)*. Their slogan is 'Live well and die well with a life-limiting illness.' My illness was limiting me and I wanted to live well. When I first entered the building, I felt like a fraud. I didn't have cancer and I could see that others were in a worse state than me. One man carried an oxygen bottle wherever he went, whilst others were visibly struggling. My illness and therefore my disabilities were invisible, but the staff treated us all with the same dignity and respect.

I accessed a six-week course on dealing with breathlessness and fatigue. Serious fatigue is painful, it is far more than just extreme tiredness. Every single muscle throughout my entire body hurt. There were some parts of the course that I didn't like, mindfulness with its Buddhist roots did not appeal to me. I referred to it as 'mindlessness' because the process involves emptying your mind. I wouldn't do it, as I always want God in my head.

The main thing that did help me was peer support and seeing others in much worse conditions. I had always said that no matter how bad a situation becomes, there will always be someone in a far worse place.

I was supported by Longfield for over a year, right beyond my transplant. Massage therapy helped to improve my dialysis and art therapy helped to prevent my head from filling with dark thoughts. I also accessed the NHS mental health service called 'Let's Talk.'

A year after that first potential transplant phone call, something else happened. I would refer to it as a revelation or even a miracle, but I'll save that story for the next chapter.

My second transplant call came after two years of being on the waiting list. It was the same as the first call, stay home and wait. This time it seemed easier, I had more resilience and more support. They also stood me down quickly and I just continued with life as it was.

I waited another eleven months before the phone rang again. This time I was called to the Oxford transplant centre, but only as the secondary patient. I waited all day, only to be sent home again.

Just ten days later, the same happened again, only this time I was the primary candidate - first in the queue. We were supposed to be going away for the weekend with the church but we had to cancel the trip and asked them all to pray.

My hope had been built up. I was prepped for surgery, gowned up, with a canular in my vein. I even had a separate room with a hospital bed and I was nil by mouth. My expectations were high, adrenalin filled my body ready for the fight of surgery. Fear had been dispelled by the hope that surged through every fibre of my very being. Can you imagine the tension that I faced?

This turned into the longest wait of my four false calls and you guessed it, I was sent home again, but the reason why caused an emotional overload. The surgeon himself came in to break the news. He explained that, even though the deceased person was an organ donor, the family still had the final say. They had taken too long to give their consent and the kidneys were wasted, no good to anyone.

I learned that day that this can happen all too often. Families hesitate in the emotional shock and no good comes from the death of their loved one. When the surgeon broke the news, I wept.

At last, my fifth and final call came soon after. The waiting game was over, but this is also another chapter.

Consider this...

1. In the UK, the law has now been updated. Everyone is now considered to be an organ donor unless the person has opted out. However,

relatives STILL have the final say. If you want your organs to be used to help another after you have gone, be sure to let your relatives know now.

Chapter Eleven

I'm Still Valued

So, what about that revelation I referred to just now? Was it in fact, a miracle? This event took place in July 2018, after I had been on the transplant waiting list for two years and five months. I was still on dialysis. Cast your mind back to chapter three, the story of the person who told me I could never be an author. I had struggled to break through that barrier, to overcome the curse and call myself an author. This is the story of how that curse was broken.

We went to a Christian summer camp festival, called, "Naturally Supernatural." This was our third year of attending. Halfway through the week, during the loud worship time, in the throng of thousands of people, I became angry with God. I sat and I cried out aloud, "O God! What am I supposed to be doing with my life? Have you given up on me? Do you no longer have any use for me? Why have you abandoned me?" That is what it felt like.

Then, amid the noise and hubbub, I heard Him! It wasn't an audible voice; it was like a brain download. Some may say that it was a thought, but it was so much more than that. It originated from a supernatural source! It was so powerful I was shaking, **"You still have skills and tools that I have given you. I want you to use them. I haven't finished with you yet."**

I felt the warming presence of the Holy Spirit coursing through me and I instantly knew that God had heard my cry and had responded. However, I still didn't know what it meant. Skills and tools? Did He want me to continue in youth work? He had equipped me for that role, but now it didn't seem right.

Later that week, a woman whom I had never met before was praying for me. She told me that she felt that God hadn't finished with me yet. She had a picture of me walking and said, "I believe God wants you to walk with your Gospel shoes on and that you will be ready to speak the good news of the Gospel."

For a brief period, once again I found myself angry and confused. I tried to explain to her, "I have end-stage kidney failure, I'm on dialysis and I'm waiting for a transplant! I don't think I'll be walking far anytime soon!" My reaction to her was a perfect indicator of how frustrated I was feeling with my whole life at that point. My tone was hurtful and attacking.

I was bang out of order, yet she humbly apologised, "I'm sorry, I'm new to this and maybe I have it wrong?"

We both returned to our seats, but something caused me to watch where she went. She was four rows immediately behind where I was sitting. Her words continued to echo around my head, just like the words from five years earlier had stayed with me, *"You can never be an author!"*

She said, *"God hasn't finished with you yet!"* God had told me the same, *"I haven't finished with you yet!"* Little did I know, this was the five-year-old curse being undone, I was being released. ***"I have given you tools and skills…"***

My mind raced through my life, *'What tools? What skills?'* My thoughts galloped backwards and stopped in the first year of knowing Jesus. Instantly I knew what He was telling me. I rushed over to the woman who had prayed for me. "I'm so sorry", I said, "I need to apologise. God spoke to me through you and I was too angry to hear or understand, but what you said was spot on. I now know that he wants me to write."

In my first year of knowing Jesus, He gave me the gift *(tool)* and the ability *(skill),* of rhyming words and I used it to become a Christian rap artist. That skill has since developed and my writing skills *(storytelling),* helped me to develop The Door Youth Project charity.

I could feel the power of the Holy Spirit already forming words in my head and I was so excited. When I went home from Naturally Supernatural, I had the idea to write some teen fiction. I had previously gathered a collection of teen fiction books, which I now intended to read, to gain inspiration. Now, as I pawed my way through the books, I came to an abrupt halt, as I once again heard God's voice in my heart, *"I have given you the tools and skills, now use them!"*

So, I left the books on the shelf, then, doubt tried to have the final word. *"You can NEVER be an author! An author writes 3,600 words an hour!"* Was that actually true? I decided to Google it and discovered that most authors write 1,000 words in a day. That was when I found a reference to the figure of 3,600. This, apparently, is how many words a copy typist can produce in an hour. An element of truth had been injected into a convincing lie. I had been cursed and lied to. I now knew the truth and I started to write my first novel. "Issues" was written in just over a month and published in January 2019. Then, as soon as it was published, I felt inspired to write, 'My Foundation for Life' *(published February 2019).* I had used the skills and the tools, but still struggled to call myself an author *(the curse was strong) – "You can never be an author!"* The fire was fading in my heart and I didn't write much apart from poetry *(recovering from a kidney transplant slowed me down).* Then at the end of my transplant year in November 2019, I realised that I had written enough poems for my first poetry book, so I published 'Rhyme Time'. I questioned if poetry qualified me as an author. The all-encompassing imposter syndrome consumed me again and I convinced myself, *'I can never be an author'.*

At the beginning of 2020, the weather turned. As it started to snow, I was once again inspired to write my first science fiction novel. I was halfway through writing it when I had a serious accident *(story coming later)*, and so I stopped writing again. When 'The INVASION of the Mimics', my fifth book, was eventually published in October 2020, I could, at last, call myself an *'author'*. The curse had been lifted and with it came a full-on release.

I must also mention another significant step that helped to remove the curse. In January 2020, I discovered and joined the Association of Christian Writers. In doing so I realised that I was not alone. I had struggled to believe in myself due to working in isolation, but that was no longer the case. I found so many supportive and understanding new friends in the ACW, many of whom had also struggled with imposter syndrome. Peer support is essential for all of us and my new-found peers were now referring to me as an author.

Just after publishing 'The Invasion of the Mimics, I was in a prayer meeting, when these words came into my head, "ONE GOD – Many names." I instantly thought that I had to produce a film *(yes, I also make films),* with this title. As the film was being made, I knew that God also wanted me to publish a book with the same title. So in November 2020, I started to meditate on the many names and titles of God. There are over 900 in the book. As I wrote my thoughts and life-related stories, I could feel God's Holy Spirit's presence growing in me. Then, after just three months and halfway through writing the book, he gave me another 'commission'.

Commission is the word that I like to use. I see it as **COM**e together on **MISSION** with God. This time, the call was to use the 'base' writing skill that he had given me *(use the skills and tools)* – 'rhyme'. A friend of mine had recently written Psalm 23 as a rhyming poem. I had produced a poetry book and several *'spoken word'* films. Now, I felt God speak to me again, **"I gave you these tools and these skills for this time, everything else that you have written was in preparation for this project. Work with me and write the "Psalms in Rhyme."**

I write to bless others and to give God the glory and so I was obedient and did as he had commanded. So, in February 2021, I also started working on 'Psalms in Rhyme.' When I started, the speed at which I was writing told me that the whole book, with 2,461 verses, would take two and a half years. I remember saying to God, "Really? You're having a laugh, aren't you?" In response, I felt God speak into my heart again, **"Just let me show you."**

Once again, I felt the Holy Spirit touch me, reassure me and reveal the words to write. Instead of two and a half years, it took just over six months before it was written and published. That was a miracle and at times, I couldn't write the words down fast enough. The writing was now flowing, like a supernatural river of words. The curse was broken, "I AM AN AUTHOR!"

Writing two books at the same time is quite incredible and only possible for me with God in the mix. Also, as if that wasn't enough, he gave me my first illustrated children's book to produce, *'The Land of Make Believe.'* He continued to pour other poems into my mind regularly, plus he gave me the first four chapters of the sequel to, *'The Invasion of the Mimics'* called *'Legacy of the Mimics.'* All this in the space of a few months.

Just a few negative words telling me that *'I CAN'T'* had held me back, but I had learned. NEVER believe it when ANYONE tells you that you can't do something or be something.
ALWAYS reject the NEGATIVE words spoken over you.

Consider this...

1. What tools and skills do you still have that God can use?

2. What or who is stopping you from using them?

Chapter Twelve

Transplant

I leapt forward quite a bit in that last chapter to cover the journey of becoming an author, but let's return to my renal failure journey. On 23rd February 2019, after a three-year wait. The phone eventually rang for the last time.

This was the call that I had been waiting for.

On that day we had planned a rare gathering of Heather's side of her family. A buffet lunch had been prepared and just as the first people arrived to eat, the phone rang. The nurse on the end of the line told me that I was 'nil by mouth' and to make my way to Oxford as soon as possible.

Within a few minutes, my bag was packed and we left the food and guests to eat and lock up when they left. We had travelled the road many times previously and knew that it would take an hour and twenty minutes on a clear run.

I now realise that life rarely gives us clear runs. Is that being negative or realistic? We hit the tailback and almost stopped, crawling along before we faced the policeman parked across the road. The main A40 approach to Oxford was blocked due to an accident. We needed to seek an alternative route along with everyone else.

I'm pretty sure everyone in the traffic jam was frustrated, but how many of them had been waiting three years for a life-saving moment in time? The diversion involved driving over an ancient toll bridge, where the queue crawled along. A man sat in a booth at the mid-point of the bridge collecting five pence from each car. Did we even have any money? We must have, as we were allowed to pass and eventually, we arrived at the hospital about an hour later than anticipated.

I questioned God, "Why does life need to be so complicated?" Little did I know then that there would be even more complications ahead. It is possible to receive a kidney transplant and be home five days later. This stay in the hospital would be eleven days before they discharged me.

Various tests took place throughout the remainder of the afternoon. At some point, a doctor told me that it was going to be a very long wait, so I should grab a snack. I was starving and when they bought me a sandwich, I did as I was told and gratefully consumed it. An hour later, I was informed that they were now ready for me. I explained I had just eaten, and was therefore told that I would have to wait another six hours. I simply couldn't believe what I was hearing and moaned about the doctor who recommended that I have some food. This was so very frustrating, but you can imagine that it would be even more so at this juncture. Remember, there is only a small window of opportunity before the organ becomes unusable. I was understandably distressed.

Anyway, I went to surgery at 11.00 pm and received the new kidney with just thirty minutes to spare! The operation was a success, but due to the delay, the kidney was referred to as sleepy. This *'delayed graft'* needed to be woken up. To put it simply, it wasn't working. My body was filling with fluid and the only way it was going to go was with dialysis, so I was manually drained three times each day for three days.

To make matters even worse, my bowel had been disturbed during surgery and I developed my second life-threatening paralytic ileus. The young student nurse with me at the time, reacted with complete shock as black vomit projected across the room and splattered the wall opposite. It was violent and probably the first time that she had observed such an event.

I managed to instruct her speaking quickly, "I have a paralytic ileus. I need an NG tube stat. Call a doctor now." My previous experience had taught me the lingo and the urgency and a doctor appeared immediately, with a tube inserted within ten minutes.

I try to find the humour in the darkest of moments and when the nurse first reacted, she found me a standard sick bowl. I glanced at the bowl, then toward her and screamed, "You're gonna need a bigger bowl." It reminded me of that scene in the movie 'Jaws' where someone says, "We're gonna need a bigger boat!"

I now had five different tubes inserted into my body *(2 drains, my dialysis catheter, my willie catheter and an NG tube)* and I looked in a right state. The room and bed looked like I had exploded, but as I sat there in my mess, I knew that God still valued me and that He hadn't finished with me yet.

Over the eleven days in the hospital, a stream of compassionate friends came to visit and it was so good to see them. Although visitors can be tiring, I feel that they also help toward the healing process.

When I eventually returned home, I chatted with my neighbour and he told me that his dad had recently died. His cause of death was a 'paralytic ileus'. It certainly highlighted the severity of what I had been through.

As people found out about my transplant, they were

genuinely happy for me and many of them said, "You are cured then?"

I lost count of the number of times that I had to explain, it's not a cure, there is no cure, it's just another treatment. The transplant works, but due to the delay it has never risen much above 30% function, it has been working for over four years and I am currently no longer in need of dialysis.

Some Christians reading this may be wondering if I have ever forgiven the doctor who told me to eat. I would say that I have, as I hold no bitterness or resentment toward him. The fact that I did eventually receive my transplant filled me with so much joy and hope that I was grateful for the entire team that had cared for me. It does none of us any good to hold grudges. I am just happy to be alive.

I had survived my second close brush with death, I had to consume a pile of pills for the rest of my life, my immune system had been suppressed, my white blood cells were low and I was labelled, 'Clinically Extremely Vulnerable' – CEV. On top of all of that, Covid was coming.

I still live with chronic kidney disease *(CKD)*, and I still have huge native polycystic kidneys *(PKD)*. This illness is still life-limiting and disabling, yet I am still able, I am capable and I am still valued.

Consider this...

1. On a scale of 1-10 how valued do you feel?

2. List out the negative things and thoughts that make you feel devalued.

3. List out the positive things that could make you feel valued.

4. We all have things that we perceive as negative in our lives but we need a good balance.

   What positive angle or twist can you put on the negative perceptions?

   How can you pray to reduce or eliminate the negative?

5. Find a helpful friend to support you in this. Remember, my hospital visitors were like a lifeline to me.

Chapter Thirteen

Crash, bang, wallop

After the long three-year wait and two and a half years on dialysis, the transplant provided an element of freedom. Life seemed to almost return to normal and for sixteen months I had no serious hospital visits. There were of course the regular check-ups and post-transplant procedures, but nothing too traumatic. Looking back, it seemed to be a much-needed reprieve and we made the most of life.

As mentioned earlier in the chapter about The Shaggy Dog Raconteurs, we were becoming more well-known as a band, travelling further afield and playing at gigs every other weekend. On 14th March 2020, we played at a venue in Wales, but there was a very strange atmosphere. Covid was being mentioned, fear was spreading and just over a week later, lockdown was enforced upon the UK.

I received notification immediately telling me that, as I am a transplant recipient and classed as Clinically Extremely Vulnerable *(CEV)*, I had to 'shield.' To be told to confine yourself to your own home for 3 months was bad news, but of course, it had to be done. Once again, I was a prisoner and Heather was trapped with me.

We all quickly learned how to use online meeting platforms and the church adapted as we all met online.

My brother had the same kidney disease as me, with additional heart complications and sadly he died just before the lockdown. With restricted numbers of mourners allowed at funerals and my shielding situation, I was advised not to attend the funeral. This was the first real indicator of just how difficult this whole process was going to be.

Part of my mental health coping mechanism is to write. So, I produced a series of spoken word videos called *'My Lockdown Series.'* My body fitness also allowed me to do some much-needed work on the house. I could still order materials for delivery.

We had been used to adjusting to health situations rapidly and we adapted quickly to the new, lockdown conditions as well. Where the general population struggled with things such as hand washing and mask-wearing, I was already used to these guidelines because of my condition. Lockdown became just another norm.

By June 2020, I was allowed to leave the house to collect goods that I had ordered online *(click & collect).* So, on 8th June 2020, I left the house to fetch a tube of decorator filler. Little did I know that that purchase could have cost me my life.

I live on a very steep and narrow country lane. I step from the gate straight into the road, there are no pavements. My view is obscured by my neighbour's overgrown hedge. One step, two steps, smash! The speeding cyclist made no sound and seemed to come out of nowhere. The human missile hit me with force. I felt my feet leave the ground and in a whirling blur, I landed some five metres away further down the hill. I later found out that the cyclist first hit our car, which was parked on the road. That helped to reduce the impact on me. It all happened so fast, too fast to notice the small details.

The initial impact hit me on my right side. During my short flight, my body twisted and I landed on my right side providing a secondary impact and more wounds.

From my waist to my head, I sustained multiple injuries. Firstly, my transplant kidney is situated just above my pelvis on my right. It had suffered major trauma. Although I wasn't aware, my kidney function was already dropping. It would soon be at 10% *(end-stage)* and I would be prepped for dialysis. I struggled to breathe with six broken ribs, I felt my whole rib cage moving. The pain was unbearable. I had sustained a fractured right wrist but other pains were so severe it wasn't noticed straight away. My right shoulder was a mess, dislocated, and broken in two places and my bicep tendon had ruptured beyond repair. Blood trickled from a wound on my head. The bones to the side of my right eye socket crunched when I touched them. I also drifted in and out of consciousness with a concussion.

I remember being led on my back, head facing downhill for what seemed an eternity. I remember my clothes being cut from my body by paramedics. The gas and air helped with the pain but my head spun even more. I remember the fire and rescue service being there due to the narrow access. I remember the neck brace being fitted to keep my head in position. Most of all I remember the surge of pain as my broken body was gently manoeuvred onto a spine board.

I assume I was placed into the waiting ambulance but I just can't remember. I don't remember the journey to the hospital and I have no recollection of being in the emergency department, but I know that I was there. I took a photograph of me there and posted it on social media, but can't remember doing so. I also don't remember having any x-rays, yet I know several were taken. I later found out about the damage to my kidney but have no memory of a CT scan. I was transferred to a ward but failed to even remember that.

Due to Covid, no one was allowed to travel with me to the hospital, and no visitors were allowed. All Heather could do was wait for the information that she received by phone. I was told that I was on the ward for two days before being taken to the operating theatre, although there is one thing that I can recall about that time.

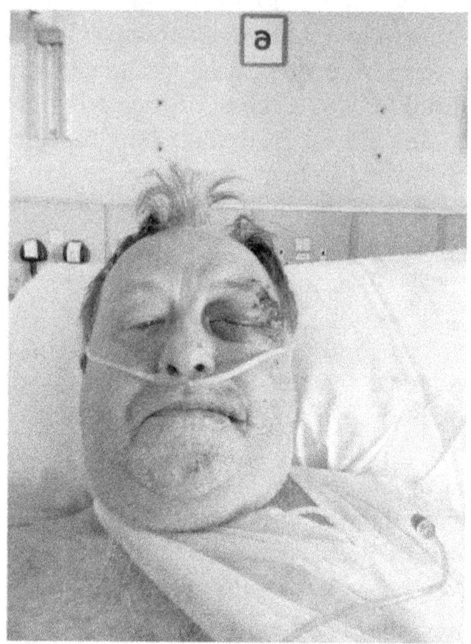

Proof that I was in the Emergency Department and bloated from years of steroids

One of my friends happens to be the hospital Chaplain. No visitors were allowed during this time, but I do remember him coming to see me every day that he was in the hospital. I can't remember much of what we talked about either, but I was so pleased to see a friendly and familiar face. I am sure that my mind was trying to shut down due to the extreme lack of familiarity, combined with immense pain.

In the operating theatre, they reset my dislocated shoulder. I'm not sure whether they were planning to repair the two shoulder breaks at the same time, as their plans had to change. Whilst under general anaesthetic, I experienced an aspiration. This is when something enters and obstructs your airway. My stomach contents had caused the problem and I woke up two days later on a life support machine. The machine breathed for me and kept me alive.

During these days, my family and friends prayed. They had been told to expect the worst. My likelihood of survival was extremely low. Remember, no one could visit. I wouldn't have even been aware if they did. The struggle for Heather must have been so tough. I often think that I had the easy part, as I had absolutely no awareness, or did I?

I started to have a realisation that my eyes were open but I couldn't speak. I have no idea when it began, but it seemed to go on for hours. The same images repeated, as if on a loop over and over. I could hear muffled voices speaking to me. A nurse with red hair walked from his desk, looked straight into my face, spoke to me and then went back to sit down. He sat a few seconds before the loop started all over again. The repetition was like torture. It could have been minutes or days that I experienced this phenomenon, but when they eventually woke me up, I recognised the nurse and knew that he was real.

As I awoke from my induced slumber, I could not speak until the tube down my throat was removed. I can't remember my first words, but I do remember being disoriented. Noises from machines overpowered the atmosphere. A doctor talked loudly to colleagues in a doorway and I remember shouting to him to shut up. The staff tried to calm me down but my brain was unable to comprehend the severity of my predicament. They decided to call Heather and allow her to see me. She was masked and gowned and had to follow a strict Covid protocol. She could only stay for a short time. We held hands and she spoke. Her voice gave me a reality check and a tear trickled down my cheek. I think that I apologised for making such a mess and causing her so much grief.

I felt something pulling on the right side of my neck, so reached my left hand up to feel the central line ready for emergency dialysis. I knew what it was and what it meant and asked if my kidney was okay. Did I need dialysis? It was then that they informed me about my damaged transplant, it had dropped to 10% function but was miraculously bouncing back up. A few minutes later, the central line was removed and I felt relief.

Shortly afterwards, I was transferred back to the ward. I remember being there for about another week and the Chaplain continued to be my visiting life-saver nearly every day. It wasn't until I was released from the hospital that I found out that many people had been praying for me. I thank each of them, whoever they may be and believe that I am alive today because of their prayers. Through the power of God, I had survived another close brush with death, in response to the cries of the saints.

The road to recovery was long and rocky. I was discharged with a serious bowel infection, C-Difficile and nurses had to come in to take tests each day. For three months Heather helped me with toilet functions and showering, and I slept propped up in a spare bed.

I waited 21 months before I was eventually allowed to undergo surgery to have my shoulder repaired. Covid closed operating theatres, my surgeon caught Covid and

I had to have cardio stents fitted before they would risk any strain on my heart. The delays resulted in further deterioration of my shoulder, as the unsecured broken bones rubbed against each other and ground themselves away. By the time I went to surgery, the shoulder was so damaged that I needed a joint replacement.

This whole story reminds me of a song from the early 90s by a band called Chumbawanba. The song is called, *'I get knocked down, but I get up again'* and this is exactly what I needed to do. Once again, I turned to writing poetry and *'When'* was the first thing that I wrote. Shortly afterwards I also wrote *'Thankful'* so here they are.

When

This is the first thing that I wrote,
following a near-fatal accident.
It was a close brush with death and of course, death does come knocking at our door eventually.
It's only a matter of WHEN

Crash,
smash,
over in a flash.
Head took a bash.
Nasty gash.
Ribs all broken.
Shoulder explosion.
Memory erosion.
Much confusion.
Operation.
Complication.
Life support.
Hello Mort.
Life too short.
No more thought.

No more light.
Need to fight.
Survive the night.
Such a messed-up sight.
Need to stay alive.
Feed the spirit inside.
So close,
I cried.
Thankful to be alive.
You never know
WHEN,
it might happen to you,
but death will come knocking.
You all know it's true,
but before it does,
there's one thing you must do.
Believe,
repent,
invite HIM in.
No more live a life of SIN.
Be protected by the
armour of Him.
Be protected by His Spirit within.

Thankful

God gave me the start of this poem
when I was in an MRI machine.

I feel so grateful, so thankful,
glad to be alive.
They say, 'Only the strong survive'.
I don't feel strong,
feel quite weak.
Struggle walking down the street,
but I'm thankful,

thankful to be alive.
Injured and deprived.
The pain lies deep inside.
Look at me the cripple.
You judge me with your fickle mind.
Open your eyes, stop acting blind.
I'm no superhero, don't wear a cape.
Tell me where to go, show me. Where's my fate?

See that I'm still capable and wholly available.
I thank you God and say amen.
Escaped the grip of death again.
Still, I face the struggle and pain.
Enough to make you go insane.
Oh why, oh why do I feel so bad?
I know, it's you, stops me going mad.
And I thank you again,
despite the pain.

Thank you for your grace,
That keeps me alive.
I look upon your face,
as you help me survive.
Above the noise of the MRI machine,
I hear your voice like a tambourine.
I question,
is this real or a dream?

Then I thank you, Lord,
for I am redeemed.
I thank you for your resurrection,
and giving me a special connection.
Watch over me,
give me protection.
Show me the way,
give me direction.
Now keep me safe from the flame.

I pray all this in Jesus' name.
Amen is all that's left to say.
So be it, that is what I pray.

Consider this...

1. Write your own poem or try journalling to describe something about you or a and give thanks.

   Pray first and allow the Holy Spirit to guide you (a poem doesn't have to rhyme)

2. Share your writing with at least one person.

   If you are able, share it with a larger group.

3. Accept the positive comments and allow them to inspire you to write more.

Chapter Fourteen

Keep Breathing

My polycystic kidneys are rather large, I always explain to people that it is like being in the last month of pregnancy and expecting twins. The only difference is, that my term will not end without medical intervention and that will not happen unless my native kidneys become a threat to my life. So, my body continues to grow and people often assume that I am fat. I am classed as overweight, and obese even, but a vast amount of my excess size is due to my kidneys.

It is easy to lose your body confidence and I often feel the need to explain to people why I am so big. On one occasion I was waiting to go on stage at a festival with the band. Another band were also backstage and as usual, I started to chat with them *(I chat to anyone).* I can't remember how it happened but we started to talk about body image and in particular being overweight. At one point in the conversation, one of the other band members mentioned that I was fat. I told them that it wasn't fat and that I suffered from cysts on my kidneys. I showed him the protrusion of my huge kidneys and he started to apologise. I told him that it is like being permanently pregnant and we both laughed it off. I do miss that backstage banter. The conversation inspired me to write this next poem.

I'm Not Fat

I hear you laugh; you think that I'm fat
It's rather sad, as a matter of fact
You say, look at that bloke, he's so large

What a joke, he's the size of a barge
If you knew, what I've been through
I mean really been through
You certainly wouldn't mock
If you knew, what's really true
You would be in shock
So, let's take stock
of why I look like a bus
I don't fuss
don't eat too much
but the truth MUST, be told
I'm not big because I'm old
Though, I am getting on a bit
Clothes are hard to fit
but **I'm NOT fat,** that's a fact
Yes, I'm over-sized
guess why and win a prize.
If you give in, then I win
even with my double-chin
I'll put you out of your misery
And tell you why, I'm a plus-sized me
My kidneys are gigantic and I mean MEGA
A diet won't help, I'm like it forever
Polycystic Kidney Disease is the medical name
If you could know what it's like
you'd never laugh again
I know that you don't mean it
when you laugh and grin
As underneath my skin
there's a mass that lies within

But God made me the way that I am
It was all part of His Master plan
I know that I'm big and not a pretty sight
But I still have fight
and the might to write
God spoke to me and said

"I've not finished with you yet."
The pen is mightier than the sword
I'm a ready-writer, that God has called
I'm not really fat, I just look that way
You may think I'm a prat
but for you, I pray
That's a fact and **I'm NOT FAT**

Why am I telling you all this now? The reason is that obesity can be an underlying factor for many other serious health issues. I had been waking up in the night for many months struggling to breathe. My snoring had increased to an extreme level of decibels and Heather told me that she would watch me sleep and every so often I stopped breathing. I was falling asleep throughout the day as a result of such a bad night's sleep.

Once again, I was having tests and in May 2021 I was diagnosed with severe and complex sleep apnoea. Sleep apnoea can be caused by chemical (drug-induced) or mechanical (body) issues and I had both. I was told that on average I stopped breathing every 45 seconds, that's 90 times an hour, all through the night and needed to use a special machine to keep me breathing at night. I now sleep every night with a mask that covers my mouth and nose, with a tube that feeds a continuous flow of air.

As obesity is on the increase, so too is sleep apnoea, with 6% of the population affected. This still seems a low percentage and the problem is easily remedied with the machine, so for many it doesn't seem a very big deal. For me though, on top of everything else that I suffer with, I questioned God, "Why me? Why is it always me?"

The next thing that I did was write this.

One more piece of straw!

On top of all my other health issues I fear
I am now diagnosed with sleep apnoea!
So now I know why I'm tired all the time.
And they tell me that I'll be just fine.
One more condition on my list.
A poor position, do you get my drift?
Let me give you the gist!
It's one more thing, on top of everything.
Am I supposed to do something?
I do the most I can do, I get creating.
Writing, biting off what I can chew,
that's what I do.
I keep it real, I know the deal,
you may know how I feel.
I'm not crying, long way from dying,
I know I'm not flying, but still.
I don't feel ill,
just tired, yet still inspired, maybe even admired?
I'm inspired to write this,
it's just one more condition on my list.
A poor position, do you get my drift?
Are you now getting the gist?
Can I take any more, it's just one more,
piece of straw
It won't break my back, I'm not a camel.
As a matter of fact, I'm a man-type mammal!
I'm spouting all my flannel!
When the going gets tough the weak run away?
Well, I'm gonna stay, not going, not today.
Did I hear you say, HOORAY?
It's just another diagnosis,
another one on my list.
Don't get me wrong, I don't dismiss,
I just persist, to exist.
Don't let it take the...

what did you expect?
A little defect, but I'm not a reject,
I have no regrets
At least now I know, way to go!
So let's get on with the show!
Just one more condition on my list.
A poor position, do you get my drift?
Do you now get the gist?

Whatever you face, and you've had enough.
Remember, get going when the going gets tough!

After writing this poem I felt better – I still felt valued. If you are wondering how just writing a poem can help, well consider this. In 2021 an interesting study was published by the American Academy of Paediatrics. They were assessing the behaviour of a group of 44 hospitalised children. The patients were encouraged to read and write poetry. The researchers saw reductions in fear, sadness, anger, worry and fatigue. The evidence concluded that poetry was a welcome distraction from stress and an opportunity for self-reflection. Poetry, or indeed any form of creative writing, will help to improve your mental health.

I believe that this is so important to all of us if we want to start to feel better about ourselves, especially if we want to understand that we are valued. Who doesn't want that? So, the reflective *(and entirely optional)* element for this chapter is similar to the last chapter. This is just me trying to encourage you to be creative.

Consider this...

1. Create something with your own hands, a painting, drawing, textile, garden or a special cake.

   Pray first and allow the Holy Spirit to guide you to your creative self.

2. Share your creation with at least one person.

   If you are able, share it with a larger group.

3. Accept the positive comments and allow them to inspire you to create even more.

Chapter Fifteen

Put your 'Blest' foot forward

In June 2022, I published my 9th book, Legacy of the Mimics. I published another poetry book later on in August that year. This brought my total to ten books so far. This is quite a significant achievement for any writer, although for me, with so many health hurdles that I had to contend with, I regard it as miraculous.

As with any miracle, there is a natural tendency to want to share your story and so I looked for opportunities. I had previously made several attempts at pushing myself out there. I'd look for any events to speak at and especially perform poetry, but it had been fruitless. I felt the Holy Spirit nudge me in this direction for years but self-promotion does seem a most unnatural thing to do.

A year earlier in 2021, I was struggling with this so much that I was inspired once again to write. As you may have gathered by now, it's what I do to try to stabilise my feelings and my mental well-being. This time I wrote...

No Honour

In Nazareth, the Nazarene,
was never believed and rarely seen.
I know a little of how it must have been,
for the Nazarene.
As those at the scene, think that I'm obscene.
But really, I am not, I'm a man of honour.
Speaking truth upon ya.
Not in it for profit.

Don't do it to fill my pocket.
No Shakespearian sonnet
Hurt, but get back on it.
Love? I want it.
Attraction of the opposite
Will you ever drop it?
Simply catastrophic.
Make me want to vomit.
No honour for the Prophet.
Not in my backyard, it really is so hard.
Disbelief, need relief.
Need hope, yes, hope.
Instead, you treat me like a joke.
But I'm not laughing.
Simply asking why?
Why can't you give me a chance?
Not asking for romance.
Allow my words to enhance.
Time now to advance.
I'm a prophet without honour,
in the town where I was born.
They treat me like a bomber
and they pierce me with a thorn.
And I? I just mourn.
No need for a storm
I just feel down.
Mourn for the town
and for the lost.
Because I do give a toss.
I care about them regardless.
A prophet without honour nevertheless.
I care about them, like the Nazarene
But when they look at me, they see Frankenstein.
Now I know that this isn't true for all,
And this does give me hope.
Pride it comes before a fall,
Get off that slippery slope.

Like a dog with a bone, I wouldn't give up gnawing away at it. I knew that God was directing my path, so continued to look for opportunities. So, in June 2022, I searched for a Christian book festival anywhere in the UK. I found plenty in the USA and one that had happened once, as a one-off event in the UK but nothing existed.

I instantly felt that there was a huge need for a Christian book festival and I knew plenty of authors that would be glad to take part. I felt God leading me, speaking into my heart, **"I have given you tools and skills to use."**

I felt that God was calling me to start a festival, so I, first of all, tried the easy option and asked the well-established, *'Stroud Book Festival'* if we could provide a Christian venue as part of their festival. This would mean that we could be included in all of their advertising. I thought that it was a good idea but it wasn't God's idea, God doesn't particularly like the easy option.

Do not be unequally bound together with unbelievers [do not make mismatched alliances with them, inconsistent with your faith]. For what partnership can righteousness have with lawlessness? Or what fellowship can light have with darkness? 2 Corinthians 6:14 (Amplified Bible).

I waited for a response but none arrived. A restlessness stirred in my heart and I became agitated. I describe it as having a stone in your shoe, it gives you discomfort and sooner or later you are going to have to remove the shoe. I eased the irritation by searching for a venue. I figured, that when the Stroud Book Festival people eventually came back to me, I could tell them that I have a venue.

I also need to point out that the festival is held annually in November, so there were already less than four months to put it all together. I had organised festivals and events in the past and I knew that this would be difficult in the time available. If it was going to happen, it would take a miracle.

I aimed to find the four different key elements that we would need.

- The venue, as already mentioned
- A keynote speaker
- Some authors, of course, and
- The necessary funding.

I knew that we would need at least three months to advertise the festival, once these things were in place, so only had a month to secure all these.

I sent one email to one church and almost immediately the Reverend Keith Rudman caught the vision. He allowed us to use Stroud Baptist Church at no cost. It was such a generous offer.

At the end of the same week, I posted a call out for Christian authors. I advertised this on the Association of Christian Authors page and their members too caught the vision. I aimed for fourteen writers in total and by the end of the weekend the response had been incredible. All of the spaces had been filled and we even had a reserve list. The call-out had attracted authors from all over the UK, from hundreds of miles away. I knew that there was a need for this event because there was nothing else like it, but I had never anticipated this level of response. I began to sense a real excitement building for this festival – a Holy Spirit buzz.

Two of the four essential requirements had been found in less than a week, which is enough to make anyone tingle with excitement. However, finding a keynote speaker was going to be a more difficult task and so I needed to find some help. Mike Juggins, the owner of Scrolleaters Christian bookshop, was keen to help, as was the Reverend Jo Regan *(she loves reading does she).* Both of these two made some wonderful suggestions, coming up with names that I would never have imagined.

Sophie Neville was suggested by Jo and I was already in contact with her through social media and the Association of Christian Writers. I chatted briefly with Sophie, agreed on a suitable fee and booked her to appear on the Friday evening of the 1st Stroud Christian Book Festival. It had taken about two weeks to reach this stage.

Three out of four of the needs had been met. I had stepped out in faith but next came what could be considered the biggest step of faith, we needed money. For that first year, we were able to work within a budget of £700. I launched a crowdfunding appeal and wrote to the local churches and a few Christian businesses. Miraculously the full amount had been pledged within a month of finding the venue. The four essential needs had been found and during that crazy whirlwind month, I even managed to buy a domain name and build a website. Things had happened so fast and I never expected that. Then, I suddenly realised, we didn't have a bank account. How were we supposed to receive the funds?

I made several enquiries and eventually settled on the bank that I already banked with, one of the main high street banks. The application was a quick process but there were two stages of approval. The first stage could take up to a week and the second stage another month. More faith was needed so I prayed and asked Jo Regan to pray. The first stage was approved the next day and the whole account was open within six days. God had worked another miracle and we were now officially in business.

After three weeks of contacting the Stroud Book Festival, they eventually responded and politely turned us down. They didn't want a Christian venue as part of their festival. I thought it only fair to tell them that they had taken so long to respond, that we had already progressed with our own festival and that it would sit alongside theirs. They were happy to hear that and we were happy not to be yoked to them.

Up until that stage, we had been using the same branding colours as Stroud Book Festival, and the team of Jo, Mike and I, now felt a need to differentiate. We discussed various suggestions for a name for the festival and settled on the **BOOK BLEST Christian book festival.**

On the 4th and 5th of November 2022, the very first Book Blest festival took place and it was regarded as a great success. We were learning as we stepped out in faith on this new venture and God provided all of our needs.

At the outset, I had established what I considered to be the aims of this festival. Primarily we wanted to give God the glory for giving us the ability to create and especially write. Our other aims had been to act as a festival of excellence and opportunity for all Christian authors. We also wanted to bring hope, encouragement and inspiration to those writers and for them to know that they are not alone. Finally, we felt that it was important to show the world that God is real, relevant and relational.

The feedback that we received confirmed that we had achieved the vision and our mission now continues. At the end of the festival, we immediately started to plan for the next year and beyond. The greater vision is to see this event replicated in towns across the UK, to give more opportunity to more Christian authors and to continue to glorify God in our writing. I recently heard from someone who lives in Northern Ireland and attended the first Book Blest. She was so impressed and inspired, that she has now started a Christian writers and book fair in her home town.

For me, Book Blest boosted my confidence and encouraged me to push myself out there more. This has resulted in numerous bookings and speaking engagements. These mainly feature my testimony and poetry. I am excited about the prospect of my venues and events and am open to wherever God leads me. I may have multiple health issues and invisible disabilities, yet I am still able, and capable and yes, you guessed it, I'm still valued and so are you.

Consider this...

1. Pray about setting up a Book Blest festival in your town.

2. Contact Book Blest, Stroud so that we can help you. www.bookblest.co.uk

3. Find a team and start to find the four essential needs – venue, authors, keynote speaker (you can always ask me) and funding.

Chapter Sixteen

The deepest valley

There is a thought that many Christians believe, when we step out to work for the glory of God, we can come under attack. I believe that is true. If and when we step onto the battlefield, casualties are possible. I say this because I have experienced it so many times that when it happens, it isn't a surprise. Often, for me, I can struggle with weariness and fatigue leading up to or after an event. You could say that this is only to be expected given my health issues. Then, during an event, I feel spiritually supercharged as a supernatural filling occurs. You could argue that this is adrenalin surging through my body, but I say this is how God equips us for the battle. This is how He strengthens us with the endurance to run the race that He has set out before us.

This is the story of the toughest battle that I have ever faced and I am currently still coping with the aftermath. The memories are fresh and the ordeal was brutal. It was the deepest, darkest valley that I have survived and I know that I was not alone. I know that He was by my side. Psalm 23 means so much more to me now, as does this poem that I wrote a few years ago.

Valley

As I walk through the valley
of the shadow of death
I don't feel fear, I feel your caress
I excite, that I might
see you this day
Then in spite, of my plight

I delight to pray
And you hear, hold me dear
near to keep me safe
From the grave, I stay brave
feel your love embrace
In my darkest depression
hear my heartfelt confession
In my tearful expression
you leave a lasting Impression
Now, in my deep despair
I feel your presence there
like you care
Despite the pain I face
you wrap me in your grace
Say run the race
set the pace
but my pace is slow
Darkness brings a deathblow

Show, me which way to go
I hear you say hello
Time to follow
yet, I feel so hollow
so I wallow in the mire
No desire
lost my fire
life soon expire
await my funeral pyre
When life is tough
I've had enough
feel like giving up
It's then he kicks my butt
my eyes had been shut
My open eyes
to my surprise
remove the disguise of night
I rise, to the prize, of light

a glorious sight
You lift me, from the valley
Saying, this is not your finale

It had been twenty-one months since I had felt any angina pains and I had done my best to get on with life. I have felt that pain so many times, it is like recognising a familiar friend, in this case not a very nice friend – not really a friend at all. It starts *(for me)* as a slight numbness, a niggle in my wrist. It morphs into an ache, escalating, and a warning is sent to my brain, this is pain. At first, it moves slowly up my arms and then it crosses my chest. I question, "Why are you back?"

I have another friend; a nice friend and I keep him in my pocket. I direct the nozzle of the little red bottle underneath my tongue and spray. It didn't work so I sprayed again. Still, I am in pain. I don't want to be so I spray the GTN spray a third time. The rules state that if I need to spray three times, I need to call for an ambulance. I wait, the pain subsides, the spray has worked, no need for an ambulance, this is not an emergency, this is my reasoning.

After a short rest, I resume whatever I was doing, it was something physical. It's always physical exercise that triggers the pain. It had been happening for a few weeks and it was beginning to worsen, with more serious pain and more often but the GTN spray did the trick. Even though it was taking longer to work, at least it worked.

It had started a few weeks before Christmas, about a month after the Book Blest festival. Christmas came and went along with Boxing Day, a restful time. Then, on 27th December 2022, I woke at 2.00am with pain. I felt pinned to the bed and couldn't move, so Heather grabbed my GTN spray. Three squirts and it eventually eased.

Exhausted, I fell back into a deep sleep until 7.00am. It had only been five hours and I knew what I had to do. My angina had become unstable. Unstable angina is unreliable and the most dangerous type. I spent most of the morning trying to speak to a doctor. The emergency services were overwhelmed and the phone systems not working correctly. It was 2.00pm by the time I arrived at the Emergency Department of Cheltenham General Hospital, where I would remain for the next 48 hours.

After two nights, I woke on the second morning with severe pain in the toes of my right foot. It was agonising and diagnosed as chronic gout, caused by dehydration and my underlying renal failure. The pain was so bad that I struggled to walk, but for a short period, it took my mind off of the more serious issue.

Everything in the hospital takes time, x-rays, blood tests, ECG, general observations, monitoring, and medication. Time passed extremely slowly but eventually, I was given a bed in the cardiology ward.

I was immediately given a five-day course of eight steroids a day to fight off the gout. I am pretty sure that this also gave me the strength that my heart needed and I felt very little pain for about a week. I began to feel a little like a fraud and that I was taking up a bed unnecessarily. I waited about two days before finding out just how serious my situation was. I needed an angiogram, a procedure that involves inserting a catheter into an artery in the groin, arm or neck. It is threaded through the blood vessels to the heart. A coronary angiogram can show blocked or narrowed blood vessels in the heart and uses X-ray imaging and a special dye *(contrast)* to see your heart's blood vessels.

This would be my fourth angiogram; two of the previous

times had resulted in having six coronary stents inserted to keep my arteries flowing and each time the dye had lowered my kidney function. It was always something of a trade-off, improved heart health at the cost of my renal condition.

I'm gowned up and wheeled to a freezing cold lab where blankets are piled on top of me, as I lay on a surgical table. I am conscious throughout the procedure and I recognise the familiar feelings of prodding and poking. The Cardiologist talks to me, reassuring me, and then he stops, the investigation is over, and now he will tell me the news.

"You have some serious blockage to three of your arteries. They are very difficult to reach. We could fix it with stents but they wouldn't last much longer than 18 months. We need to discuss the best way forward with the surgeons."

I struggled to take it all in and a surge of emotion caused the tears to well up. When I returned to the ward the nurses were surprised to hear the news as I didn't appear to be ill. Their reaction made it seem even more real and I knew then that I was facing a triple bypass – open heart surgery.

I knew many others who had gone down this treacherous road including my dad, mum and brother. I had witnessed their struggles but had no idea of the level of pain and suffering that lay ahead. I tried to stay positive, I tried to write... but it was not easy. I wrote this before my surgery.

Bad News

Bad news arrives
I decide to try to stop the slide,
the subside
Into the divide so wide
I take care to avoid the despair,
lingering just there
I fail
It surrounds, all around, as my soul is bound
I scream aloud, muffled by darkness shroud
Covered, smothered, food for the Buzzard
I tumble and stumble into the divide,
look to the skies
Try to get a grip, as I slip into the miry pit
More bad news crushes my head
Filled with dread, depression being fed
Let it in, under my skin, will I ever win?
In a bad news spin, lights are dim
Things aren't great
Help me to escape
Before it's too late
No time to debate
What is my fate
Just need a mate
Before it's too late
To listen and care,
To lift me from despair
Is there anyone there?

I stayed in the ward in Cheltenham until a bed could be found at the Bristol Heart Institute. Each day that I waited my pains were increasing, more frequent, more severe, lasting longer and mainly at night. I cried out to God and questioned Him, "Why am I here? Why is this happening?" Then I started to speak into the opportunities that arose.

On New Year's Eve, I wrote a poem and dedicated it to the nurses and staff. I recorded it as a spoken word video and posted it on my YouTube channel *(all from my hospital bed).* I performed the poem to other patients and visitors. I had numerous conversations about being a Christian and at one point I even performed one of my old rap songs. Why was I here? The answer is always the same, no matter where you are. The answer is, to be wholly available and ready to be used by God. Even whilst seriously ill and waiting for major heart surgery, God chooses to use me and He will do the same for you because you are still valued.

Consider this...

1. Are you struggling with a difficult situation?

   Do you question where God is in all of it?

   Discuss how you are feeling with a friend or group.

2. Wherever you are and whatever you are facing, ask God why you are there and expect an answer.

3. Offer yourself to God, ask Him to use you and say, "Here I am Lord, wholly available."

Chapter Seventeen

Endurance

I spent a total of two weeks in Cheltenham Cardiology Ward and on the day that I was due to leave they tested me for any communicable diseases. My Covid test was negative but I had an indicator for Flu. On arrival in Bristol, they put me in isolation with a sign on the door, 'Flu Infection Control.'

A nurse quickly did my general observations, then hastily left. For a few hours, it seemed as if I was being ignored, I mean, who wants to catch the Flu? Someone later brought me a sandwich and a cup of tea. Then, I later found out that some of my paperwork was missing and they were, therefore, uncertain how to process me.

The Flu is exhausting and I eventually went to bed very late. I must have slept for about three hours before being woken abruptly with chest pain, at about 2.00am. It was serious pain and I struggled to move to reach the call bell. The attack was the worst that I have ever experienced and took lots of GTN to make it subside.

After a routine ECG, I fell back to sleep until the same happened again at about 4.00 am and 6.00 am. This time, after the ECG, I was asked to sign a consent form, met with the anaesthetist and was prepped for theatre. The nurse shaved my chest, arms and legs. She explained that I had been bumped up the list for an emergency operation and told me to advise my family.

I called Heather and told her. In a hurry, I had forgotten to hang up the phone and left the line open. She could hear me talking as I was taken to the operating theatre. I remember multiple cannulas being fitted, and then my body started to feel fuzzy and the lights dimmed. I woke up two days later.

I had been on a life support machine since surgery, which was a familiar experience. As before, they woke me up with the tube still down my throat. It is a disorientating and disempowering experience. I wanted to ask questions, but couldn't. When the tube was eventually removed the first thing that I asked for was pain relief. I couldn't move, I didn't want to, the pain was more than anything that I had previously experienced. A device with a red button was placed into my hand and the nurse instructed me to press it. The pain was reduced with the injection of morphine, but it was still bad.

I was in an isolation room because of the Flu and a nurse never left my side. He was so reassuring and explained everything to me. I couldn't see the monitors and the stack of equipment that my body was connected to, as it was located behind me. Later that day when Heather arrived with Steve Woodcock, they described it to me. Their faces looked shocked by the sight before them.

The morphine messes with my memory but I do remember every day I vomited a lot, I struggled to keep food down. Every day more tubes were removed from my body as progress was made, but I still battled with pain.

The decision was made to stop my morphine and give me Fentanyl, a far more powerful opioid and easier going on my kidneys. Fentanyl is approximately 100 times more potent than morphine and 50 times more potent than heroin as an analgesic. It certainly was extremely efficient at stopping pain and in the space of 24 hours, I pressed the little red button enough times to inject three whole syringes into my body.

It just so happens that delirium is one of the side effects of this potent drug. The feeling is rather pleasant and very similar to morphine. I felt relaxed and at ease, sleepy and as if I was floating. I can't recall how long I had been on Fentanyl when the hallucinations started. At first, they were quite enjoyable, euphoric even. In my tiredness, I closed my eyes and immediately found myself in what I can only describe as an alternate reality. I use the word reality because that is how it felt – REAL.

I was transported to a joyful place full of fun and had a great time sliding down huge sand dunes. It was amazing and felt so real. After a while, I opened my eyes and I found myself back in my bed, in my isolation room with a nurse by my side. I briefly closed my eyes and was transported back, then opened them and returned. Through this action, I had the belief that I could control the journey between the two realities. After numerous trips to the sand dunes, confusion set in and I struggled to determine what was real and what wasn't.

Eventually, I found myself trapped in the alternate place. I remember someone telling me that I had to be on the transport to return by midnight, but I was enjoying being there so much that I didn't want it to end, so I stayed. I heard the chime of a clock indicating that it was midnight and saw a car whizz past me with people escaping. At that moment, I was sucked into a wall and became a concrete figurine in a grotesque grotto. I tried to move and cry out, but I was trapped. Fear began to fill my thoughts and it seemed to last forever.

Eventually, my eyes opened and I was back in my bed. I'm not sure how I had been behaving in my unconscious state but the nurse looked a little concerned. I closed my eyes for a moment and nothing happened, I felt safe. The hallucinations had stopped... I hadn't been pressing my little red button.

As I returned to reality, so too did the pain, so I pressed the button. Every time I was allowed, I pressed it. Soon a new reality appeared whenever I closed my eyes. This time I saw a basic computer screen. It looked very similar to a spreadsheet and was mainly green. In the top left was a large green button with the word 'exit'. I watched the mouse arrow move toward it and click it. I opened my eyes and was back to reality.

I visited this computer screen reality several times before I was once again, trapped. This time the cage was different. As I opened my eyes expecting to return to the room, I could still see the computer screen, the two realities had merged.

The screen was on the wall. On the left were letters and at the top a communication box. I could see the mouse arrow and wondered if I could control it. The usual hospital table stretched across my bed in front of me. I placed my right hand on the table and moved it. The mouse moved with it. I was in control. With my left finger, I tapped the table and found out that I could click and select letters. I was watching the screen on the wall opposite me and a nurse was watching me.

I typed words like 'hello' into the box until I could no more. Somehow my mouse disappeared, just like it does in reality, only I couldn't find it. In reality, we always eventually find it but it was impossible. I felt trapped again.

I frantically tried to find the mouse, one hand sliding, the other tapping on the table. I thought to myself, "If only I could click the exit button, as I had before, then I could escape." I was biting on my tongue with the anxiety and the nurse called for help.

I tried to explain calmly, "I know what you are thinking. You think that I'm having a fit, but I'm not. I just need to find my mouse. Can you see it?" I asked as I stared at the wall opposite. She seemed even more confused than me.

Suddenly, words started to materialise in the communication box, and slowly they faded in and out. Slowly they calmed me down. **"YOU... ARE... DYING."** It should have been alarming but instead, I just had peace.

I read each word out loud, then questioned who said that. One word appeared in the box, **"GOD."**

Shocked and stunned, I spoke out loud again, "Is that really you God? Am I really dying?"

"YES... YES", came the reply.

"I'm dying", I said quietly, then I asked the nurse, "Have my family been called." To which she replied, "Yes."

"Wow, I'm talking to God", I said. The nurse looked at me as if I was bonkers. "Where am I going, God?" I wanted to know.

"STANDBY... DESTINATION... COMING UP......HEAVEN"

"Wow, I'm dying and I'm going to heaven", I spoke quieter as a sense of peace filled me. Then, without any prompt, words that listed my life's work appeared.

"THE DOOR... MASTER'S MC... POETRY... GOLDEN... THREAD..." and other books appeared. There were many things mentioned and I can't remember them all. This was my life before my eyes.

Suddenly, I wondered how I could let Heather know about this conversation, so I asked and the answer came on the screen, which only I could see.

"JESUS..." she would know because Jesus would tell her.

Just then, I thought that I needed to see my family before I died, so I asked the nurse when they would arrive.

I'm not sure why the nurse had previously answered 'yes' when I asked if my family had been called. Now she told me, "It's two o'clock in the morning. You are not dying and we cannot phone them."

More words appeared on my screen and I repeated them, shouting them out in desperation. **"LIES... CONSPIRACY... TREACHERY..."**

At some point, another nurse entered. She had been waiting for a doctor to prescribe some medication. The anti-psychotic worked quickly, it calmed me down and the computer screen on the wall faded, and then it was no more. The brain is a powerful organ and my conversation with God felt so real. Was it real? Who knows, but I can recall so much of it, which, it seems is rather unusual.

I closed my eyes and saw traces of green lines, like the green 'code rain' in the film, 'The Matrix'. I quietly whispered to myself, "Wow, I'm in The Matrix." The lines disappeared and I think I slept briefly. As I slept, I saw the typical scene that many people have talked about.

I was in a tunnel that was lit with light. People waited in a queue and made their way towards an even brighter light. I didn't recognise anyone. I remember thinking, surely, I must know someone.

I awoke and the nurse smiled at me. I smiled back and drifted off again. The same happened again, the same scene. Again, I didn't recognise anyone and I didn't feel as if I belonged there. I assumed it just wasn't my time and the scene faded. I must have slept for the rest of the night and awoke to find the day nurse was back looking after me. I was so pleased to see him, it felt normal and real.

What seemed to be a close brush with death or a near-death experience (NDE) left me feeling extremely emotional. I still feel that same emotion months after surgery. When Heather arrived later that day, I shared my experience with her. I struggled through tears. I shared the same story with others and now, I have shared it with you. It was an incredibly believable experience, but I am so glad to be alive.

The next day, despite still being infectious with the Flu, my regular day nurse asked me if I would like to go outside. I relished it, even though I knew that the January air would be bitterly cold. So, he sat me in a wheelchair and smothered me with blankets. My face was obscured with a mask, so I must have looked a very odd sight, with just a pair of blue eyes peering out from the blue blankets.

Once outside I could remove my mask. The cold air was exhilarating. The nurse told me to look up between the buildings and see the sky. There was a reason for all that he did for me. This time, because I had been in the hospital for nearly three weeks, my body needed sunlight and vitamin D. As I glanced toward heaven, snow started to land on my face and I was overwhelmed by the emotion. Tears and mucus flowed freely as the nurse handed me some tissues. He was prepared. He had seen it in many patients before, but I wondered how many of them thought that they were dying. How many were feeling the joy that I now felt?

It had been a slow road to recovery and I was discharged from the hospital with a serious chest infection. Months later, after antibiotics, I am still suffering the effects of that infection and I am still taking regular pain relief.

Less than two months after surgery, I spoke at the Full Gospel Businessmen's dinner in Bath and God used me. He is still using me and I still feel valued.

I still fight health battles every day and expect to do so for the rest of my life. Less than three months after my heart surgery, I was admitted to the hospital with a chronic kidney infection. It is not unusual for someone with polycystic kidneys, but this was my first kidney infection. After another week, lots of prayer and antibiotics, plus of course more sharing of my faith with the nurses, I was allowed to go home.

Consider this...

1. Thank God for the endurance that He gives you to persevere.

2. Start to list the blessings that you have in your life, especially the little things like sunshine and a snowflake on your skin.

3. Think again about someone who is struggling with health or other issues and befriend them. My nurse was like a lifeline to me.

Chapter Eighteen

The future?

The stories in this book may make you wonder whether my life is like one long drama. After all, my tales are rather dramatic. I am pleased to say that I do experience long moments of peace between the battles, though even on peaceful days, I live with the symptoms of a broken body. This is my normal. Twenty pills a day and a constant supply of morphine *(I wear a pain patch),* help to maintain my normal. I praise God for the peaceful, average days, the mundane days, without any form of crisis. I thank God for every day that I have breath in my lungs and regard each as a bonus. It may sound strange to say it, but I am also grateful for the difficult days, for every scuffle, conflict and battle; the big and the small ones. I think of the caterpillar that has to fight with all their might, just to get out of their cocoon. All this, merely to stay alive and move into the next stage of metamorphosis. Without any struggle, there would be no beautiful creation, such as this emerging butterfly. Their wings wouldn't have become strong enough to fly and so they'd soon die.

My health skirmishes actually inspire me to create. Words are my weapon of choice. How do you fight your battles? What inspires your creativity?

What does the future hold for any of us? How can any one of us answer that question with 100% certainty? I know 100% that I am going to heaven, although I don't know when. Who does?

My experience of stepping out of my gate and being hit by a speeding cyclist tells me that the unexpected happens. My triple heart bypass tells me to be prepared for the worst. My God tells me that I am still valued. How do I know that? Quite simply because He keeps using me as His instrument. As long I say, "Here I am Lord wholly available", I know that He will continue to show me more of what He wants me to do.

Ultimately, He wants each one of us to have a deeper, more meaningful relationship. He wants us to spend time with Him, to chat with Him, to listen to Him and be obedient to His desire for each one of us.

We all fail dismally with this as we are distracted by other tasks and hindrances. We allow our selfish desires to sideline the will of God for our lives. We are all guilty of this. As mentioned earlier in this book, I wrote the book of 'Psalms in Rhyme' alongside writing 'One God Many Names.' At the time, I was saturated in scripture and I felt this was the closest that I have ever been to God. I want you to experience some of that.

What does the future hold? I want that Psalms experience again. I want it more and more. I want to communicate with God daily, 24 hours a day, 7 days a week. I want conversations just like I had when I was under the influence of mind-altering substances. Yet, we don't need drugs to achieve this. Romans 12:2 says, *'We are being transformed by the renewing of our minds.'*

What does the future hold? I want my mind to be transformed.

I want to push myself out of my comfort zone and beyond, to get out of my comfortable boat and walk on metaphoric water. Is that what you want?

The Reverend Steve Chalke used to ask this question. If

you could know what God is doing and be part of it, would you want to? Some of you may say, "Yes, I want to know." Others may say, "Yes, I want to be part of it, whatever it is." How many will say, "Yes I want to know and be part of it, no matter what it is."

You may have already heard the story of tightrope walker Charles Blondin. He stretched a tightrope over a quarter of a mile, spanning the breadth of Niagara Falls. The thundering sound of the pounding water drowning out all other sounds is fearful enough, but then he stepped onto the rope and walked across.

This stunning act made Blondin famous in the summer of 1859. Several times, he walked 160 feet above the Falls, back and forth between Canada and the United States as huge crowds on both sides looked on with shock and awe. Once he crossed in a sack, once on stilts, another time on a bicycle and once he even carried a stove and cooked an omelette.

On July 15, Blondin walked backwards across the tightrope to Canada and returned pushing a wheelbarrow.

The story is told that it was after pushing the wheelbarrow across again, this time while blindfolded, that Blondin asked for some audience participation. The crowds had watched with great expectation. He had proved that he could do it and they all believed in him; of that, there was no doubt. Then, he asked his audience, "Do you believe I can carry a person across in this wheelbarrow?"

"Of course", the crowd shouted back, "Yes, you can do it, we believe."

However, when he asked for a volunteer to get into the wheelbarrow and take a ride across the Falls with him, no one came forward.

Later in August of 1859, his manager, Harry Colcord, did ride on Blondin's back across the Falls.

This story is sadly very similar to our Christian lives, we say that we believe but do we have faith? Are you ready to put your trust in God for whatever future lies ahead for you?

Proverbs 3:5-6 says,
'Trust in the LORD with all your heart and
do not lean on your own understanding.
In all your ways acknowledge Him and
He will make your paths straight'.

Lack of trust and doubt are massive barriers that hold us back. Low self-worth, disbelief and imposter syndrome will prevent you from achieving what God has planned for you. Another barrier is apathy and I see it all around me. Humanity is infected with it. I say 'infected' because I have seen it spread like a deadly contagion.

If you don't believe me, try asking for volunteers for a worthy cause and take a look at how society has changed in the last ten years. In 2012/13, 70% of people volunteered at least once a year and 44% at least once a month. Those figures have since fallen to 55% and 34% respectively.

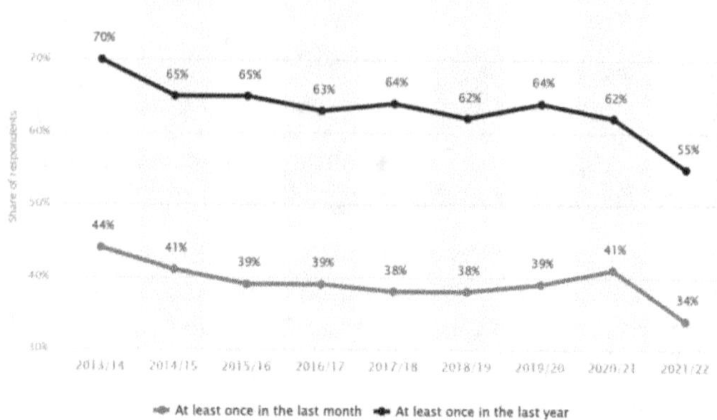

Whatever your future holds, I urge you to consider volunteering your time and skills. This will help you to understand that you are still valued. I am pretty sure that I have already mentioned that a few times, but do you believe it? Do you realise that God looks at you in a completely different way? He sees your potential. He wants to use your strengths, that is obvious, but he can also turn your weaknesses into His opportunities. If that makes you fearful, don't worry He can also eliminate any threats.

This next poem is a bit of a riddle, you already know the answer. The question is, are you a prisoner?

Prisoners

These people are so dumb.
Deluded by their so-called freedom
They are secluded as my captive
Restrained from being active
My invisible bonds are wound tight
They don't fight, no need to show my sight
I don't use fright to capture my prey

I simply delight them to stray
From what is right and how to pray
My prisoner puppets avoid all action
My weapon of choice is simple distraction
I steal their voices fraction by fraction
I tempt them with subtle attraction
I fill them with self-satisfaction
I am the killer of vision
Destroyer of mission
I take one life at a time
I deceive, you believe all is fine
I am jailer of the multitude
The never failure to intrude
You know who I am
I am all around
Wherever you look
I am found
Do you know who I am?
Will you have a guess?
I know you can
But you don't care less
I am the captive taker
Church breaker
World shaker
You are slave to me
You will never see
I am apathy
You know my name
I am the bad stain
I am always there
And you don't care
You are my prisoners under my spell
You all believe that all is well

As I come to the end of my story so far, I hear the news that Christian singer-songwriter, Dave Bryant has just passed away. I am certain that he is now spending eternity in the glory of God. One of the songs that Dave penned was 'Jesus take me as I am' and I wonder how many of us pray these words and mean them. Look at some of the other words.

Jesus take me as I am
I can come no other way
Take me deeper into you
Make my flesh life melt away

Make me like a precious stone.
Crystal clear and finely honed
Love of Jesus shining through
Giving glory back to you

Can you say these words and mean them? Do you want to go deeper with God? Will you allow Him to hone you? We are all pretty much like rough diamonds that have just been dug out of the ground. We are not that impressive, yet we have potential. Rough diamonds are covered in filth, yet when they have been transformed, the light sparkles from them. In our raw state, God looks at each one of us and says, **"You are valued and I take you as you are. Let me wash away your flesh life as you come deeper into me. You will be my instrument, my precious stone."**

Not one of us can know clearly what the future holds, there is just so much that cannot be predicted or prepared for. We all face uncertainty, but for me, I seem to have an abundance of the unexpected. These are mainly health-related. They could prevent me from making plans. For example, if I agreed to be somewhere and then ended up in the hospital again, I would be letting people down. Thoughts like this, but maybe not as extreme, do hold people back from making any commitments. Potentially this is preventing some people from being wholly available, to be used by God.

Of course, I don't want to let people down, but more importantly, I don't want to let God down. So, I push myself out there, I knock on doors and I go to where God leads.

I continue to write however God leads me and I am open to all of the opportunities that He reveals to me. I am now taking bookings for speaking engagements, which are mainly testimony and poetry. I am looking beyond the present and faithfully booking dates months in advance. I pray that God will watch over me and protect me and that He will use me to inspire and bless others. I hope that you have found my story inspiring and that you will now let God show you what to do next with your life.

Future

What does the future hold?
Would you like to be told?
What is around the next corner?
Do you want an informer?
To predict a verdict
To avoid conflict
To know what lies ahead
To know what will be said
Before it's said
Would it be good to know?
To know which way to go?
To know what will happen every hour
It would be like having a superpower
But life would be so predictable
No longer excitable
No surprises
No fun
Boring

We need a mix of fearlessly and fearfully
To live carelessly and purposefully
We need certain and uncertainty
We need a balance to enhance
To be still and dance
To walk and run
Variety is fun
Only God knows what the future holds
He watches as it unfolds
We simply behold

Consider this...

1. Start each day by praying for God to show you and lead you and say, "Here I am wholly available, make me like a precious stone."

2. Keep a list of your options and pray over them, asking God what He wants from you.

3. Keep a daily journal, you never know, your story could become a book to inspire.

Bonus Book

"Satan's lies have a little truth mixed in, which makes them harder to recognise. We need to refute them by saturating ourselves with the truth... it's only by learning the scriptures that we can sort them out".

Anne Peterson

Jesus talked about the wise and foolish builders (Matthew 7:24-29). The wise man built his house upon the rock and when the rains came down, the streams rose and the winds blew, but the house did not fall. The foolish man took the easy option and built his house on the sand. Then when the storms came, the house fell with a great crash.

Our paths are seldom straight forward life always throws its storms at us. How we all weather those storms varies. Some of us will struggle with the slightest little worry, whereas others are able to show far greater resilience.

What is it that makes some of us more resilient than others? I am sure that psychologists will have several long-winded explanations to answer this question, but I believe that we can increase our resilience by building our lives on a foundation of truth. The truth that I am referring to here is more than living honestly, with integrity and never telling a lie.

They came to him (Jesus) and said, "Teacher, we know that you are a man of integrity. You aren't swayed by others, because you pay no attention to who they are; but you teach the way of God in accordance with the ***truth."***
(Mark 12:14)

I am referring to building our lives on a foundation of "truth" which is The Word of God. How many of us have truly done that? How many of us have a firm foundation which is like rock?

I am now 58 years old and have been a Christian for 32

years. If you have read my auto-biography book, The Golden Thread, you will know that God called me into a life of working with young people and you will know of some of the "storms" of life that I have had to face and struggled with.

Throughout my life, God has given me various scriptures to help me through the storms. Each verse was so relevant at the time that it was given and they remain relevant to this day, whether they were given 32 years ago or just in the last year. The point is that we **never** stop building our foundation, because the storms never stop and we need to constantly be reinforcing not just our foundations, but also shoring up the battlements of our mind and fighting off spiritual attacks with the word (that is the sword) of God.

Take the helmet of salvation and the sword of the Spirt, which is the word of God – Ephesians 6:17

I now have fourteen key passages from scripture upon which I have built my life. Some of you reading this may have a lot more than my fourteen and others may have far less. The number of scriptures isn't really important, you could build your life on just one scripture if it is right for you and means something to you. However, I believe that as you start to build on one scripture, God will lead you into more for you at specific times of your life, scriptures that will speak to you with a sincere relevance to the storm that you are facing.

If you are just starting out in your Christian walk, then start to keep a record of the scriptures that you want to build your life upon. If you are further on in your walk, then I urge you to start to think back over your life and to make a list of the scriptures that have carried you through the storms.

As an exercise, I ask that you consider three things about each of the verses that are precious to you:

1. When was it given? – What were you facing at the time?
2. Why was it given? – Consider this carefully, there could be many reasons.
3. What does it mean to you now? – The relevance never dies, it always grows stronger.

Consider writing these down with an eplanation of why they are part of your foundation.

I will now share with you my fourteen foundations for my life, with stories that are associated with them. I hope that this will encourage you to do the same. If you would like help to collate your foundation and write your stories, I would be more than willing to help you. I look forward to hearing from you. My contact details are at the back of this book.

My 1st Foundation

Therefore, if anyone is in Christ, he is a new creation. The old has passed away; behold, the new has come.
2 Corinthians 5:17

I invited Jesus into my life in 1986 and at my baptism, which happened within the first year, someone gave me a beautiful poster. It had a picture of a butterfly which had metamorphasised from a caterpillar. The scripture verse was in the corner and the poster was put on the wall where it could be seen every day. I still believe that this is one of the best ways to learn a scripture and to have it constantly building a foundation for your life.

Although, the best way for me to learn scripture, has been when it is presented in the form of a song.

I am a new creation,
No more in condemnation,
Here in the grace of God I stand.
My heart is over-flowing,
Your love just keeps on growing,
Here in the grace of God I stand.
Dave Bilborough

I was a new Christian, a baby Christian and with the newness came the excitement. I wanted to tell everyone that I met about the amazing love of God that I had discovered. It was like discovering a cure for cancer and wanting to share this newfound knowledge. It was like an overflow, I couldn't keep it in or like a bottle of Champagne, the fizz just wanted to come out. Another song would reinforce this feeling and stimulate my actions.

I get so excited Lord every time I realise,
I'm forgiven, I'm forgiven.
With the past behind grace for today
And hope to come
I'm forgiven, I'm forgiven.
Hallelujah Lord, my heart just fills with praise,
My feet start dancing and my hands rise up
And my lips just praise your name
I'm forgiven, I'm forgiven, I'm forgiven

.I later discovered that the way that I was feeling is referred to as my "first love." The way that I felt when I first became a Christian, the way that I behaved, the things that I said, it was like a new energy was in me and pouring out.

Paul in his letter to the Ephesians praised them and recognised that their first love was zeal and enthusiasm for their salvation. The Ephesian church was made alive together with Christ and realised that they loved Christ because He first loved them.

This was their "first love" and we could all learn so much from the way that the Ephesian church behaved. Yet we can later read in Revelation:

But I have this against you,
that you have abandoned the love you had at first.
Revelation 2:4

The Ephesian church was known for their good deeds, their hard work and their perseverance. They didn't tolerate wicked people and tested false prophets. They had an impressive track record, an outstanding reputation and incredible credibility. Yet they had lost their "first love".

How many well-meaning projects, organisations and charities do you know that have fallen into this trap? How many times have you said of yourself, that you have lost your "first love"?

Maybe you have never said that, but then maybe you have never realised.

I am a long way from my "first love", from the enthusiasm and excitement that bubbled over when I was a baby Christian. I cover up my lack of enthusiasm and excitement by saying that I am wiser and therefore more restrained, more in control.

Who am I kidding by believing that? My self, that's who. I have come to realise that control is nearly always associated with fear. The more that we fear something, the more we want to be in control. I know that this is the route of all bullying. All bullies are fearful of something and they bully people to take back control.

So, are we afraid of our "first love" and going back to the way that we were? We can never go back to exactly the way that we were and quite frankly it's probably best that we don't. However, to recapture some of the lost passion and stimulate it with a new fizz, we could all benefit from that.

There are great movements of people praying for the revival of God's Church across the land, but revival starts with one person at a time. That person is you. That person is me. We all need revival and the fizz of our first love.

I am reminded of that old joke - How many psychiatrists does it take to change a lightbulb? Answer - One, but the lightbulb needs to want to change.

Do you want to change?

If anyone is in Christ, he is a new creation. The old has passed away; behold, the new has come. If we really believe in this foundational scripture then we need to change and allow God to revive us. The church of Ephesus was told to repent and do the things that they did at first. If they didn't do this they would have their "lampstand removed" (Revelation 2:5). So, there are serious consequences if we fail to remember our "first love".

I am a new creation. I still believe that, and this first foundation is still so important to me, but I also realise that it takes time to make a new creation. It is important to remember that we:

"do not conform to the pattern of this world, but we must be transformed by the renewing of our minds"
(Romans 12:2).

I live next door to a Potter and recently had the privilege of filming her making a teapot. It was an incredibly long process, but it was so interesting to watch. The lump of clay was transformed, slowly, gently and carefully. This is how God moulds us and changes us, but we have to want to change and get back to our "first love".

We are the clay, you are the potter;
we are all the work of your hand.
Isaiah 64:8

My 2nd Foundation

Unless you change and become like a child,
you will never get into the kingdom of heaven.
Matthew 18:3

I can remember reading this verse for the first time and the words just jumped off the page. I felt that this verse was so important to me, but didn't have a poster this time, so I just scribbled it out on a scrap of paper and put it on my fireplace mantelpiece.

The one main thing that struck me when I first read this verse was that I wanted more than anything to "get into the kingdom of heaven".

The disciples had been arguing about whom they thought was the greatest in the kingdom of heaven, and then they asked Jesus for his opinion. He responded with this verse and called a child to him as an example.

He wasn't impressed by the way that the disciples were behaving and his response said, "none of you will get into the kingdom of heaven in your current state".

He told them that they needed to change. For many years I missed that important word as I memorised this verse as, "unless you become like a child....".

Now though I understand that the word "change" is the most important part of this verse. It is the same as the word "repentance", which means to turn from and change your mind. Jesus was telling them that they had to turn from worldly, carnal views and desires.

Jesus wasn't telling us to become childlike and do childish things. Paul in his letter to the church in Corinth affirms this when he wrote:

It's like this: when I was a child I spoke and thought and reasoned as a child does. But when I became a man my thoughts grew far beyond those of my childhood, and now I have put away the childish things.
1 Corinthians 13:11 (TLB)

So, what did Jesus mean when He said that we had to "become like a child"? I believe that Jesus was referring to the way that a child thinks. A child's mind is innocent. It is free from pride, covetousness, and selfish ambition. It is humble, sincere and disengaged from affection for a materialistic life.

Jesus was telling His disciples that they needed to transform their minds if they wanted to get into heaven.

Is it any coincidence that the first two scriptures that I was led to as a baby Christian involved the transformation of the mind? Our minds are vulnerable, they can be so easily influenced in the wrong way. I have met some people in my life who have had their minds so twisted that they have lost understanding of what is right and wrong. Some that I have met have lived a life of fantasy and lies and they have become so deeply engrained that the person now believes it is true.

No matter how "messed up" a person's mind may be, I

do believe that God can free us from the mind-sets that we can easily fall into.

Some will say that if you want something bad enough, then you will make it happen. Well, I do want to "enter the kingdom of heaven". I want it so much that I am open to the transformational power of God's Holy Spirit, as He gently changes me to become like a child.

My 3rd Foundation

The stone the builder had rejected
will become the Capstone.
1 Peter 2:7

If you have read my previous book "The Golden Thread", then you will already know how this scripture was given to me, but here is an abridged extract.

Becoming a Capstone
It wasn't long before we were attending mid-week small group meetings. These could be in the form of a Bible study, a short course, a prayer meeting or simply a social gathering.

This scripture was given to me at a prayer meeting, which was being held at Derek Morris's house. Derek said, "I have been praying and asked the Lord to give me a word for you."

He read out the scripture from 1 Peter.

I had previously had a short period in the building industry, but a fall from a roof had left me in fear. After the fall I took a sales job, which seemed to have fewer hazards and health risks. Now though, I had recently ventured back onto the building sites.

He knew nothing about my previous attempt to try to run a building business. He knew nothing about my fall (which also involved my first angel encounter) and he knew nothing of the fear that I had first experienced when I tried to climb back onto a roof. He didn't know that I had (or so it felt) been rejected, but God knew and he understood. This was God speaking directly to me through his word and channelled via Derek's obedience, sensitivity and discernment.

That word would also be fulfilled, as over the next two years my business would grow on the wave of the building boom which was now in place. I always say that God's timing is absolutely perfect and this was the perfect time for the construction industry. By 1988 I would be employing a team of twenty-seven men and managing projects over nine different sites.

God was now leading and guiding us on an amazing journey. That journey would see many signs and wonders. We would witness miracles and see prayers answered, but through all of this we would learn to trust God, grow in our relationship with him and be built up in faith.

I left the building industry after ten years as I followed God's call into youth work. It would be easy to say that this scripture was for then, for that period only, but that is not how it works with "Foundation for Life" scriptures. Foundations are what we build upon and they should never move. So, this scripture came with me into youth work.

I poured my life into the work at The Door Youth Project in Stroud and developed it for 23 years. In everything that I did and all that I achieved, I always gave God the glory, as it was Him working through me.

The whole project was under-pinned and soaked in prayer and I believe it was this that led to the success. We saw numerous prayers answered and even more so when the prayer was sacrificial, we had given up our own time and struggled out of bed at 6.00am in the dark, depths of winter. These prayers were like another layer of foundation.

So many people now saw me as the "capstone" of this project and I received several awards, which I suppose happens naturally. Although this work was developing supernaturally, it was built on a base of prayer and scripture, the most powerful foundation.

Of course when Peter wrote his letter to the scattered churches this verse had a completely different meaning. The builders that he referred to are:

> *The rulers of the Jews, both civil and ecclesiastical, and especially the latter, the Scribes, Pharisees, and chief priests; who set up for builders of the church of God, but were miserable ones; they built themselves, and taught others to build, on the observance of the ceremonial law, and the traditions of the elders; on their carnal privileges and moral righteousness; and these disallowed of Christ in the building, rejected him as the Messiah, refused him as the Saviour and Redeemer, and set him at nought, had him in the utmost derision, and reckoned him as a worm, and no man; but, to their great mortification, he is not only laid and retained as the foundation and cornerstone, but made the head of the building, and is exalted at God's right hand above angels and men; he is the head of the body, the church; he is higher than the kings of the earth, and angels are subject to him.*
> (John Gill's Exposition of The Bible)

The Bible is full of references that use building terminology to express a point. Paul wrote to Timothy and referred to the church as the pillar and foundation-stone of the truth (1 Timothy 3:15).

Again, writing to the church in Ephesus Paul describes Jesus as the "chief cornerstone". He explains that we are all being built together for a dwelling place of God in the Spirit (Ephesians 2:20-22).

Why is it that when we look around the World we can find areas where the church is in decline or plateaued and in other areas we see growth? We can see old churches dying, but we also find new churches being planted. As we become complacent we stop trying, we give up and we stop affecting the lives of others. This is why some churches die and others are given life.

It is time that we removed our complacency. We need to continue to build on what has gone before. For some of us that will mean returning to our "first love" and changing to "become like a child."

One American church denomination recently found that 80% of its converts came to Christ in churches less than two years old. I find this news both exciting and at the same time upsetting. It is exciting that so many lives are still being saved, but sad to think of so many churches that have lost the vision to grow.

During my time as a builder, God gave me a picture of a toolbox and He said that His kingdom is like this toolbox. That we are all the tools in His box. Some of us, He will use more often than others, but we all have a set purpose. A knife is used for cutting, but you wouldn't dream of using it to hammer a nail or tighten a screw.

Having said that, my toolbox, contained a very old, very large screwdriver with a large wooden handle. We jokingly referred to it as the "multi-tool". It was used for: levering lids off of paint pots, stirring paint, chiselling wood and sometimes stone, hammering things that needed hammering and of course screwing screws. It was an abused tool and my point is that we can all be at risk of being misused similarly.

We all have a purpose and a role to play within the church. For some that purpose, that calling will be clearer than others, but it is there. We all need to seek God for what he wants us to be. None of us should be everything to everyone. As much as we may feel more valued if we do more, we can't be like the "multi-tool", it will only lead to burnout.

So, asking God what He wants you to **BE** is more important than asking what He wants you to **DO**! We are all called to be "Human Beings" and not "Human Doings".

Some will also be called to become "capstones", but remember, every stone in the building is important. Your role is important.

My 4th Foundation

Whatever your hand finds to do,
do it with all of your might.
Ecclesiastes 9:10a

I spent ten years of my life working as a builder and it was as I was finishing a job on my friend John's house, that he gave me a small card with this verse on it. I used that card for many years as a bookmark or carried it in my wallet, applying those words in every area of my life.

I spent twenty-five years of my life writing and performing rap music in local schools. It seemed quite easy when I was twenty-six years old, but as I hit my forties and on into my fifties it was more of a struggle. There were times when I would dread going on stage for an assembly in front of 300 young people, so I learnt to do two things.

Before an assembly, I would lie on the stage with my eyes closed and imagine how I felt after the event. I always felt excited, energised and full of joy, it was a real buzz. I would also meditate on this verse. A car can't run without fuel and this verse was like fuel in my tank. It boosted my spirit.
As I previously mentioned I was at The Door Youth Project for 23 years. In my final year, some people from a local youth club came to visit the project. They were interested in how we could help them and happened to mention that they would like me to work with them, to save their struggling youth club.

One of my team informed them that I hadn't been involved in frontline youth work for over five years. The implication was that I was past it. The statement was also false it had only been three years.

It is easy for all of us to make throw-away statements, but these words can often be so damaging. I started to question my ability as a youth worker, could I ever go back to working hands-on with young people? How can one simple negative statement cause so much doubt?

The fact is that words are powerful and when negative words are spoken about you or over you, they impact you deeply in a negative way.

When Jesus was tempted by Satan in the wilderness, He used the words of scripture to fight back. We need to remember this and do the same.

So, when I left The Door Youth Project, I went to work for that struggling youth club. At first, I had a developmental role, but as new funding started to pour in and a youth worker was needed to drive the delivery work, I stepped into that role.

I remembered this foundation verse of mine, "whatever your hand finds to do, do it with all of your might." I became a frontline youth worker again and realised that I wasn't past it. The result was that I saved that youth club from closure.

Sometimes we don't need other people to say negative things over us to put doubts in our minds about our abilities; we can also do it ourselves.

As we become older it becomes easier to doubt yourself. It is also made even easier if there are medical conditions that may start to hinder you.

If you have read my biography book, The Golden Thread, you will know that I was diagnosed with polycystic kidney disease in 2008. Now ten years later my condition has worsened. I am now in end-stage kidney failure, on dialysis and have been waiting for a transplant for over two and a half years. As a result, my energy levels are low and I can often feel quite unwell. I can also struggle to remember the words that I want to say, as "renal fog" takes hold of my brain.

So it would be easy to look at this foundational verse, especially the part that says "Do it with all of your might" and say "I don't have any might left".

Hopefully, you have read the story behind my writing and this book, at the start of this book. If you missed it go back and read it now.

The lady that had prayed for me at Naturally Supernatural was reassured and I had felt so blessed and ready to use the tools and skills that I had with **all of the might** that I had left.

Three things have happened since returning from Naturally Supernatural. The first was when a mother approached me in a church that I was visiting. She knew me and told me that her son would like a mentor, a Christian male role model to help direct him. I jumped at this opportunity without hesitation and it made me feel valued.

Secondly, a local school had recently lost the person that was leading their Christian Union and I was asked if I would like to be part of a new team that was being put together to continue this work. Again I instantly jumped at this opportunity. It had been ten years since I had been involved in a similar lunchtime club in another school, but it felt great knowing that God could still use me.

The third thing was being asked to "preach" in church. It had been over two years since I had previously brought the word in any church and I wasn't feeling very confident, instantly found myself saying "yes". I had tools and skills and that would be enough to ensure that I could do this with **all of my might**.

I also started to write this book, to share how my life had been underpinned by so many powerful scriptures. Recognising these fourteen scriptures was only the start, the most important thing is to share what we have learnt and to be prepared to wear the Gospel shoes with the readiness to speak out about the good news and witness to the world what God has done for us, with us and through us.

Whatever your hand finds to do, do it with all of your might:

- Whatever you have the opportunity and ability to do, do it.
- Whatever is the duty of your calling, do it.
- Whatever you do, do it for the glory of God.
- Whatever you do, do it for the good of mankind.
- Whatever you are doing, whether it work or play, do it with all of your might.

Our might can come in many forms, but here are just a few that spring to mind:

- Unwearied diligence
- Vigour
- Enthusiasm
- Energy
- Power
- Strength
- Wisdom
- Love

My 5th Foundation

Commit your plans to The Lord
and they will succeed.
Proverbs 16:3

This is my third and final foundational scripture related to my time as a builder. Somebody gave me a poster with a cartoon man scratching his head looking at The Leaning Tower of Pisa. It had this verse on it. At that time I was just starting as a builder again and I suppose the person who gave me the poster wanted to make sure that I committed everything that I was embarking on to God.

I prayed this into everything that I did, but I also used it in a daily practical way. Proverbs 16 3 became my password for when I visited the local petrol station. Every time that I filled my tank on my business account I told the cashier "Proverbs 16 3".

I ran that business for ten years and when I moved from building into youth work, this scripture was used at The Door Youth Project as a password for many things. It was used for the whole of the 23 years that I was there. I'm pretty sure that they would have changed it by now though.

The foundations of The Leaning Tower of Pisa were not adequate, which is why it leans. As Christians, we need to build our lives on an adequate firm foundation and the only thing that is good enough is scripture.

The scriptures that you choose need to be relevant to your life. You can't build your life on my foundation. Some of my scriptures may be relevant to you and if that is the case that is fine, but you need to build for your life.

Try writing out each of your foundational scriptures and what they mean to you.

When we look at all of the things that we have to do in life, we can often feel that it is all just too much. It's not surprising is it that 25% of people on the planet today suffer from some form of mental illness, mainly depression and anxiety.

The "commit your plans" part of this verse translates as "roll your burdens onto me". So we don't have to struggle with all of our burdens, God is prepared to carry them. Then no matter what it is that we are doing we must depend upon God's providence and grace for assistance and success.

Of course, the plans that we make for our lives also need to be the plans that God has for us. This verse could very easily become abused and used like a wishing well, but that is not how it works.

We can't just say that we want to be successful, drive a Mercedes Benz, wear a gold Rolex watch and dress in the finest tailored clothes. No, we are all different and success for one person will look different to success for someone else.

We need to all be constantly looking to where God is leading us and not telling Him where we want to go. This takes patience as many of us want something immediately, but we also grow through waiting.

I try to commit all of my plans to The Lord. I try and fail, but at least I try. I'd rather die trying and sometimes failing, than never trying and therefore always failing.

My 6th Foundation

Your old men will dream dreams,
your young men will see visions.
Joel 2:28b

This scripture is so true, when I was younger in my late 20s through to my 40's I had amazing visions. God would give me pictures of how something would look or a way to meet an identified need. Now though in my late 50s, I can have some incredible dreams.

I first read this verse when I was about 29 years old and soon afterwards received the vision for The Door Youth Project. It is amazing when two people have the same vision and Andy Morris had the exact same vision.

Extract from The Golden Thread:
Twenty-six Gloucester Street had recently become vacant and the two of us found it impossible to drive past without seeing the building overflowing with young people. This was not just an idea, more than just imagination running wild, this was a physical picture of what this place was going to become. Not what it could be, but what it would be! The two of us talked about this shared 'vision' that God had given us both. We agreed that this was going to be the place where someone would set up a coffee bar for young people. It would be fifteen months before we realised that God was speaking to us and eighteen months before we actually did anything.

Looking at our situation now I think that we were a little like Jonah. God spoke to Jonah and told him to go to Ninevah, but he went in exactly the opposite direction. Similarly, we did nothing about it, we just talked!

I now know that when God gives us a vision we need to cast that vision out. We can't keep it to ourselves if we want people to catch the vision.

I often play catch the ball with my grandchildren and at 3 years old they struggle, but every so often they succeed and their face lights up. Obviously, as they become older they find the task a lot easier.

Casting a vision is not so easy. It can often fall on deaf ears. People become complacent with situations and will often have an attitude of, "It's a good idea, but it's not for me". Just like my grandchildren learning to catch the ball, Christians NEED to learn to catch visions. It doesn't seem to come naturally, but it will come supernaturally.

When we start to cast our visions in God's supernatural power, then we will see a supernatural catching of the vision.

Where there is no vision, the people perish.
Proverbs 29:18

Now I would like to share with you the most amazing dream that I have ever had, it happened on the night of ***30th January 2016.***

Earlier that evening I had been in a prayer meeting where someone asked God to speak to us in our dreams. On the way home in the car I mentioned to Heather, my wife that I can sometimes become a little concerned about the future, especially regarding things such as work, health and church. This is anxiety. That night I had a dream, but it didn't feel like a dream, it felt real.

In the dream, I was at my mum's funeral, although it wasn't as her funeral was. Someone was singing and people were finding it so emotional, some people were leaving the building, as they found it all too distressing. This was representative of a time in my life when I had thought to myself, "What happens now? What is the future?" It had been 14 months since I left The Door Youth Project, I was just about to be placed on the kidney transplant list and I would be starting dialysis later this year, so it was a very difficult time in my life.

In my dream, I sensed a presence to my side and I turned to see who it was. I was somewhat surprised to see my dad standing there, as he had been dead for 23 years. He was wearing a Gabardine Mack and a flat cap. He spoke to me saying, "Don't worry, everything is going to be all right."

I replied to him by saying, "I love you dad." I had never told him that when he was alive and have always regretted not doing so.

He responded to me by saying, "You little Tinker." I was surprised to hear this, as I then remembered that it was something that my dad used to call me when I was about 5 or 6 years old.

Then I woke up and ran down the hill to tell my brother Chris. He was excited to hear what I had to tell him.

Then I woke up again, I had had a dream within a dream. I hadn't actually told my brother, but I did go to see him later that day and told him all about it.

I do believe that this was God in my dream, telling me that everything was going to be all right. He appeared as my dad and was so real.

I will finish this section with this entry from my prayer journal:

13/02/16

Yesterday I was praying and chatting to God (as you do) and he was chatting back (as he does). Now, I am predominantly a visual learner and God knows that, so he will often speak to me in pictures. Yesterday he gave me two very brief, but amazing pictures. These were for me, but I also feel that they could be for others out there.

So, here's the first picture. I saw a person drowning and they were thrashing around, panicking, struggling to keep their head above water. A swimmer approached (maybe a lifeguard) and was attempting to rescue them. The lifeguard said, "Stop struggling, relax, let me save you." Just in case you hadn't realised, God is our lifeguard.

The next picture was one of an Orchestra and the members were all blindfolded. None of them could therefore, follow the Conductor and the music sounded terrible. God said, "I am the Conductor, keep your eyes fixed on me and together you will make a beautiful sound."

If these pictures relate to your situation in life, I pray that God will scoop you up out of the depths that you are sinking into and that he will open your eyes to the journey that he has planned for you.

My 7th Foundation

I can do all things through
Christ who strengthens me.
Philippians 4:13

In January 1992 I felt God was calling me into full-time youth work and to live by faith (no income), but it wouldn't last.

Extract from The Golden Thread:
After just six months of living by faith and dealing with some of the most serious and unexpected issues that you could imagine, I couldn't handle any more. At the time there was a saying that the average life span for a Christian youth worker was about two years. On average burnout would hit and you could cope no more. I like to think that things have changed since then and that youth workers who are employed in Christian settings are now properly managed, resourced and supported.

It's easy for me to look back now and realise that there was another reason why I was on the edge of burnout. I had worked by faith, but I had also carried out all of my youth work duties and beyond, in my own strength!

For now, I felt that God was saying, "You have done enough." He was calling me back out of working for him, living by faith. Six months after standing up in front of the church and telling everyone that God was "calling me", now I was telling them, "God is calling me back out." They had understood when I told them that God had called me, but now many of them struggled to understand why I should be called back from where he had led me.

So, I couldn't survive any longer than 6 months on my

own strength, but three and a half years later, in January 1996 it was a different story.

The Door had now been open for five years and it was felt by the trustees that it was time to employ somebody to drive the work forwards.

Extract from The Golden Thread:
I was asked if I was willing to take that step of faith and I accepted in a flash. Then after that flash came the doubts, the hesitations and then the "what ifs?" Doubt is the enemy's way of chipping away at faith. I have seen it happen in many projects where doubt has crept in, chipped away and eventually blown faith out of the water. Did I have the faith? I had been called before, my 'taster calling'. Looking back now, it was as if God said, "The previous time was your audition, you were good, but you needed a little more time. Now is the time, this is your 'CALL BACK'."

I asked, "What can I do this time that will help me? How can I be better?"

God reminded me, "Don't do things in your own strength and trust in me. Yes my Word says that you can do all things, but it doesn't say that you WILL do all things.

With this new-found knowledge I started to work differently. Looking back now I think that my first attempt to move into youth work was all about me. I can admit that now, now that I realise that we all have to make ourselves vulnerable at times and that starts by admitting our vulnerability. We all have vulnerabilities and we all need to understand them and admit we have them. I couldn't make it all about me, God had to be in the centre of EVERYTHING that I was doing. I now knew that unless I invited God in and worked in His strength and not my own, I would not see any success.

So, once again I committed my plans to The Lord, knowing that it was the only way to succeed.

*****

We know that Paul suffered so much more than many of us ever will have to and yet he remained strong in Christ.

From Barnes' notes on the Bible:
Let us remember these points –

1) That we need not sink under any trial, for there is one who can strengthen us.

(2) That we need not yield to temptation. There is one who is able to make a way for our escape.

(3) That we need not be harassed, vexed, and tortured with improper thoughts and unholy desires. There is one who can enable us to banish such thoughts from the mind and restore the right balance to the affections of the soul.

(4) That we need not dread what is to come. Trials, temptations, poverty, want, persecution, may await us; but we need not sink into despondency. At every step of life, Christ is able to strengthen us, and can bring us triumphantly through. What a privilege it is, therefore, to be a Christian - to feel, in the trials of life, that we have one friend, unchanging and most mighty, who can always help us! How cheerfully should we engage in our duties, and meet the trials that are before us, leaning on the arm of our Almighty Redeemer! Let us not shrink from duty; let us not dread persecution let us not fear the bed of death. In all circumstances, Christ, our unchanging Friend, can uphold us. Let the eye and the affections of the heart be fixed on him; let the simple, fervent, believing prayer be directed always to him when trials come, when temptations assail, when duty presses hard upon us, and

when a crowd of unholy and forbidden thoughts rush into the soul: and we shall be safe.

My 8th Foundation

The joy of The Lord is my strength
Nehemiah 8:10b

Once I knew and fully understood that I had to do EVERYTHING in God's strength, I wanted to know how to find that strength. I was led to this verse and realised that if I want strength from God, then I need to be full of his joy.

I prayed this verse into my life and though there have been times when I have struggled with depression, I still generally have a joyous disposition.

The work at The Door was at times extremely challenging and I believe that it was the combination of all of my foundational scriptures that carried me through.

We were always looking for money to run the project and on one occasion things were so bad that we couldn't pay everyone's wages. I went without money for a few weeks, knowing that God would provide and He did, He always did.

It was a real joy to be doing God's work and most of the time I like to think that that joy was infectious. When we acknowledge God and allow His joy to fill us, it flows out of us and impacts all of those that we meet in our daily lives.

I did however find that the joy of The Lord landed me in trouble a few times. I found that at times of hearing someone's bad news, I would still be smiling with joy. The person that was telling me their news would ask why I am smiling. I had to learn to change my facial expression, to use a kind of poker-face, but the joy was still there.

I am sure that it was this over-flowing joy that people saw in me that intrigued people. I like to think that they could see Jesus in me and there were a few times when people actually said that to me.

Once again we can take a look at the Apostle Paul as an example. Regardless of all the hardships that he endured he always remained joyful.

Rejoice in the Lord always: and again I say, Rejoice
Philippians 4:4

My 9th Foundation

And my God will supply every need of yours according to his riches in glory in Christ Jesus.
Philippians 4:19

Yet another scripture, from this wonderful letter of Paul's to the Philippian church.

I can't remember when I first started using this scripture as a foundation, but I do know that it has been many years. We used to sing a song:

Jehovah Jireh
My provider
His grace is sufficient
For me, for me, for me
Jehovah Jireh
My provider
His grace is sufficient
For me
My God shall supply all my needs
According to His riches in glory
He will give His angels
Charge over me
Jehovah Jireh cares for me, for me, for me.
Jehovah Jireh cares for me.

It is important to remember that this verse says that God will provide all of our needs, not our wants. I have met people throughout my life that for various reasons are confused over what God should provide for us.

Somebody could say that they need a four bedroom house, but they only have two children and therefore only need three bedrooms, the forth one is a want.

The needs that God has provided for me have taken many forms, financial, practical, hands on help and even the miraculous. When I worked for six months by faith, with no wages, God provided. Running a charity for 23 years with most of the time no more than three months funding ahead, but God provided. He used people to step in and provide funds, He spoke, they obeyed and we received. We were blessed.

I could share many stories that highlight how God supplies all of our needs, but I will share just a few. The first comes from a time in my life when I was a young Christian and God had led us to build a house. I had to focus a lot of my time on this project and as a result was unable to attend church.

Extract from The Golden Thread:
At the start of 1987, my friendship with Andy Morris had developed and I was now helping him with youth work in the church. He had asked for anyone to help him and I just felt that it was right to offer a hand.

Andy was a practical, helpful friend and he knew just what he had to do, as he came to see me. My lack of attendance at the church meant that I hadn't been able to help him for a while, but he didn't judge me for not being there. "What can I do to help you? Give me a job! I'm here to help!"

I hadn't even asked him for help but he just knew that I needed it. He helped me to clean up the foundation trenches, wheeling wheelbarrows and shovelling. He was the only one of my new found Christian 'friends' that turned up to help me. I have always had a bit of a problem with asking for help, but they all knew what I was doing. I also have the attitude that a good volunteer is worth ten 'pressed men' and Andy worked hard. We were a team! He gave me a few days of help, which in the scale of the project, didn't sound like much, but it was enough. It was practical and it said, "I understand."

God used Andy to provide me with the help that I needed to drive the work forward.

There have also been a couple of times in my life when I didn't have a car or the means to buy one. I needed a car and on both occasions God spoke to people telling them to give me a car. Both of these cars were amazing blessings, though they needed money to maintain and keep on the road, but God provided that.

Extract from The Golden Thread:
This car was a real blessing, however it wasn't long before we needed to replace the exhaust pipe which had almost broken in half and sounded like a tractor. In a short space of time we would be unable to drive it. We told nobody of this specific need, we had already been given so much, but I did enquire how much a new exhaust pipe would cost. I was told that it would be £76.32 and realised that this was money that we didn't have! Most of what we were being given as gifts was being used to pay off debts and the mortgage, with any left being used for basic foods.

I decided to just pray and ask God to help. I told him that without the car it would be hard to work. I was living in faith and in faith I knew that God would listen and step in, if it truly was a need. So I asked him to provide the money for the exhaust and then went to bed.

The next morning an envelope was lying on the front door mat. Someone had obviously delivered it in the night. When I opened it and counted how much we had been blessed with, I was amazed to see that it was £76.32 the exact amount that was needed for the exhaust pipe, not a penny more, not a penny less! We hadn't told anyone about this need, but obviously God had and we were so grateful to once again have transport.

When we needed £60,000 to buy the building that The Door Youth Project was operating from, we started an appeal and half of the money was dropped through our letter box in just one anonymous banker's draft. That was an incredible answer to prayer, but I believe that the story I am about to tell you is even more incredible.

One day a girl came to me and told me that she wanted to do a sponsored slim in aid of The Door. I gave her some information leaflets so that she could tell people about the charity. She went home and showed the leaflets to her mum.

Her mum was impressed with what we were doing and especially how we had supported her daughter, so she took the leaflets to work. She worked for the local branch of Provident UK who were in the process of looking for charities that they could support.

We had recently launched our mentoring service for young people and one of the leaflets that they were now reading was telling them all about it. They could see the potential in this fledgling service and wanted to help with a financial donation.

I was surprised to receive a call from the Regional Manager, Ian, who wanted to visit us. I was always glad to show people around, to let people see the passion in me for the work that we were doing.

I had no idea what would happen at this meeting, I had shown so many people around the project and they all kind of went the same way, lots of smiles and affirmation that we were doing a good job, and then people would leave with, "Keep up the good work" type of comment."

This meeting was following the same path as all previous meetings until we came to the end of the tour and we sat in one of the small meeting rooms. Ian told me that he would like to support our mentoring service and gave me £5,000. It was just what we had needed at the time and I was reminded that God provides all of our needs.

Of course I was very happy, but that wasn't the end of God's provision through the generosity of Provident UK. Ian would regularly call in with donations of things like tea, coffee and biscuits to keep our staff happy. Then after three months he called to tell me that some of the "top brass" wanted to visit the project. They were travelling all the way down from Bradford in Yorkshire.

Ian told me that they wanted to know how we had used the £5,000 and what difference it had made. He also told me to show them what we could do with even more money.

So I prepared for the meeting with an easy to follow power point presentation. They were impressed with the professionalism of the organisation and how we could demonstrate what their money had achieved. They were even more impressed when I showed them what we could achieve with a further £27,000.

They became the main financial supporter of our mentoring service and soon increased their support to £30,000 per year. We launched the mentoring service in 2006 and in 2014 when I left The Door Provident had given over £240,000.

We hadn't specifically prayed for this, but we had prayed a lot generally that God would provide all of our needs.

There have been moments (very small moments) in my life lately when it has felt that God has abandoned me, but I know that he hasn't. When I have those moments of doubt I can look back at my life and the way that He has provided and I know that He will never give up on me. I know that He will continue to provide all of what I need and if there is something that I am not given, then that is something that I don't need yet.

My 10th Foundation

For God hath not given us the spirit of fear; but of power, and of love, and of a sound mind.
2 Timothy 1:7

This is another scripture that I just picked up on my journey through life. Remembering it was made easy once again by a song:

God has not given us a spirit of fear,
But of love, power and a sound mind.
God has not given us a spirit of fear,
But of love, power and a sound mind.
Love for one another,
Power to overcome,
Overcome the enemy WHOO!

Throughout my life I have faced fear several times, as I am sure that we all have. There are different levels of fear and I believe that we all need fear in our lives to a degree. Fear keeps us inside boundaries. I used to climb a lot of mountains and it was good to have a little fear inside to keep you safe. That type of fear gives you an awareness.

Can you imagine what the World would be like if there was no fear in it? People would continuously put themselves into serious danger and many people would doubtlessly be killed.

The Bible tells us to "fear God".
Fear God and keep His commandments, for this is the duty of all mankind.
Ecclesiastes 12:13

This is a different kind of fear. We fear God in awe and reverence, but we shouldn't have a spirit of fear.

A spirit of fear is all consuming. A good example of this is a person who suffers from agoraphobia. They are afraid to leave the confines of their own home, afraid of wide open spaces. In effect they become prisoners, trapped in and by their fear. Their fear is very real and extremely over-whelming.

Perhaps the polar opposite to agoraphobia is claustrophobia, the fear of enclosed spaces. Again the person that suffers with this condition is a prisoner. They may feel though, that because they are ok in wide open spaces they are free, but they are not free in the mind.

I believe that when we come under spiritual attack it is the mind that becomes the target. As I mentioned earlier when talking about my 1st Foundation scripture;
"do not conform to the pattern of this world, but we must be transformed by the renewing of our minds"
(Romans 12:2).

If God wants to transform us by renewing our minds it stands to reason to Satan will want to destroy our minds and fill us with a fear that completely controls us. That is not what God does when we are called to fear Him, he doesn't control us He gives us our free-will and allows us to make choices.

In order to combat the over-whelming fear of a spiritual sense we need to put on the full armour of God as Paul mentions in Ephesians 6:14-17.

He first mentions the belt of truth, which highlights that all that we say and do should be true, honest and with integrity. From the word true we have the word trust and if we behave truthfully, then people will trust us.

The breastplate is there to protect our hearts, which from a purely anatomical point of view keeps the blood circulating in our bodies and therefore keeps us alive. However, in a more poetic sense our hearts are what allow us to care about others. Without the breastplate of God our hearts can become hardened and desensitised.

Next comes the Gospel shoes. I have already previously mentioned these in my 4th foundation of scripture. We all need to wear the shoes, be prepared to speak out the truth of the Gospel in love.

We need to carry the shield of faith and understand how to step out in faith. A wooden shield would be soaked with water before battle, so that it can easily extinguish the flaming arrows of the enemy. A good shield can also interlock to form a wall and as Christians we need to learn to stand together, that way we are stronger. So why do we see so much division and disunity within the church?

The sword of the spirit, which is the word of God, can be used for defence and attack. There is power in the name of Jesus, at his name demons will flee. That's just at the use of His name, so imagine the force contained in an entire scripture passage that contains His name.

Finally, the helmet of salvation protects your mind and I have already mentioned how important it is to protect our minds. This is where we can allow a spirit of fear to creep in, but it is also where we can tell it to go in the name of Jesus.

*****

A study asked a number of teenagers what they feared the most and their most frequent answer was “the future”. Perhaps the reason being is the fact that the future is unknown for most of us and as a teenager the road to the future is a long one or at least we would perhaps like to think that it is.

Many of us live with a fear of the unknown. We are afraid to step out of our comfort zone into the unknown.

Surely the younger a person is then the more unknown exists for them to step into. Though we all have some form of unknown that we need to step into.

I have spent most of my life helping and enabling young people to step into their unknown. At times I have been scared and had to step into my own unknown areas, to push myself, but I have done so without a spirit of fear. I have stepped into my future with power, love and a sound mind.

My 11th Foundation

I came that they may have life
and have it abundantly.
John 10:10b

When I first of all read this as a young Christian and being slightly influenced by the "prosperity gospel", I thought that this verse meant that God would bless us with materialistic wealth.

Don't get me wrong, I still do believe that God can bless us with the things that we need for a comfortable life, but we shouldn't worship those things. We shouldn't allow those worldly things to come between us and God.

In the book of Job, we can read that he lost nearly everything, his health, wealth and family, but he still stayed focused on and worshipped God.

In August 1993 I too felt a little like Job, I felt as if I was losing everything, but actually I gained more than I was losing.

Extract from The Golden Thread:
Five months later we eventually found a buyer for our house. They had negotiated us down considerably in price, but at least we could now pay off our debts and start again. It took a few weeks for all of the legal bits and pieces to be done and we were set to move out in August 1993.

We now had to find somewhere to move to, but couldn't find anything. To make matters even worse, we had now become so far behind with our mortgage payments, that the building society told us that we were too high a risk. We would not be offered another mortgage. We therefore had no alternative but to move into rented accommodation; it was as if God was teaching me some new lessons.

I had always looked down on the thought of renting property. My parents had brought me up with the understanding that it is better to have a mortgage and buy a house, rather than live in someone else's and have nothing to show for the money that is spent. Now, moving into rented accommodation was my first lesson in humbling. I had also personally never wanted to buy a house on the new housing estate which had been built near to us. In my head I would think, "That is where all of the losers end up!" Little did I know that after eight months of living in rented, I would also end up on the Manor Village housing estate. My opinion has now been well and truly changed!

It was the day of moving into the rented house and I was the last person to leave Zion House, the house that God had led me to build. The rest of the family had left just half an hour before and I had just thrown the last few final items into the back of my clapped out old pickup (another humbling experience to drive this).

Now I felt angry with God. He had led us to Zion House and we were losing everything or so it felt. As I sat in the pickup I was shouting out loud with anger, rage was taking over and I didn't care if the neighbours heard me. "GOD WHY HAS THIS HAPPENED? You tell us in The Bible that if we turn to you we will have life in ABUNDANCE (John10:10). ***I DON'T CALL THIS ABUNDANT! I'VE LOST EVERYTHING!"***

I kept shouting as I pulled out of the drive and heading down the hill I continued, with the rage building. The journey was only about two minutes drive and I felt like I was going to explode, but as I arrived at my destination I felt a calming peace touch me. God spoke into my heart and said, "You do have life in abundance, if you have Jesus in you he is the abundance, everything else is insignificant. You do have life in

ABUNDANCE!"

My view changed instantly as if a download had just been placed straight into my head and my heart. I had been thinking materialistically all of this time, now I had had my eyes opened. I had lost nearly all of my material wealth in order to allow me to have a new outlook and to enable me to value that which cannot be seen more than that which is seen.

Now in 2018, some 25 years later, I can look back at my life and see that I have been so blessed.

I am not rich, though I do have some money in the bank. I am not the healthiest of people, as I have already mentioned in my 4th Foundation, I have polycystic kidney disease, but at least I am alive. I don't have many really close friends, but the ones that I do have would do anything for me, most of all I know that they pray for me.

I have been blessed with three children who have given me four amazing grand-children. These four are such a blessing, more than money, more than possessions, more than everything else.

None of this though is abundance, when I die I can take none of it with me into eternity. Only Jesus can provide true abundance and when I die I will become even more abundant in him, for all eternity.

Of course our earthly possessions can bring us an element of happiness, but it doesn't last. I believe that inside each one of us is a God shaped vacuum. We can spend our entire lives trying various things to fill that void, maybe drugs, alcohol, fast cars, lavish holidays, incredible experiences, the list is endless. There is though only one thing that fits perfectly into that God shaped vacuum... God.

If you have managed to read this book this far, then maybe, just maybe you can identify a little with what I am saying?

If you don't know Jesus and you want to get to know him, there is no time like the present. Just invite Him into your life, say sorry for the way that you have been and turn away from sin in your life. Don't forget to say thank you. You may be giving up your old life and your old ways, but you are about to have an abundant life.

If you already call yourself a Christian, but you can relate to what I am saying, then say the same prayer. He came that you may have life and have it abundantly.

My 12th Foundation

I press on toward the goal for the prize of the upward call of God in Christ Jesus.
Philippians 3:14

In 2001 I climbed Mount Kilimanjaro, the tallest free-standing mountain in the world.

I had known this verse from Philippians for a number of years and once again had learnt it with the help of a song.

I'm gonna fight the fight,
Gonna run the race,
Gonna press on towards the Goal.
I'm gonna fight the fight,
Gonna run the race,
Gonna press on towards the Goal
For I will take hold of that for which
The Lord took hold of me.

Kilimanjaro is the tallest free standing mountain in the World, so it is no mean feat. It is an active volcano and its tallest peak, Uhuru stands at 5,896M (19,343ft) above sea level.

At that altitude there is very little oxygen, which means your muscles have to work a lot harder. People have likened it to walking through treacle, every single step takes great physical and mental effort. Plus of course there is also the added risk of altitude sickness.

The final assent to the summit starts at mid-night in the freezing cold and pitch black darkness. After several hours of a very slow and relentless climb the route becomes steeper. The scree slope starts several hundred metres below the volcano crater and it is the most difficult scree slope that I have ever climbed. It is deep and full of volcanic ash.

Every step was so hard and made even harder by the fact that your foot would just slide back more or less to where it started. This was such a mental challenge and it was this song, this verse that kept me going. I meditated on it and used it like a mantra, repeating it over and over.

Since climbing Kilimanjaro I have used this mantra at times when I have been faced with extreme challenges.

It's been a while since I climbed a physical mountain, but starting dialysis is a huge mental mountain. In my early days on dialysis I had to undergo a great deal of physical pain and this verse helped me to press on through.

*****

Of course the prize that Paul is referring to here is the prize that awaits us in Heaven. Despite all of the struggles, persecution and prison that Paul faced, he never lost sight of the goal.

At times when we are faced with life's struggles it is so easy to just give in and say that we have had enough. I have been in that place so many times that I have lost count. I have wanted to give up, that means give up life, but I have kept going.

This verse and the other foundations that I have kept me on track they kept me going and kept me sane.

Nobody ever said that life was going to be easy, but with the right foundation, it is made a little easier and all together more bearable.

Do you not know that in a race all the runners run, but only one gets the prize? Run in such a way as to get the prize.
1 Corinthians 9:24

The way of life is above to the wise, that he may depart from hell beneath.
Proverbs 15:24

I recently had a conversation with a group of young people based around the question, "why do we exist"?

They had some interesting points that included doing good things and looking after the planet that we are on.

I shared with them that I believe we all exist to have a relationship with God and to worship Him. This of course is true, but there is even more to it than that? We exist to press on towards the heavenly goal.

Life is full of choices and every choice that we make can have an impact on how we run the race. If we choose to lie about something, that will affect use. Likewise if we choose to care about something, that will also make a difference.

However you choose to run your race, make sure that you never lose sight of the goal which is heaven.

My 13th Foundation

But God will never forget the needy, the hope of the afflicted will never perish.
Psalm 9:18

My Kilimanjaro verse became a foundation in 2001 and this next verse didn't come along until 2018.

Between my 12th and 13th foundational scriptures there was a 17 year period where I didn't have any new scriptures to build my life upon. It would be easy to jump to conclusions and say that God had given up on me or that I had given up on Him, but that wasn't the case.

My first twelve verses were given to me between 1986 and 2001. Over a period of 15 years, I had on average a verse every 15 months. So why was there a 17 year gap with nothing?

Quite simply I had all that I needed, after all how many foundational verses do you have? How many people do you know with any foundational verses that they stand on, let alone have 12 of them?

I used those first 12 verses often on a daily basis. I interweaved them in my mind along with other supporting verses, as I have done so throughout this book. The combination of these initial 12 had provided me with the foundation that I needed for the season that I was in.

In January 2016 I feel that I started to fall into a new season. You will recall the story that I told earlier of my dad appearing in a dream. I believe that this was the start of the new season and although I already had 12 foundational scriptures, God knew that I needed reassurance, so He appeared as my dad in my dream.

When I had left The Door in November 2014 and had been given a 12 month contract to go to work for Frith Youth Centre. It was such a blessing to be able to help them, as this was the youth club that I had gone to more than any other when I was a teenager. When I was 16 years old I was the Chairman of the Junior Committee, so it was a real joy to go back and help save it from closure. My contract with Frith though had now recently ended, so there was uncertainty.

I also knew that my kidney disease would only continue to deteriorate. I was due to attend the Churchill Transplant Hospital in Oxford and it was imminent to that I was about to be put on the waiting list for a kidney transplant.

In additional all of this uncertainty of what the future held, my Consultant had already told me that I had just over six months before I would need dialysis in order to stay alive.

Now this may sound a little over dramatic, but it is true, dialysis does keep people alive.

Waiting for a kidney transplant is not easy, you never know when the phone is likely to ring. When the call does eventually come I am likely to only have four hours in which I have to make my way to Oxford. This impacts on every area of your life.

If I go away on holiday, I have to be close enough to Oxford, so foreign holidays are out of the question. I can't do work that would take me too far away. Not that I now have much energy for work, but I try to do what I can do. The lack of energy can often be difficult to handle, as I was once so active. It is so easy to fall into the guilt trap and start to condemn yourself.

Eventually most people that are on the waiting list can start to struggle mentally and I was no exception. Despite having my foundational scriptures, despite the dream where God appeared as my dad, despite the great support of my church family, it eventually became too much.

I found myself crying, especially at night when I had to attach myself to my dialysis machine. I would often cry myself to sleep, lying in the dark, with uncontrollable tears soaking into my pillow. When you are attached to a machine you in effect become a prisoner in your own bedroom. Now though as I cried myself to sleep, I looked forward to being asleep, as it was the only time that I could escape the anxiety caused by the waiting.

Eventually I started having "dark thoughts". Every night when I was preparing to connect to the machine I would pray that the phone would ring (most transplant calls come in the night). My first dark thought was, "I am actually praying for someone to die, so that I could have one of their kidneys. I discussed this with one of the renal nurses and they told me that people die all of the time, but they did notice that I was struggling mentally and told me that they would refer me to the Clinical Psychologist.

My dark thoughts changed into, "what happens if one of my daughters had to die?" Both of them had been checked for this horrible disease and they were clear. This was a whole new level of anxiety and the crying into my pillow increased with it. It wasn't long before the darkness started to absorb me and I started to think that I would be better off dead and that my family would be better off if I were dead.

I visited my GP in the summer of 2017 and explained the way that I was feeling. She prescribed Prozac. At first these started to take the edge off of how I was feeling, but after a few weeks I was having strange side effects. It felt like I was in someone else's body so I told my GP. She changed me onto Mirtazapine and they seemed to work better, though they only took the edge off.

I still had dark thoughts and still had thoughts of wanting to die. Eventually I started to visit the Clinical Psychologist and she helped me to see things in a more positive way. I worked with her for about three months. I learnt to harness my new positive thinking into creative thinking.

Many therapists will use creative techniques as a way of refocussing the brain and switching off from the trauma. In November 2017 I started to make films in a serious way. I had had to make a short film earlier in the year as part of a funding bid for a charity that I was working with. Now my friends, the Morris family, were in the process of setting up a suicide support charity in memory of their son Pete, who had tragically taken his own life.

I made two films for Sunflowers suicide support and once again my life started to feel as if I had a purpose.

*****

By February 2018 I had been on the kidney transplant waiting list for two years. I had previously been told that the average waiting time for Oxford is two years, so it was only inevitable that my anxiety started to build again.

We had been attending Five Valley's Christian Fellowship also for about two years and one Sunday morning when we were meeting at Tetbury (we meet in mainly four different venues), I was given this 13th foundational scripture. It had been so long since my foundation was added to.

Claire was leading the meeting and she asked us to find a verse in the Bible that meant something to you. I wanted something new, I could have easily fallen back onto my old foundation, but I just felt that it had to be something new.

The word HOPE came into my mind, I believe God put it there. In my waiting, the waiting game as the nurses call it, I have always felt hope. Hope that one day the call will come. Incidentally I have already had three calls, but neither of them progressed to an operation. To have a call and then for it not to proceed can be very hard mentally and our hope can be lost.

I opened my electronic Bible on my phone and searched for the word "hope". Almost instantly this verse jumped out at me, "*But God will never forget the needy, the hope of the afflicted will never perish*".
Psalm 9:18

On that day my verse was added to many others and a new song was created using them. I held onto my piece of paper with the verse scribbled on it. It was a new foundation for my new season.

My 14th Foundation

Do not be anxious about anything, but in every situation, by prayer and petition, with thanksgiving, present your requests to God. And the peace of God, which transcends all understanding, will guard your hearts and your minds in Christ Jesus.
Philippians 4:6-7

We return once again to the book of Philippians for the third time. We can draw so much from this book. Paul suffered so much hardship, including being beaten and imprisoned, but he was never anxious.

This last foundation came to me in the summer of 2018 and unlike all of my other foundations, this one was two verses, therefore longer than any other.

Incidentally, these two verses are the most highlighted in the Kindle e-book Bible. Therefore we can only assume that they are some of the most popular.

When you consider that one in four people in the UK suffer from some form of mental illness, we can only assume that this is the same all over the world. I believe the problem is even worse than these figures, as this just highlights what is being reported. Even though nowadays more and more people are feeling more comfortable opening up about their mental health there is still a stigma attached and the true figures I believe will be much higher. So it's no surprise that people all around the world turn to these two verses.

There is so much in these two verses, but for me, there are two main things that hit me when I read them:

1. Do not be anxious.
2. The Peace of God.

Do not be anxious or be careful for nothing in some versions is an exact mirror image of when Jesus told us, "Do not worry.
"

"Therefore I tell you, do not worry about your life, what you will eat or drink; or about your body, what you will wear. Is not life more than food and the body more than clothes?
Matthew 6:25

From McLaren's Exposition:
It is easy for prosperous people, who have nothing to trouble them, to give good advices to suffering hearts; and these are generally as futile as they are easy. But who was he who here said to the Church at Philippi, 'Be careful for nothing?' A prisoner in a Roman prison; and when Rome fixed its claws it did not usually let go without drawing blood. He was expecting his trial, which might, so far as he knew, very probably end in death. Everything in the future was entirely dark and uncertain. It was this man, with all the pressure of personal sorrows weighing upon him, who, in the very crisis of his life, turned to his brethren in Philippi, who had far fewer causes of anxiety than he had, and cheerfully bade them 'be careful for nothing, but in everything by prayer and supplication, with thanksgiving, make their requests known unto God.' Had not that bird learned to sing when his cage was darkened? And do you not think that advice of that sort, coming not from someone perched up on a safe hillock to the strugglers in the field below, but from a man in the thick of the fight, would be like a trumpet-call to them who heard it?

I can still become anxious at times when I hear the phone ring, but it is nowhere near as bad as it used to be. Nowadays I try to just press on with life, on towards the goal. I know that I am to still use the gifts that I have been given and especially the wisdom and love that God has blessed me with.

I know that as well as these fourteen foundational verses I have a whole Bible full of words that mean something, but I also know that there are people around me that care enough to listen.

One of my favourite expressions is, "I don't care how much you know until I know how much you care". I know that I have people that care about me, whether it be my family, my friends or the renal team. I know that I can turn to them and just knowing that makes a huge difference.

I have a peace which transcends all understanding, at least most of the time. There may be the odd day when it takes a wobble, but with my foundational scriptures and my support network it doesn't wobble for long.

The "peace of God" was first announced to the shepherds when Jesus was born.

"Glory to God in the highest, and on earth peace,
and goodwill toward men."
Luke 2:14

Jesus also mentioned it as some of His parting words.

"Peace I leave with you. My peace I give to you. Not as the world gives do I give to you. Let not your heart be troubled, neither let it be afraid".
John 14:27

*****

I believe that we all need scriptural foundations for our lives. Some of you may already have some that you use to support and strengthen what you do.

I would like to encourage you again to start building your own foundation of verses that are for you for your life.

You may feel that some of the verses that have supported me are also for you. That's ok, I don't own them, they are for all of us. However, you are different to me, as we are all different. So I would encourage you to seek the words that are for you.

Perhaps you will find that, like me, there are certain words for certain seasons, but bear in mind that a foundation never moves. Once you have selected it, it is there for life.

I have discussed this with a number of friends that are Christians and nearly all of them could quote a verse or two that had been with them for many years. Now I would encourage you to write them down. Perhaps you can remember how that scripture came to you and what it means, what is the story behind it?

You might start with your favourite verse, though personally I would struggle to pick a favourite from my fourteen foundational verses.

Start writing now and take ownership of your foundation. Use the blank pages at the end of this book for your own foundation and if you need help then please contact me, I would love to hear from you.

Brendan Conboy has an active speaking MINISTRY for GOD And is looking forward to hearing from you

Contact Brendan at the following:
Email – bmconboy@gmail.com
Phone - +44 (0)1453 731008
Mobile – 07980 404873
www.brendanconboy.co.uk

The following pages contain information about Brendan's book titles (Bibliography).

Song lyrics not previously mentioned In The Golden Thread

I truly believe that all of my song lyrics are the inspired Word of God, given to me over a period of time from the late 80s to the mid-90s. These songs all have a powerful message, as Kimberley did when she stole the tape.

These songs were used in school assemblies (mainly at Archway School, Stroud) for 25 years and were heard by thousands of young people. This also helped to fulfil the prophecy from Duncan White.

Inspired by God

I been thinking 'bout the good times,
been thinking 'bout the fun,
Been a wandering in the darkness
and a wondering what've I done.
(repeat)
Feeding off the memories but memories fade and die,
Doom and gloom and darkness overhead
in an ever-changing sky.

Chorus:
Inspiration come, inspiration go,
Exactly where it go, ain't nobody know. x2

I hear the sound... I hear the sound,
I hear the sound of the nightingale
as it sits away up high,
Unaware of darkness looming, looming in the sky.
Riders on the backs of horses running from the storm,
No inspiration's needed now
we must be home by dawn!
Yeshua Adonai we love you!

People, people, people, people everywhere,
Hurrying, scurrying without a care.
On their way to nowhere, walking in their sleep
People keep looking, people keep searching,
searching to stay alive.
People keep looking, people keep searching,
for that feeling good inside.
Are you searching for that feeling
that feels good inside?
Are you searching for that feeling
to make you stay alive?
Yo, people!
What are you searching for?
Are you searching for inspiration?
Well, I'll tell you.
When you find your inspiration
then take some good advice.
Are you inspired by good?
Are you inspired by bad?
Are you inspired by Jesus Christ?
God gave his Holy Spirit, inspiration to us all.
So don't give up, just ask yourself,
What's that inspiration for?
[Chorus]

*****

Reality

The dream generator keep on dreaming the dream.

Chorus:
Reality, reality, it happen to you and
it happen to me.
Reality, reality it happens to us all. X2

The dream generator is the major dominator,
Influencing the way of life.

You gotta keep dreaming, dreaming a dream,
A big car or a beautiful wife.
Hey there mister average what is your dream?
Are you just another dreaming fool?
Do you gamble, do you bet,
are you a millionaire yet?
Do you dream about winning the pools?
Is there a pot of gold at the end of the rainbow?
A yellow brick road showing you which way to go?
Is there a pot of gold at the end of the rainbow?
A yellow brick road showing you which way to go?

[Chorus]

If you dream about loving,
then you dream about giving.
If you dream about giving,
then you dream about living.
If you dream about living,
then you dream about lying
If you dream about lying,
then you dream about crying.
If you dream about crying
you dream about love!

Now reality happens to us all,
Just as pride comes before a fall.
Whether you dream or whether you don't.
Whether you will or whether you won't.

[Chorus]

Are you looking for a high, when you're feeling low,
Escape into a chemical and life begins to glow.
It's easy to say "yes", but you'd rather answer no.
You've tried all of the rest, but this high is the best,
So why is there an element of doubt?

I'll tell you now for why,
cuz when you're flying high,
You're the one that's really losing out!

[Chorus]

Are you a running and a hiding
from the things you have seen?
Hiding your face in a video screen.
Take a look at the dream in your head if you can,
The dream in your head's about a little man.
Are you a Mario or Sonic, Street Fighter Two,
Lost in a world where nothing is true?
. Are you a Mario or Sonic, Street Fighter Two,
Lost in a world where nothing is true?
Get real, stop dreaming a dream!
Get real, stop dreaming a dream!
Get real, stop dreaming a dream!
Get real and stop your dreaming!

Now there is the ultimate game,
With your helmet on it's inside your brain.
But the helmet of salvation,
Is the helmet of the nation.
Virtual reality or reality that's absolute,
The choice is yours,
put the helmet on and get to know the truth!
Get real you know what I'm saying!
Get real you know what I mean!
Get real you know what I'm praying!
Get real and stop your dreaming!
Get real you know what I'm saying!
Get real you know what I'm praying!
Get real you know what I'm saying!
Get real and stop your dreaming!

*****

Poetic Justice

Chorus:
If you could rap your way into Heaven.
If you could rap your way out of hell!
The whole world would be rapping,
The good the bad as well. [repeat]

You can't try to justify the things that you still do.
You might die, might even fry,
unless you find what's true
So, I rap, let's rap, c'mon rap, let's rap, GO!
If you are a kid or you are a child,
Get poetic get justice get reconciled
You gotta get in the light get poetic.
If you follow the dark, you're pathetic.

So, I rap in time, I rap with rhyme,
but there's something I've gotta say,
I rap for good and I rap for God
cuz there's something I've gotta say
I rap for good and I rap for God
and I get down on my knees and pray.
When He speaks to me, it's shear poetry,
but words just can't explain.
The way that I feel, I know that God is real
so, I rhyme in time again.

Though I've told you before I'll tell you again.
I'll tell you again and again and again.
I'll keep telling you just as long as it takes,
You to realise we all make mistakes.
Rapping is easy, but you know it's not the way.
You gotta pray to God in Heaven
and this is what you say.
Please forgive me God
for the things that I have done.

I believe in Jesus your one and only Son!

[Chorus]

*****

The Word

Baby craving, craving baby, craving to be fed,
Gotta keep craving, gotta keep feeding,
else you wind up dead!
Don't matter if you're rich, don't matter if you're poor.
Starvation hits the nation and it happens to us all.

Chorus:
You gotta feed on the word.
You gotta feed on the word.
You gotta feed on the word of The Lord
You gotta feed on the word.
You gotta feed on the word.
You gotta feed on the word of my Lord God.

There's a feeling of hunger deep inside,
I don't wanna eat because of my pride.
But pride it comes before a fall,
That feeling of hunger happens to us all.
Satisfaction, satisfaction, never can get enough,
Of the right stuff, you know what I'm saying?
Nuff said I've said enough!

[Chorus]

If you wanna feed, you gotta have a read!
If you wanna feed, you gotta have a read!
If you wanna feed, you gotta have a read!
You gotta water the seed!
But don't get choked up on the weed!
Do you read or do you not?

You gotta water the seed when the sun is hot.
You gotta water the seed and let it grow.
You gotta water the seed and more seed sow!

Spiritual nourishment,
it's the Word of God, there's no supplement.
If you feed the word, your spirit will grow,
Feed the spirit within and more seeds sow.

[Chorus]

If you're feeding on the word,
you get closer to The Lord.
Check it out this word is living.
So, take a look inside, get a new start to life,
From a God that is forgiving.
Can't judge a book by its cover,
get into the word you'll discover.
There's a God in Heaven that you can call Dad,
With a Son that you can call Brother.

[Chorus]

Baby craving, craving baby, craving to be fed,
Gotta keep craving, gotta keep feeding,
else you wind up dead!
[repeat]

*****

Keep on mocking

Chorus:
Hear you laughing, laughing at me,
Laughing with a heart of misery.
See you mocking, mocking what I do,
You mocking bless me don't you know it's true!
[repeat]

What d'you think you're laughing at now?
Gonna let us in on the joke?
Are you laughing at me? Are you laughing at him?
Are you laughing at some other bloke?
Everywhere I go, everything I do,
I hear the sound of laughter.
Faces smiling and fingers pointing
people heading for disaster.
Nothing wrong with having a laugh.
Nothing wrong with a bit of fun.
If no one in the world ever had a laugh,
No work would ever get done.
If you have a laugh it ain't that bad.
All work and no play it make Jack bad.
If you have a laugh it ain't that bad.
All work and no play it make Jack bad.
[Chorus]

Just wait a while before you smile
and ask the question "Why?"
Do you laugh at my belly?
Do you laugh cuz I'm smelly?
Can you look me in the eye?
When I ask you do you know what's true?
Do you know what is a lie?
When I ask you are you laughing at me?
Are you laughing at the man in the sky?

[Chorus]

Are ya laughing by yourself?
Or ya laughing with your friends?
If ya laughing for a reason
keep on laughing to the end.
If ya laughing by yourself?
Or ya laughing with your friends?

If ya laughing for a reason
keep on laughing to the end.
If ya laughing cuz someone else does,
And you don't want to look out of place.
Just think again, what you're laughing about,
About the look upon my face.
If you laugh at me because I'm free,
All I feel for you is sorry.
They laughed at the Boss
as they hung him on the cross,
All his thoughts for your tomorrow.

[Chorus]

Now this is nearly the end of this song,
Or the end of you if you wait too long.
Don't laugh at me anymore,
You can laugh with me; you know the score.
Don't have to be weak, like the rest of the sheep,
if you know what's true.
You can be blessed, just forget the rest,
And let them laugh at you.

Blessed are those who are persecuted in my name. x4
Woe to you who laugh now,
For you will morn and weep. x2
Blessed are those who are persecuted in my name. x2

*****

Cross the line

Chorus:
There's no time to wait!
No more hesitate!
Think about it no more time,
Jump up step out and cross the line!

Check it out this life of ups and downs,
Of in and outs and merry-go-rounds.
A life of good, a life of bad,
A life of happy sad and mad!
Some people are crazy, some just lazy!
Work hard, play hard, live hard, die hard.
Filthy dirty, squeaky clean,
All questions and answers, you know what I mean.

[Chorus]

Black or white, short or tall,
Fat or thin, or large or small.
God loves you all.
God loves you all.
Summer, winter, rain or shine,
You gotta get on up and cross the line.
Get up a, get down.

Some things are happening, but some things ain't,
Do you know what happens to all wet paint?
Starts off wet, but it ends up dry,
You gotta cross the line if you don't wanna die.
Now I'll explain to you the words of this song,
Some things are right, some things are wrong.
One hand is left, the other is right,
Work all day and sleep all night!
[Chorus]

Now the words of this song that I rap to you
is communication through and through.
You may not understand it,
but you know what to do,
Get rid of the false and follow the true.
The truth that I am talking about,
Is the kind of truth that leaves no doubt.
No doubt of what is in your mind,

Jump up step out and cross the line.
[Chorus]

The Golden Thread – Biography

A true story of fear, forgiveness and faith

First published – 1st September 2015

Brendan Conboy grew up in fear and confusion, struggling with many personal issues. These experiences formed a foundation that could have ended in disaster, but instead, became the motivator to want to make a positive difference.

Issues – Teen / YA Fiction

We all have issues… Can a bully change?

First published – 23rd January 2019

Marcus Daniel was a caring, intelligent, larger-than-average ten-year-old. His parents changed and then so did he. Now Marcus is thirteen years old and a spiteful bully, full of anger, rage and pain. His actions have changed others. Will the fear, pain and rage win?

My Foundation for Life – Semi Biog / Scriptural Teaching

14 underpinning and impacting scriptures

First published – 19th February 2019

What is it that makes some of us more resilient than others? I am sure that psychologists will have several long-winded explanations to answer this question, but I believe that we can increase our resilience by building our lives on a foundation of truth

Rhyme Time – Poetry

Poems with a message for you to read.
Poems of truth that plant a seed.

First published – 13th November 2020

The Invasion of the Mimics
Science Fiction / Dystopian / Fantasy
They're already here… Invading your country…
Dwelling in your home… Living in your body!
First published – 21st October 2020

Climate change had been predicted long ago, but not one person could foresee the events that had unfolded. Humanity is defeated, civilisation lost, all hope has gone. Enlightenment is the new belief, but there are those who refuse to believe.

The Land of Make Believe – Children's fantasy in rhyme
Based on the story of doubting Thomas
First published – 4th March 2021

ONE GOD Many Names
First published – 14th July 2021

When we meditate on the many names of God, something powerful can happen to us. Brendan Conboy shares his thoughts and personal stories of what some of these names mean and how they had a transformational impact on his life.

The Book of PSALMS in Rhyme
First published – 24th August 2021

POWERFUL...
POETIC...
RHYTHMIC,
RHYMING
PSALMS...
A fresh expression to ignite your soul.

Legacy of the Mimics
First published – 20th June 2022

Book two in the Mimics series.
Her eyes told her everything was calm, as it should be. Her eyes deceived her. Her mind sensed something else.

Beyond the void

Popcorn Poetry
First published – 30th August 2022

75 Poems that pop with rhythm & rhyme
The concept of **Popcorn Poetry** is simple, popcorn is made for sharing, just like the rhymes in this book - read them out loud and share them with friends.

Half Man Half Poet
First published – 2nd April 2023

An enzyme of rhyme designed for this time Life – Health – Social issues – Christian message. This book has something for everyone

The End is not The End
First published – June 2023

Poems for end of life and beyond – There is no avoiding death, it happens to us all. These poems will hopefully bring peace in the struggle.

The Gift

First published 25th September 2023

A compilation of four of my poetry books.

Rhyme Time

Popcorn Poetry

Half Man

The End

I'm Still Valued

First published – November 2023

Brendan's continuing life story featuring a life-limiting and disabling kidney disease. He has faced many life-threatening battles and persevered. Almost died and been in the well-known, tunnel of light.

Yellow
DOG
Publishing

www.ingramcontent.com/pod-product-compliance
Lightning Source LLC
Chambersburg PA
CBHW070341170726
48291CB00001B/130

9781739368470